something
for the weekend

Ruth Watson

something

for the weekend

with eight around the table

Photography by Peter Cassidy and illustrations by Toby Morrison

Quadrille

For Max, and everyone at the Crown and Castle, who held the fort while I wrote this book

contents

On the first page of my first book, *The Really Helpful Cookbook,* I blithered on about how the world really didn't need any more cookery books. I believed it then and have continued to believe it ever since. I believed it before, too, but as I am beginning to sound more Tony Blair than Tony Blair – or even Rory Bremner – I think I'll put a stop to this credo excursus. Anyway, the point is I was wrong: the world (or Britain, at least) does have need of another cookery book, and it's the one you're reading now.

My bibliographical epiphany came after a friend had rung to ask me for some culinary advice because he was having eight people round for dinner, and the recipe he wanted to use only catered for four. 'Could he double up on the quantities', was the question. As it happens, the ingredients in that particular recipe tolerated multiplication quite happily, and the preparation wasn't affected in any significant way. But the question got me thinking, and prompted me to start browsing through my extensive cookery book collection. To my real surprise, I discovered there was hardly a book in it that contained recipes to feed eight people. There were a few that gave detailed instructions on how to plan and cook finger food for a hundred, and some that catered for two to four, but the majority of recipes were for four to six people, a number I presume cookery writers must feel constitutes the 'norm'.

the weekend
starts here

Well, rather like Prince Charles answering 'yes' to the question of whether he loved Diana, but then adding that infamous rider, 'whatever love means', I feel similarly equivocal about the idea of four to six being the 'norm'. Of course, I am no statistician, and it's entirely possible that the average household comprises two adults and two children, but so what: the point is who bothers to look through a cookery book before rustling up the average weekday meal? I don't think it's overly cynical to suggest it's the potential presence of people outside the core family unit that prompts most cooks to roam beyond their usual culinary repertoire, and to seek new ideas. If so, it also stands to reason that recipes need to cater for more than four to six.

Personally, I seldom use a cookery book unless we have asked people round for a meal (note the word 'use': I read food-related books constantly), and then it will be for inspiration or to check quantities. Like most working women, there is a significant difference between what I knock up for a casual supper and what I cook for dinner at the weekend. One major difference is that we hardly ever eat meat during the week, or certainly not big tranches of it. Cooking a sirloin of beef is likely to cause an eclipse of the fridge if there isn't sufficient ravenous company ready to make serious inroads into the joint while it's hot. My husband loves cold roast beef sandwiches, but even he runs out of enthusiasm after a day or two, and the sirloin just sits around in an increasingly chilly sulk. Stews, ragouts and casseroles also need a number of people tucking into the pot to make them worthwhile, and no sane person makes a chicken pie for two.

During the week, there's none of the formality of a 'proper' meal, either; supper for the two of us is likely to be a one-plate salad, perhaps tumbled with rags of chicken or chunks of feta, or a bowl of linguine tossed with garlic, olive oil, anchovies and purple sprouting broccoli. The ingredients may be similar – identical even – to those I'd use in a more formal dinner, but I simply wouldn't feel comfortable serving friends who'd travelled halfway across the county with only an avocado splashed with lime juice and a Caesar salad. As for dessert, well, does anyone make a proper pudding to serve on a weekday evening? I often cut up a mango or a pineapple, and occasionally my husband will delve in the freezer for a tub of his favourite vanilla ice cream, but the idea of actually *cooking* a pudding – you're more likely to see moles wearing sunglasses.

Mind you, when friends come over I don't go to the same ridiculous lengths as I did when I first started 'entertaining' (the inverted commas indicating that I've long ditched that ridiculous concept in favour of just having some fun). Back then, I felt duty bound to produce a gastronomic performance of coruscating extravagance whenever anyone came over for dinner. The food tasted fine, but the hideous amount of work involved was certainly not good for my temper and I doubt whether our guests had a better time because I'd run myself ragged.

Nowadays, I might hand round some good olives (especially big green *gordal reina* olives stuffed with *marcona* almonds), small wedges of pizza (bought-in, but of decent quality), or little crushed artichoke and mozzarella crostini – all easy stuff that people can pick at while they have a pre-prandial drink. If it's a sit-down starter, the likelihood is that it will be something that's quick to assemble and makes relaxed, unfussed eating. Hence the 'starters to go' chapter, which is stuffed with ideas for starters of honest provenance that won't take long to rustle up but will still taste jolly good.

So, in a somewhat Brobdingnagian nutshell, that's why I decided to write *Something for the Weekend*. It's intended to bridge the gap between the copious number of undoubtedly excellent cookery books that cater for the 'norm', and what I think is reality: that when you invite friends and family round for dinner on a Saturday night, or for Sunday lunch, more often than not there are *eight round the table*.

being prepared

The recipes here don't just feed eight people, they are also intended to please a disparate group of people – you may notice the absence of sweetbreads and tapioca. Perhaps even more importantly, they are recipes that won't cause you misery of heart in the preparation. Most of the dishes can be partly prepared ahead of time, if not completely finished, without coming to any harm. In fact, many of the recipes *must* be made in advance and will actually improve with some maturation.

To help you see at a glance whether the recipe is something that fits the time you have available, or whether you'd be better off leaving it for another occasion, you'll find a bit at the beginning of each recipe that clearly indicates how far in advance the dish can be made. It will also be clear what – if anything – you will need to do at the last minute. As an example, I wouldn't make the chicken pie if I was short of time: it's not only quite a long-winded recipe (probably the lengthiest one in the entire book) but it patently lends itself to the pleasures of a leisurely cooking session, rather than a last minute stove-top scamper.

Being absolutely ready before guests arrive is as much a practical issue as it is a psychological one. Trying to whisk egg whites for a soufflé to start the meal, while simultaneously willing the main course duck to (*please*) crisp up, while dashing in and out of the kitchen with fiddly home-made canapés for guests who are already on to their third drink – breathe – is *not* a recipe for calm happiness. I should know, I was that (very young, over ambitious and hyperventilating) woman – and the dinner was a catastrophe.

Throughout this book you'll keep coming across the gentle (I hope) admonition to 'keep it simple'. I repeat this mantra because it really is the secret to health, harmony and a bloody good meal that everyone – including the cook – truly enjoys.

deciding what to cook

One of my greatest joys at the Crown and Castle is writing menus, with all the complex gastronomic and culinary choreography it demands: elements such as making sure one section of the kitchen isn't madly overworked while another remains idle; that the deep-fat fryer isn't straining under the welter of hand-cut chips while the salamander remains untested by a single glazed steak; that the seasons are respected; that the menu offers not only a good balance of ingredients, but of dishes that range from the creamy and rich to the robust and meaty; that the cooking methods are various and not everything is dry-fried, with nary a gravy-slopped casserole in sight.

It's also important to guard against the same ingredient continually cropping up: yoghurt dolloped in the Middle Eastern soup, then on the barberry and pistachio pilaf, and again on the blueberry cake; that herb-marinated and spiced dishes don't proliferate at the expense of pleasingly quiet dishes; that the colour of the food is varied and neither all dark and dramatic, nor pale and listless; and, finally, that the menu is balanced between dishes that will hold particular appeal for men and dishes that women will prefer. (You may well be thinking this notion is sexist and distasteful, but I've been taking customer orders for over 20 years and I *know* that more women will choose plaice than steak, and more men game terrine than quiche. And, while I am being stereotypical, more fat people will order pork belly than thin people. Like it or not, it's true.)

Even though you are not running a professional kitchen, it's every bit as important to consider the structure and content of the meal you're proposing to serve. I am not going to insult your ingenuity or intelligence by telling you exactly what you should cook – if I find my brain dulling over at the mere thought of those school textbook-like appendices with lists of menus for every occasion, why wouldn't you. I am looking at one now: apparently, a 'a sophisticated supper' for eight comprises cheese soufflés to start, followed by stuffed beef chasseur, Touraine potatoes, green salad, meringue petits fours and coffee. For a number of practical reasons, I think not.

Without getting too anal about it, however, I do have three cautionary bits of advice to give. First, don't overstretch yourself. Hold hard to that mantra 'keep it simple', especially if you're a novice cook, an anxious cook or a downright useless cook. Choose a cold starter that's easy to put together well ahead of time, followed by a good-tempered stew or baked dish, and a simple, (perhaps uncooked?) pudding: I am a huge fan of fresh fruit salad, which is wildly underrated but, you'll find, is usually greeted with surprised and delighted appreciation. Practice your cooking on a loving partner, rather than a group of friends who deserve better than blasted to buggery pheasant or soggy lemon tart. In fact, be a real friend and take them out to supper – there's not a person alive who wouldn't rather go to a pub or Pizza Express than toy miserably with boiled-to-rags mackerel.

Secondly, think about the colour and texture of the entire menu. Do a quick, mental check: is every course of ghostly pallor or have you unwittingly planned on serving pink prawns followed by pink salmon with pink rhubarb fool pavlova for pudding? It's all too easy to develop gustatory tunnel vision. I well remember an occasion when I'd decided to make guineafowl, leek and girolles pie for the main course. In the nick of time, I realised that it was probably better to skip the onion quiche I'd planned on serving before the pie. Obviously my brain was thinking, yum, something creamy, beige, mild and pastryish would be just the ticket: it didn't consider that creamy, beige, mild and pastryish served twice was rather more yuk than yum. Beware the ides of starch.

Consider the richness (or meagreness) of the meal, too. If you've decided on a menu that starts with a fairly austere salad, then a light chicken and squash stew, it's perfectly all right to go mad on a big, creamy meringue cake for pudding. But if the starter is a rich smoked salmon paupiette, it's probably wise not to follow it with a fatty (albeit toothsome) roast goose or an aioli-enriched fish bourride.

Thirdly, do take note of the 'done and dusted' advice at the start of each recipe. This will give you a clear idea of the timings involved and will allow you to plan a menu suitable for the occasion and your skills. Then you can balance out the workload so if the starter needs a bit of pre-prandial fiddling you can choose an accommodating main course that merely needs sticking on the table. There's no need to worry about the desserts because practically all of them can be made well ahead of time. In the few instances when this isn't possible – apple pie for example – you can either take it out of the oven when you sit down, and keep it warm, or put it in the oven as you sit down and leave it to chug along until you're ready to eat it.

treating food with kindness

not everything likes being pre-prepared... Schools, hospitals, football clubs and rubbishy pubs may roast meat and poultry the day before and then 'regenerate' it, but you may not. The reason has nothing to do with hygiene and everything to do with pride. Reheated roast meat is crap, and you don't want to serve crap; you want to serve a beautifully tender, juicy roast that has people whimpering with pleasure.

Anyway, why do it when there's no need? The roast will be quite happy burbling along in the oven until just before you sit down to eat. It then needs to rest in a warm place (perhaps with a bit of cooking foil loosely draped over its shoulders) before it's fit to eat, and all the while you can be eating your starter. It's the accompaniments that can cause the trouble – but not if you use my *side orders* recipes.

...salads definitely don't Never, ever, be tempted to dress a fragile leaf or herb salad until it is absolutely ready to be served: the leaves will turn to sludge faster than a tissue in the shower. French bean and shallot salad, roast red peppers – or anything similarly robust – will put up with more brutal treatment.

refrigerating food Ha! I'll bet you're thinking, 'I know what this means', and indeed you do. But there are a couple of rules concerning the refrigeration of food that need to be emphasised. First, all foods (or the dishes they're stored in) must be either wrapped in cling film or sealed in some way that prevents dehydration, cross-contamination, or tainted flavours. Remember, too, that hot food should not be left lurking around for hours while it cools – especially in summer – and that only cool food should be put in the fridge, otherwise it can raise the temperature inside and jeopardise the safety of the food already there. Where appropriate, plunging the base of a saucepan or dish into a sink full of ice-cold water is an easy way to get the temperature down quickly.

bringing food to room temperature Unless there is a specific instruction to do otherwise, you should *always* bring food to cool room temperature before serving it. With the possible exception of cucumber, cream, salad leaves and hard-boiled eggs, most food tastes of zilch when it's served fridge-cold. Tuck into a terrine just released from the fridge and you will only get a fraction of the flavour and none of the rich, unctuousness of the meat – on the other hand, the terrine shouldn't be so warm the fat starts to glisten. *Cool* room temperature is the thing.

reheating food One of the advantages of refrigerating a stew is that before reheating it you can remove any fat that has risen to the surface and congealed…mmm, what a gloriously revolting word – it definitely gives phlegm a run for its money. Having dealt with this little detail, remember that most food must be brought to room temperature before it is reheated. Although you can deep-fry chips that have come from the freezer, if you try to reheat a big casserole that's gone straight from fridge to oven, it's doomed to disaster. Nine times out of ten the casserole will look piping hot on the surface, and nine times out of ten it will be as chilly as Hull on a February night in the middle.

For the same reason, always use a mild-tempered oven or lowish flame. If the food is being reheated in the oven, keep the dish covered so it warms through evenly, and neither dries up nor burns. (Dishes such as duck confit and pork belly are exceptions to the rule. They've already had a gentle cooking to render them tender and need a big, belting blast of heat to finish them off.) Whether you're reheating food on top of the stove or in the oven you will still need to give the pot an occasional stir – and, in the case of mash or a thick purée, an almost continuous stir to prevent any scorching on the bottom. In addition, anything thick and sauce-like, that has been refrigerated, will probably need a bit more liquid to bring it back to the right consistency.

some culinary advice and explanation

One of the biggest problems for any cookery writer is just how much detail to go into. Delia has won a loyal audience by presuming her readers know absolutely zilch, and offers so much information you end up feeling quite distressed if she doesn't let on how many bubbles per square inch (definitely not centimetres) there are in a chocolate mousse. Diametrically opposed in style, Nigel Slater assumes his readership is pretty savvy about technique; he's far more interested in conjuring up evocative descriptions about food than handing out prissy instructions.

I hope I'm somewhere in the middle. To this end, I've decided to shield the confident cook from possible irritation by corralling up the explanations for a number of cooking techniques here, rather than larding the recipes with them. (How's that for wilful use of two conflicting verbs.) So, if you have any doubts about what it means to fold egg whites into a cake mixture, then this next section could be pretty handy.

deglazing a pan Nothing to do with defenestration, but a simple way to make a sauce or add extra flavour to a stew. Here's how it works: after a foodstuff has been seared, browned or fried, the food is removed and liquid (often alcohol and/or stock) is added to the hot, unwashed pan. This is brought to a fast boil over a high heat, while the residual (tasty) debris from the bottom of the pan is scraped up and stirred in – and that's 'deglazing'.

There's more: for food that was merely browned – e.g. meat destined for a stew – the results of this deglazing (the icky-bitty liquid) go into the casserole to enrich the gravy. However, if the foodstuff was cooked completely – e.g. a pan-fried chicken breast – the deglazing can segue into a little sauce, perhaps by adding double cream and boiling it down, or taking the pan off the heat and whisking in some scraps of butter.

making a roux This is an amalgamation of melted butter and flour, cooked over heat to form a smooth paste. For a classic white sauce, add milk and keep stirring (or, better still, whisking) until the makings come to a boil and thicken into a smooth, creamy sauce.

seasoning... Everyone is so wised-up about using freshly ground black pepper and fine (or coarse) sea salt these days, I'm not sure I need to make it clear that every time I suggest a dish needs seasoning it means adding this quality and type of salt and pepper ...but I just have.

...seasoned flour I don't really think this needs an explanation either – it's simply flour that has had ground black pepper and fine sea salt added to it. If the recipe requires extra flavouring – say nutmeg, chilli or paprika – it will say so.

blanching... Forget Marlon Brando doing brutish things to a neurotic woman, this is a cooking term which involves boiling a very large quantity of water, throwing in something vegetal (but not exclusively so) and leaving it to buffet around for anything from a few seconds to a few minutes. The purpose may be to mitigate the texture (particularly when the ingredient is going into a baked dish where it won't cook readily, such as a lasagne or gratin) or to ease the peeling of, perhaps, tomatoes, peaches or shallots.

...refreshing After the food has been blanched, it's scooped out and 'refreshed' by being plunged into ice-cold water, which stops the cooking process and fixes the colour, particularly in the case of green vegetables and herbs.

folding This is a balletic form of stirring, in which it's as important to incorporate (or keep) air in the mixture, as it is to combine the ingredients. Any recipe for an airy mousse, soufflé, sponge cake or meringue will command you to 'fold' rather than stir. First, take a very large metal kitchen spoon, then cut down sharply with the side of the spoon to the bottom of the mixing bowl, and bring it back and over the surface in a large, light, looping action – rather like swirling a sparkler in the air on Guy Fawkes' night.

blind-baking Fortunately you don't have to wear a paper bag over your head to cook an empty pastry case (lined with parchment or foil and weighed down with baking beans) for 12-15 minutes at 170C fan/gas mark 5. Nor to remove the lining and beans and bake the case for another 5-6 minutes, or until the pastry is neither raw-looking nor golden brown – a dry, blonde appearance is what's needed.

napping To 'nap' something means to spoon a small quantity of thickish sauce (savoury or sweet) over a piece of food, partly covering it. For example, in a classic poire Belle Hélène the pear is 'napped' with chocolate sauce, rather than smothered with it.

concassée A French term, much used by chefs, this describes chopped tomato flesh after a whole tomato has been blanched, skinned and de-seeded. In other words, you can't carelessly chop up a tomato without some preparation. (See *chair de tomate* opposite.)

what is it?

There aren't any particularly esoteric ingredients in this book, but there may be the odd item you haven't come across before, and which needs some explanation…

chair de tomate 'Chair' means 'flesh' in French. The only place I've found these small ringpull cans of chopped Provencal tomatoes with tomato purée is in Sainsbury's. The flavour of tomatoes is intense, but without the unpleasant (slightly metallic?), bully-boy strength of regular tomato purée. If you can't be fagged to make fresh tomato concassée, (see the previous page) it makes a useful substitute.

sugocasa Sometimes known as passata, this is just sludged-up tomatoes: it comes in bottles, cans and Tetrapacks. I wouldn't bother buying chopped tomatoes (not *that* lazy) but puréed tomatoes can be very useful for stews and suchlike.

Marigold Swiss vegetable bouillon powder I have been recommending this stock powder for over a decade. At first it was difficult to unearth, but now the green cardboard tubs with bright orange lids are everywhere from health food shops to (good) supermarkets. I am not ecstatic that it contains hydrolysed vegetable protein but on the other hand it doesn't have any preservatives, colourings, artificial flavourings or genetically modified matter in it. (HVP is a mixture of gluten, soya meal, acid and water, heated and pressurised to break down the proteins into amino acids. After further processing to render it safe by international and FSA standards it's used to enhance flavour.) My only real gripe is the appallingly long-winded name: for the sake of space, I refer to it as Marigold vegetable powder whenever it crops up in a recipe.

funghi porcini stock cubes Such a clever (and obvious) idea: these stock cubes will save having to buy expensive little packets of dried porcini (aka ceps or cèpes) then soaking and chopping them. Buy the stock cubes from Limoncello (see the suppliers' list) and add them to any stock where you need a real boomph of extra flavour – and not only flavour, but that vital, earthy base note essential to a brown, gutsy stew.

vanillin (aka vanilla flavouring), vanilla essence and vanilla extract Any decent cook rightly reviles vanilla flavouring which is derived from *vanillin*, a lookey-likey chemical that replicates natural vanilla – supposedly. Vanillin, the crystalline component, was first isolated from vanilla pods by Gobley in 1858. Twenty years later, chemists had found out how to synthesise it from glycosides of pine tree sap. Just to confuse the issue, what's called vanilla essence in the USA is often actually this fake stuff, but in Europe vanillin has to be described as *vanilla flavouring*, so it's easy to avoid here.

True vanilla is far more complex and less sickly than the ersatz stuff. It comes from the pods of a tropical orchid – hence the tell-tale little black seeds that speckle proper vanilla ice cream. The *vanilla extract* sold in most good supermarkets (in brown bottles) uses alcohol to 'carry' the essential oil. A few drops of *vanilla essence* (which is normally sold in very small, clear glass bottles) equals two or three capfuls of the extract. As ever, the secret is to go gently, and keep tasting.

cake lifters These flat, plate-sized sheets of metal are just what is needed to transfer a delicate-but-huge cake, tart or meringue from its tin to a serving plate. Available from Lakeland Limited, they are cheap, incredibly useful, and all cooks should have one.

does it matter? (yes)

if it's cheap to buy, it's costly to make I'm talking about costly in time, of course. The undeniable fact is that expensive foods such as fillet steak are the quickest and easiest to get on the plate. In contrast, a relatively cheap cut of beef undoubtedly saves money but requires a good deal of careful preparation time. Take any beef stew, casserole or pie as an example: it's vital that every scrap of unappealing tissue is trimmed off, otherwise the finished dish will border on the disgusting. How you value your time is up to you. You may relish the thought of spending a day fidgeting away in the kitchen, or it may appal you. You may not even have a choice in the matter. Whatever your stance, cheaply bought food costs time in labour. Honour that fact and all will be well.

spices should smell divine Every year I root through my spice collection and chuck out any that are old and stale. Except I obviously don't. Why else would there always be jars at least two years older than their 'use-by' date in the cupboard? I also used to buy the vast majority of my spices in the supermarket, my major concession to 'freshness' being a willingness to grind whole spices myself. Well, if you take no other advice in this book, purchase your spices from Steenbergs' (or any other dedicated spice merchant). The aroma, fragrance, pungency and complexity of their spices is astoundingly superior to anything I've come across before and really shows in the finished dishes.

large pans should be very large It stands to reason that if you're cooking enough to feed eight people in one hit, you are going to need some decent-sized equipment. However massive the initial investment may seem, the money will never be wasted because good pans last for ever – mine are coming up for 30 years old, still look beautiful and perform perfectly. Anyway, there will always be an occasion when you want to cook a whole ham or a big chicken or enough raw spinach to feed two (just joking, but only just). In any case, and I say this with feeling, any cook worth his or her salt will positively relish the idea of spending money on a brilliantly engineered pan. Conversely, anyone who resents the thought should put down this book and go and splurge on a pair of diamanté-encrusted jeans instead. We used a fabulous SKK stewpot to test almost all the *urban peasant food* in this book, and I give details of where to buy it (and other equipment) in the list of kitchen equipment suppliers that follows.

Most good-quality, modern ovens come equipped with sturdy, metal oven trays that slide on to the built-in runners, and offer a large surface area. I used this type of oven tray for many dishes, including the *Asian-spiced potatoes and onions* and *tray-baked potatoes*, but you will still need a couple of large, heavy baking sheets, as well as normal, large roasting tins. On this subject, a word of warning about nomenclature: for some arcane reason, Mermaid, a UK (hurrah) company that makes large-sized, sturdy cookware, describes what I would call a roasting 'tin' as a roasting 'dish', even though I am quite sure most people think of dishes as being ceramic, rather than metal. Don't be put off as the 'dishes' are indeed metal, and with one being a generously sized 37cm x 26.5cm, and the other an even mightier 42cm x 30.5cm, these 'dishes' are the kind of roasting tins you need for many of the recipes that follow.

measuring your equipment It'll probably take the grin off your face when I tell you that for all your culinary life you've probably been measuring your cake tins, flan cases and pie dishes incorrectly. The horrible fact is that the measurements supplied by bakeware manufacturers and cookery writers are taken *across the base of the equipment, not the top*. If you constantly end up with far too much mixture for the cake tin specified it may answer the mystery as, invariably, the base is smaller than the opening.

As in *Fat Girl Slim*, I have not suggested a single ingredient that can't be bought either online, or by mail order, or in a good supermarket. But, as a few people got all screwed up because they didn't realise there was a suppliers' list in FGS, I am making damned sure you notice this one.

fresh fish and shellfish

www.martins-seafresh.co.uk jeff.martin@martins-seafresh.co.uk
✆ 01637 889168 or 0800 027 2066 A lively, up-to-the-minute website, with the Martins offering punctilious service – in season, they supply Cornish crab, lobster, cockles, red gurnard and other locally caught fish, e.g. turbot, mackerel, sea bass, etc., as well as frozen fish and shellfish.

www.fishworks.co.uk enquiries@fishworks.co.uk
✆ 01225 465126 or 0800 052 37 17 A fashionable restaurant and fish shop-company co-owned by chef/cookery writer Mitchell Tonks – the choice and quality are undeniably good, but the prices can be a bit on the rich side, not that good fish is, or should be, cheap.

smoked fish

www.butleyorfordoysterage.co.uk info@butleyorfordoysterage.co.uk
✆ 01394 450277 In the same village as our hotel, the Crown and Castle, the Oysterage supplies locally reared oysters and a great variety of smoked fish, including the best cod's roe you'll ever eat.

www.smokedeel.co.uk info@smokedeel.co.uk
✆ 01458 250875 Award-winning Brown and Forrest is the place for smoked eel, as well as other smoked fish, duck, chicken and lamb.

Richardson's Smokehouse
✆ 01394 450103 No website as yet, but Steve Richardson smokes – and mails out – anything from chicken and pigeon to trout and eel, using a fairly intense 'smoke'.

meat and game

www.guildofqbutchers.co.uk Check this website for a directory/map of British butchers who care about the meat they sell.

www.graigfarm.co.uk shop@graigfarm.co.uk
✆ 01597 851655 I bought an excellent (pricey, but worth it) organic turkey crown from these people last Christmas. They sell other organic produce (including dairy, greengrocery, etc.) but are here because of their lamb, mutton, beef, pork, chicken and wild boar, supplied in every cut imaginable.

www.pipersfarm.com

✆ 01392 881380   You'll find locally reared meats with impeccable provenance on this website, e.g. Ruby Red beef, Exmoor lamb, venison and pork.

www.richardwoodall.co.uk admin-@richardwooodall.co.uk

✆ 01229 717237   Mr Woodall has long been famous for his Cumbrian air-dried ham (as well as bacon and sausages) which is every bit as good as parma ham.

www.britainsbestbutcher.co.uk eric@britainsbestbutcher.co.uk

✆ 01507 568235   Also known as FC Phipps, *Country Life* magazine honoured this mega-busy, Lincolnshire butchers with the award now used as their website address. Specialities include Lincolnshire chine, Lincoln Red beef, Hebridean lamb, game, bacon and pies.

www.edwardsofconwy.co.uk

✆ 01492 592443   This is the place for sausages, particularly the lamb (merguez) ones you'll need for the stuffed saddle of lamb (see page 92).

www.wellhungmeat.com sales@wellhungmeat.com

✆ 0845 230 3131   A highly rated, family-run company selling tenderly reared South Devon beef, lamb, organic chickens and award-winning, rare breed pork.

www.lanefarm.co.uk Sue@lanefarm.co.uk

✆ 01379 384593   Specialising in Suffolk pork, Lane Farm's sausages and bacon are used for (our award-winning) Full English Breakfast at the Crown and Castle.

www.caleyco.com enquiries@caleyco.com

✆ 01750 505100   Aberdeen Angus beef, Blackface or Border Cheviot lamb, venison, game and organic chicken, as well as regional specialities, can all be purchased from this Scottish collective.

Seldom Seen Farm (use foodloversbritain.com website for information)

✆ 01162 596742   A specialist goose producer, that also supplies pheasants and turkeys.

cheese

www.lafromagerie.co.uk moxon@lafromagerie.co.uk or highbury@lafromagerie.co.uk

✆ 020 7935 0341 or 020 7359 7440   My admiration for Patricia Michelson (and Danny, her husband) knows no bounds. Hugely knowledgeable and unflaggingly enthusiastic, she sells the most beautiful cheeses, as well as specialised deli products of the most wonderful nature.

www.nealsyarddairy.co.uk mailorder@nealsyarddairy.co.uk

✆ 0207 500 7653   Another fantastic, honourable and hugely respected cheese supplier, Randolph Hodgson, almost single-handedly restored British and Irish cheese-makers to their current high status and financial viability. Randolph employs really good girls and boys who know their stuff and not a single cheese goes out unless it's in season and at the peak of perfection.

groceries – and smart, restaurant-type stuff that's difficult to find

www.solstice.co.uk food@solstice.co.uk

✆ 020 7498 7700 or 0800 328 7701   Originally catering solely to the trade, this company supplies fashionable, seasonal foodstuffs from red chicory to goose foie gras but the highlight for me is Poilâne sourdough bread.

www.funkin.co.uk

✆ 020 7328 4440   There's a fair chance you're thinking, 'hey-ho, another fcuk wheeze; how very amusing,' but if you are, you're doing Alex Funkin an injustice. He's the bright spark who thought we needed amazingly good quality fruit purées (joined now by juices), and we did. You can buy by mail order, but Selfridges, Waitrose, Harrods, Tesco and Harvey Nichols, also stock some or all of the flavours, which range from pear, banana and white peach to morello cherry, passion fruit and apricot – with lots in between.

www.limoncello.co.uk

✆ 01223 507036   We first started using this Cambridge-based deli a long time ago when we needed some limoncello (the varyingly marvellous or crass Amalfi lemon liqueur) and couldn't find it for love or money. The service is excellent and they now supply far more than limoncello. Buy Star funghi porcini stock cubes (for gravy, or any stews), as well as squid ink, dried borlotti beans, pancetta in a piece, or loads of other good (mostly Italian) produce.

www.esperya.com

Produce is flown in directly from Italy and arrives about three days after ordering online. Esperya is a great favourite of mine, offering superb artisanal-made – and very much seasonal – Italian foods, whether it be the best (softest, almondy) amaretti you've ever tasted, gorgeous panettone (or Easter cakes and tarts), truffled mortadella, fennel salami, extra-virgin olive oil or drippingly fresh buffalo mozzarella. I think the prices are extremely reasonable for the quality of the food – and the fact it's been shipped all the way from Genova.

www.machiavellifood.com info@machiavellifood.com

✆ 020 7498 0880   A small company offering personal service, with a limited but good-quality range of Italian produce, e.g. salami, cheese, pasta and rice.

www.portobellofood.com

✆ 020 8980 6664   For fabulous Italian cheeses, including fresh buffalo mozzarella and hard-to-find burrata, as well as beautiful butter, de Cecco pasta, breads, polenta, salumi – in fact, for all things Italian, it's hard to think of a better source.

www.provender.net

✆ 01460 240681   A Somerset-based company that's good for 'fancy' goods especially from the West Country (biscuits, chutneys, cider, etc.), and seasonal produce, e.g. haggis for Burns' night.

www.merchant-gourmet.com

✆ (free phone) 0800 731 3549   A long-established company stocking high-quality, predominantly French and Italian groceries, such as peeled chestnuts, mi-cuit plums (similar to Agen prunes), polenta, black lentils (most of which you'll find in leading supermarkets), but their online site also allows the purchase of fresh meats, charcuterie and cheeses.

www.trenchermanandturner.co.uk

✆ 01323 737 535   Based in Eastbourne, this outfit has a good retail mail order range, that includes all the usual Spanish suspects, including chorizo, lomo, serrano ham, anchovies, olives and almonds and much more besides.

www.purespain.co.uk

✆ 01962 774942   A really nice company, importing good Spanish foods, from chorizo iberico Bellota to good bottled chickpeas and wood-roasted red peppers. They also sell wonderful cast iron pans, hand-painted ceramics…and Spanish holidays.

www.mountfuji.co.uk sales@mountfuji.co.uk

✆ 01743 741169   For a really extensive selection of Japanese foods, this is the place to shop.

bread, cakes and desserts

www.handmadecake.co.uk sales@handmadecake.co.uk

✆ 01628 770908   A friendly, enthusiastic company that supplies moist, dessert-style cakes, e.g. St. Clement's cake, as well as more traditional tea-time cakes, brownies and flapjack.

www.cocoamoi.com nicepeople@cocoamoi.com

✆ 020 8864 0952   Owned by a really nice woman who makes possibly the best chocolate brownies you can buy.

Maison Blanc info.maisonblanc@lyndale.co.uk

✆ 020 8838 0848   You can't order online from this smart patisserie but there are a number of London and regional branches for those able to purchase in person.

Paul

✆ 020 7224 5615   Again, no online service from this French boulangerie-cum-patisserie, but the branches in London continue to burgeon and while the tarts and pastries are quite superb, their bread is truly to die for.

www.parkersmenu.co.uk

✆ 01963 250570   Apparently their chocolate roulade has been served at Highgrove. Whatever, this West Country family firm has won many awards for its hand-made, frozen and chilled puddings, including lemon pavlova roulade and Dorset apple cake. They supply savoury dishes as well.

Caroline's Real Bread Company

✆ 01874 690378   I honestly don't know much about this person but she comes recommended so it's probably worth a phone call to see what she has to offer.

www.wildyeastbakery.co.uk

Run by two bread fanatics, Peter and Simon, this is the place for great sourdough and Eastern European-style bread, such as Borodinsky and Volkornbrot. They also sell numerous, authentic sourdough cultures, if you want to make your own bread. Truly a company to cherish.

www.village-bakery.com

✆ 01768 881811   Founder Andrew Whitley is a pioneer of good bread-making in this country and over the last 30 years the business has developed into one of the major organic brands in the country. Waitrose sell Village Bakery breads, cakes and biscuits (as do many health food shops), but you can buy almost anything online including a large gluten-free range of products. And, as we know to our own benefit, Andrew also runs fantastically useful bread-making courses.

spices, preserves, chutneys, etc.

www.wendybrandon.co.uk

✆ 01239 841568   As she proudly states on her website, Wendy Brandon is a real person, and the company is very much family run. We buy her marmalades for our restaurant but she also makes excellent chutneys and preserves.

www.steenbergs.co.uk enquiries@steenbergs.co.uk

✆ 01756 640088   A specialist supplier of fabulously potent (mostly organic) spices and herbs, packed stylishly and sensibly in little metal cans.

chocolates

www.rococochocolates.com web@rococochocolates.com

✆ head office 020 8761 8456   An immensely stylish London-based company, Rococo supply us with their chocolates for the Crown and Castle. Having tried many suppliers, we have found their service to be the most reliable, their prices relatively modest – and the chocolates not only look fabulous, they taste fabulous too.

www.artisanduchocolat.com artisanduchocolat@hotmail.co.uk

✆ 020 7824 8365   Again, a stunningly stylish company, and if there is a chocolate more strangely seductive than their liquid salted caramels, I've yet to find it. Too expensive for us to use on a regular basis at the C&C, I do buy their piss-elegant chocolates to serve at home.

equipment suppliers

www.divertimenti.co.uk

✆ 0207 935 0689 We tested a huge number of recipes for this book in a 28cm SKK stewpot with lid, code 14105, that I bought from Divertimenti at the initially terrifying price of £141.50. It's good-looking, non-stick, yet tough enough to withstand metal utensils, and cooks evenly on all hobs except induction. In a nutshell, it's quite fantastic and worth every penny. (After that ringing endorsement, I'm looking forward to a free 24cm stewpot arriving by courier.) Like David Mellor, see below, Divertimenti also stock a huge range of stylish china, bakeware, utensils and table linen.

www.davidmellordesign.com

✆ 01433 650220 David and Corin Mellor are highly renowned product designers (DM designed the traffic lights you whizz past – or stop at – on every junction). There's a surprisingly large and useful range of equipment on this stylish site – everything from David Mellor's eponymous cutlery to hand-crafted ceramics, bakeware, glass, china and wonderfully crafted wooden boards. You can also buy the marvellous Kaiser cake tins here, and Alan Silverwood's traditional aluminium range of loaf pans, quiche tins and baking trays.

www.nisbets.co.uk

✆ 0845 140 5555 A website that's about as utilitarian and glamourless as you can get, but which offers every conceivable item of cookware, crockery, barware, glassware and machinery. They also stock sundae glasses, albeit they go under the strange and completely unhelpful description of 'ice cream cup' and 'knickerbocker glory goblet'. The service is very fast, if totally impersonal.

www.lakelandlimited.co.uk

✆ 01539 488100 One of the best retail and mail order cookware suppliers in the country.

www.traditionalwares.co.uk

✆ 08456 121273 A little disconcertingly twee in its design, nevertheless a jolly useful website that majors in supplying traditionally-made/styled kitchen equipment, hence the name. Go here for white enamel dishes (for apple pie).

www.samuelgroves.co.uk

✆ 0121 554 2001 For serious cookware, of a professional size and nature, this is the site. Not glamorous, but immensely practical stuff.

www.cookware-online.co.uk

✆ 01877 889900 You'll find a huge and comprehensive catalogue of cooking equipment here, from food mixers, weighing scales and coffee machines to baking tins and casseroles.

www.goldleafsupplies.co.uk

✆ 01656 860109/860344 Hardly an everyday necessity but, as the name suggests, this is where you can buy edible gold leaf in varying forms, from dust to petals. One day you'll want to know this.

I know there many people who think that it's enough to bung a bit of mozzarella, tomato and basil on a plate and call it a starter. Well, I am not trying to create complication where none exists but the fact is that this kind of simplicity requires both excellent quality ingredients and an understanding of how to combine them. Assembling a starter requires every bit as much care and attention as cooking a recipe written by some highfalutin chef (or his 'ghost', if I am being very bitchy – and truthful). Just-flown-in, spanking-fresh buffalo mozzarella and sun-ripened tomatoes will, indeed, make a fabulous starter: Danish half-fat mozzarella and hot-house tomatoes will not. If you keep it simple, it must be flawless, whether you're dealing with clothes, interiors or food.

As an example, I recently ordered a prawn cocktail in a local pub. A plate was dumped in front of me, bearing a small handful of barely defrosted 'cocktail' shrimps, a little pot of cash-and-carry Marie-Rose sauce and a welter of indifferent greenery. Of course, prawn cocktail is a cliché but made with decent-sized, hand-shelled North Atlantic prawns, a home-made sauce (even one based on bottled mayonnaise) and authentic cos or romaine lettuce, it's very enjoyable. This travesty of the real thing was mean and meaningless junk.

starters
to go

The problem is that while it's becoming increasingly easy to source and buy excellent artisanal produce, the degradation of 'normal' foodstuffs continues apace. I am genuinely horrified by the ecological damage wrought by pesticides and herbicides, air-transportation and monoculture; the unjust and punitive trade agreements controlled by the Superpowers; the emphasis on producing new plant strains that have everything to do with novelty, looks and stability, rather than flavour…I could go on, but this is meant to be an upbeat, cheerful cookery book, not a political harangue, so I'll leave all that to courageous (and better informed) food writers such as Joanna Blythman and Judy Bevan.

It's not difficult to list some of the foods that should be avoided: I have yet to eat anything from Israel, South Africa, Holland, Belgium (and I really, really do include their chocolate), Kenya, Turkey and most South American countries that has much distinction: figs from Israel – dry and tasteless; peaches from South Africa – woolly and tasteless; blueberries from Holland – flaccid and tasteless (and scarily gargantuan).

Contrast this lacklustre produce with in-season figs from Cyprus – squidgy and honeyed; peaches from Italy – juicy and scented; blueberries from Poland – tart and firm;

peas from Britain – hard and tasteless. Ha! Gottya. Well, you don't need me to tell you that it's practically impossible to find a sprightly fresh pea nowadays – unless you grow them yourself. (And when did you last buy a beautiful fresh apricot? About the time Tiny Tim was tiptoeing through the tulips, I reckon.)

From past experience, I can already hear the moans about the difficulty and time it takes to source and buy good food. Rubbish, is my succinct and not overly polite answer. I know not everyone has a Waitrose close by (the best supermarket of the bunch, but an hour's drive away in my case). Nor do many people live in close proximity to a farmer's market or Marylebone High Street. My God, how I envy the locals there, what with the Ginger Pig, Total Organics and La Fromagerie in one tiny side street. But there are other ways to obtain good produce.

I rely hugely on the numerous online companies that stock excellent fresh (or frozen) produce, and are delighted to ship it out to me – they are also notable for being quick to phone and check on any details that need clarifying. Admittedly you have to know where to find them, but I've made that part very easy – just leaf through the preceding chapter. The other secret is to build up a good store cupboard – not one filled with crisps, chocolate cup cakes and cook-in sauces but a cupboard from which you can snatch a useful bottle of artichoke hearts, pesto or French peas. (I know there'll also be a jar of a cactus and wildebeest sauce bought in Nairobi airport, that's long past its chuck-out date, but we all have skeletons in the cupboard.)

It's getting on for 15 years since Nigel Slater's iconic *Real Fast Food* appeared. For the first time a cookery writer had recognised that we were living in an ever-increasing whirlwind of activity, leaving precious little time for rustling up a meal – especially in the evenings after work. But the best bit wasn't just that the recipes were quick to cook, they were also modern, inspirational and free-ranging. With not a pasta bake, tuna melt or sweet n'sour pork chop in sight, here was a food writer as keen on promulgating the sublime pleasure of *Yesterday's Roast Chicken Sandwich* as he was *Warm New Potato Salad with Melted Taleggio and Rocket*. The idea that one could make a decent meal just by buying a few simple, in-season ingredients from the deli and the greengrocer, then spending a little time arranging them in an attractive and apposite way, was a revelation.

His book certainly came at the right time for me. For years I had thought it my bounden duty to produce a 'proper, cooked' three-course meal every night. A burgeoning weight problem coupled with an ever-increasing work load meant I had begun to question this convention. So, it came as true liberation when I realised that there was nothing wrong with boiling a hank of linguine and tossing it with garlic, crushed tomatoes and anchovies, or scrambling a few eggs and piling them on some sourdough toast, and calling it supper. Even more extraordinary, if mildly exasperating, was discovering that my husband didn't give a tinker's cuss whether his evening meal comprised soup and a baked potato, or game terrine, sole Walewska (blimey, I'd forgotten how much I adore that particular retro dish) and lemon meringue pie.

The only drawback to the idea of throwing food together in double-quick time, rather than subjecting it to prolonged preparation and laborious cooking, is that you might have to spend a few minutes longer shopping as it's also essential to keep some sprightly, adaptable basics in the fridge. Mine is rarely without Italian salami and dry-cured ham, buffalo mozzarella, parmesan, free-range eggs, natural yoghurt, fresh herbs, garlic, green vegetables, mushrooms and salad leaves. With these fresh ingredients and some pulses, pasta or bread, you can make an entire meal, not just a starter.

There's no doubt, though, that a carefully judged preface to a meal confirms that everything is, indeed, all right with the world. A starter isn't intended to fill every ravening gap: however, it is meant to break the ice (should it need any fracturing), titillate the palate and generally reassure your guests that going out to dinner was worth the row about who's driving/forgot to order the taxi/left the cleaning at work/didn't set the video/left it too late to buy any decent flowers… well, you get the drift. And, unless you're hell-bent on making unnecessary work for yourself, starters are the one part of the meal where you can happily rely on the expertise of others. Yes, you need to be a careful shopper and, yes, it helps if you can throw things together with a marginally artful eye – but that's all. Save your energies for the main course. But before we get there, your guests first have to sit down…

…and in the beginning there was good bread

Nothing gives out a better signal of whether one's in for a decent meal – or not – as the generous provision of really good bread. Nothing except having some beautiful butter to go with it, that is. Unfortunately, you're more likely to find a hundred *X-factor* hopefuls lounging around the average supermarket than properly made bread. To be sure there will be a plethora of golden brown, farinaceous stuff, baked in a wonderful array of shapes and sizes. The trouble is that ninety per cent of it will be made from the same wheat, the same (hydrogenated) fats, and the same fast-action raising agents. The only real variation will be in the appearance.

You probably already know the enticing smell of fresh bread that drifts around the back of most supermarkets is usually created (or enhanced) by adding synthetic aroma to the air circulation system. You may also be aware that the vast majority of freshly baked bread is merely finished off in store, and has no more integrity than the part-baked bread you yank out of the freezer and bung in the oven at home. Add all this to the paucity of neighbourhood bakeries, and it's easy to see why this most basic of food commodities is really quite difficult to obtain.

My own way round the problem is to use either an online baker or the freezer (or both). Whenever I find myself walking past a proper baker's shop – the sort where there are people who know how to create a dough, knead it, prove it, and bake it on the premises – I dive in and stock up on a variety of different loaves. What they will all have in common is a really demanding, crackling crust and a deliberately chewy, yeasty crumb: the kind that engenders a serious tussle between teeth and hand to disengage; the kind that doesn't atrophy as it ages, but offers itself up for transformation into the most splendid toast.

I am hugely partial to sourdough bread, occasionally stern, uncompromising Poilâne, but more often a lighter San Francisco-style sourdough. I also like to keep some Middle Eastern flat bread in the freezer, as well as crisp-crusted Pugliese and proper ciabatta – which is not the same as the oil-free, slipper-shaped, supermarket ciabatta that so despicably uses the same nomenclature. On occasions when I manage to get to Carmelli's in Golders Green – heartland of the triple-parking brigade and the most lawless driving this side of the Gaza strip – I'll buy a crusty, light rye loaf, teeming with tiny caraway seeds, or a bag of proper bagels. You will find a list of good bakeries in the suppliers' list: it's by no means exhaustive and probably rather too London-based, but that's because Suffolk and the metropolis are the two areas I frequent the most. I am quite sure Aberdeen has just as much to offer if you can be bothered to make the search.

Getting hold of good butter is far simpler than obtaining good bread. Almost all the supermarkets stock at least one brand of well-made unsalted butter. Although it's not impossible to find British-produced, unsalted butter (such as Rachel's organic, St. Ivel or Country Life), there's a greater likelihood that the unsalted butters on offer will be Danish, Dutch or French. Personally, I am not a huge fan of Lurpak (Danish) or Wheelbarrow (Dutch), because I think they lack the clarity of French unsalted butter and – to me – taste slightly greasy. President and Bridel are respectable French brands but my favourites are the AOC L'Echiré, Longman Farm's butter (as stocked by Neal's Yard Dairy) and the Beppino Occelli butter (currently on offer at Waitrose). The latter is Italian and wonderfully sweet and pure-tasting. I also like the fact that someone thinks it's worth bothering to emboss a picture of a cow on each pat, and pack them in dear little envelope-style wrappers, the ends secured with steel rivets. It shows both care and pride – no bad thing when it comes to food.

You may be wondering why I'm banging on about unsalted butter, especially when many recipes demand extra seasoning. Well, it's pretty obvious that if you're making a cake or dessert the absence of salt is desirable. But even if you're not, unsalted butter has a sweet, creamy, daisy-fresh quality that is absent from salted butter, and quite delectable. Simply spread on bread, unsalted butter adds a wonderful textural presence and distinct flavour; used in cooking, it is far more subtle than salted butter.

If a basket of good bread fills the spirit with hope, and beautiful butter adds faith, the whole meal should be prepared with charity which, as you know, means love. There really is no point in asking friends and family to break bread with you (and forgive the Christian overtones here: I am entirely ecumenical in my beliefs) unless you are prepared to devote time and attention to the food you are serving. If you're not, let me remind you again about Pizza Express or the pub.

...and all the way through there was water – please

It's so easy to serve decent wine nowadays; every supermarket in the land has a good selection that's labelled with useful tasting notes to guide the most vinously naïve of hosts. But I'd like to plead that you give as much thought to providing water for your guests as you do the wine. It doesn't have to be bottled water, although if you live in Suffolk you'll know our mains water tastes utterly vile. The main thing is to make sure the water is freely available and that people don't have to keep asking for it. Whatever quantity you think is required, double it – even more if it's a hot summer's day. Not only will those who are driving thoroughly appreciate your sensitivity to their situation, but so will those of us who end up as babbling inebriates if we don't sup two or three draughts of water to each one of wine. (And, if it is bottled water you are serving, *please* don't add ice and lemon, both of which completely negate the point of having bottled water in the first place.)

prawn cocktail

If you've bothered to read the preamble, you'll understand why I am beginning with this immensely popular, tried and (far too often un-) true first course. Prawn cocktail is a real delight when made properly, and just a mass-catering con when carelessly put together. Having said that, you can fake a pretty good 'pink' sauce as long as the mayonnaise is of decent quality. Read the list of what's in the jar, and eschew anything that doesn't include eggs and oil (part olive, part vegetable) as its main ingredients. Obviously prawns are available all year round, but in summer you could always replace them with (600g) fresh white crabmeat or lobster, if you're feeling very flush.

mayonnaise · tomato purée · dry sherry (or brandy) · Worcestershire sauce · Tabasco sauce · double cream · two or three romaine or cos lettuces · about a kilo of whole North Atlantic prawns · two lemons

Tip about 300ml good mayonnaise into a bowl and stir in a small squirt of tomato purée (the sauce should be pale baby's-ear-pink, not Jordan's-wedding-pink), a fairly frugal slosh of dry sherry (or even less brandy), a dash of Worcestershire sauce and Tabasco, and enough cream to convert the mayonnaise into thick pouring consistency – plus some seasoning, of course. Taste the sauce as you're going, stirring in a little of the flavourings to begin with, then adding more if necessary.

Pile shredded lettuce into small bowls or large glasses, then add the peeled prawns and finish with a spoonful or two of the sauce – not too much, or it will smother the flavour of the prawns. Serve with quartered lemons, the seeds removed, and thinly cut brown bread and butter. (For a stand-up starter, separate out some Little Gem lettuce leaves and put a spoonful or two of the prawn cocktail into each one, for guests to pick up and munch on.)

prawn, dill and cucumber cocktail

Really this is just a variation on the prawn cocktail theme but perhaps slightly more palatable to those who find the classic Marie-Rose dressing a wee bit too sweet and sickly. As I love sourish foods, particularly yoghurt, this is right up my street: I also like the crunchy little bits of cucumber. Just as above, you can serve this cocktail in individual lettuce leaves, and let everyone help themselves while they're standing around the kitchen talking to you.

half a large cucumber · light herb dressing · sour cream · two or three romaine or cos lettuces · about a kilo of whole North Atlantic prawns

Chop the cucumber into small dice, discarding the seeds. Make a light herb dressing (see page 157) but add chopped fresh dill instead of the mixed herbs, then whisk in a little sour cream to thicken it up a touch. Pile shredded lettuce into small bowls or large glasses, add the cucumber and peeled prawns muddled together, then nap with a spoonful or two of dressing.

big prawns

First, we need to sort out the nomenclature of these prawns. I am most decidedly not talking about tiger prawns, of any hue or provenance. Their quality seems to deteriorate with every passing year (with commensurate devastation of Asia's coastal mangroves due to out-of-control shrimp farming), and they are far better eaten heavily disguised in a curry (Indian or Thai-style) or a lively stir-fry.

What I am suggesting you use are the giant prawns that used to be called Mediterranean prawns, but are now more often described as Madagascan crevettes. You'll find they are always sold cooked (unlike tiger prawns), and they make an easy, luxurious, summer starter.

garlic · mayonnaise · hot chilli sauce · four to six prawns (depending on size) per person · two lemons · baguette or crusty bread

Stir two or three finely chopped (but not crushed) garlic cloves into a jar of good-quality mayonnaise, and stir in a dab of hot chilli sauce. Spoon the spiced mayo into little pots and put one on each plate, together with a bouquet of prawns and quartered lemons, the seeds removed. Hand round a basket of scrunchy warm baguette and some cold butter. (And put out finger bowls or, much easier, packets of lotion-impregnated wipes.)

prawn, avocado and melon salad

An ultra-retro combination of ingredients that goes down as well today as it did 30 years ago, when I first started cobbling this fresh-tasting salad together. Don't make it unless the melons are in tip-top condition – in other words this is something for the summer when the melons from Spain and France are at their best. Even still, you're probably better off buying them a couple of days ahead so you can nurse them to perfect ripeness in the warmth of your own (delightful) home.

about a kilo of whole North Atlantic prawns · a sweet, juicy honeydew or piel de sapo melon (or two heavy, honey-fleshed charentais or canteloupe) · three ripe (but not squishy) avocados · light herb dressing · chopped fresh tarragon, chervil, parsley and chives

Peel the prawns. Cut the melon into bite-sized chunks and the avocado into smaller chunks. Season, then toss all the ingredients in the light herb dressing (see page 157). Sprinkle with chopped herbs (all or some of them) just before serving.

avocado, spinach and bacon salad

Another hoary number but everyone still enjoys this salad; it simply does what it says on the can. You can, of course, cook your own dry-cured streaky bacon – it matters not a whit if it's smoked or unsmoked – and the salad will be all the worthier for it. As for the spinach, even if the packet does say it's washed and/or prepared, it's still worth a good rummage to get rid of any damaged, yellowing leaves or ungainly stalks.

about 200g baby leaf spinach · a bunch of watercress · three ripe (but not squishy) avocados · strong, nutty dressing · about 120g crisp, cooked, streaky bacon · chopped chives

Mix the spinach and trimmed watercress in a large bowl. Cut the avocado into large dice. Gently toss the leaves and avocado with enough strong nutty dressing (see page 157) to leave a fine film – but not so much you could run a diesel engine on it. Divide the salad and avocado among the plates, then scatter on shards of bacon and some chives.

other things to toss with spinach and watercress (dressing recipes on page 157):
– allow a few peeled quails' eggs per person and toss with crumbled (supermarket) cooked streaky bacon, parmesan shavings and the light herb dressing
– combine grapefruit segments (no peel or pith), orange segments (ditto), cubed avocado and toasted pine nuts with the sweet-tart dressing
– toss shreds of cold roast chicken breast with thinly sliced (raw) button mushrooms, a few blueberries and the sweet-tart dressing
– toss a few handfuls of ripped-up, cooked duck (or game) with a handful of toasted pecan nuts (or walnuts), some orange segments and the strong nutty dressing

smoked salmon and blinis with dill and caper crème fraîche

There aren't many people who don't like smoked salmon, but I'm one of them. Well, that's not quite true, I simply don't like the bright orange stuff with slimy band-box-wide stripes of fat running through it that's sold by many supermarkets (and quite a lot of Scottish suppliers, who should know better). Give me properly cured wild salmon and I can quickly change my opinion. Anyway, if you're trying to disguise the less than perfect provenance of your smoked salmon, or want to gussy up some good stuff, this simple combination works a treat.

24 cocktail blinis · about 800g smoked salmon · about 300g crème fraîche · a handful of chopped fresh dill (or tarragon) · a tablespoon or two of capers

Tuck the blinis into a cooking foil package and warm them up in a hot oven for 5-10 minutes. Meanwhile, furl the smoked salmon on to the plates, and mix the crème fraîche with the dill, capers and seasoning, to taste. Put some warm blinis next to the smoked salmon and spoon on a generous dollop of the crème fraîche.

smoked salmon and guacamole

Guacamole also makes a dandy accessory with smoked salmon, even if it seems odd that something innately fatty should taste so good served with something equally fatty. Two wrongs do make a right, occasionally. Make sure the cherry tomatoes are really tiny (or quarter bigger ones), and that the guacamole is fresh and chunky looking – avoid the stuff that looks like green mayonnaise.

three limes · about 300g guacamole · a handful of halved cherry tomatoes · fresh chives · fresh basil · about 800g smoked salmon · a bunch of watercress

Cut two limes into quarters and use one lime for its juice. Mix the guacamole with the tomatoes and some chopped chives and torn basil leaves. Add seasoning and lime juice to taste. Arrange the smoked salmon on the plates and add a dollop of guacamole. Serve with a wedge of lime, and a generous tuft of watercress.

other things that go with smoked salmon:

– grated horseradish (or use creamed horseradish, first checking that the main ingredient is indeed horseradish, and not cheap turnip) stirred into a blend of crème fraîche and mascarpone
– French bean and shallot salad (see page 153)
– a dollop of Avruga caviar (or the real stuff, of course) and sour cream thickened up with a little mascarpone
– free-range scrambled eggs with a little chopped smoked salmon stirred in, served on half a toasted bagel, with a slice of smoked salmon alongside

smoked salmon paupiettes

Very rich and very Eighties, but so what, they taste good. Make sure what follows is on the lean side, though, or you'll have your guests gagging (what an attractive image).

about 500g white crabmeat (or smoked trout or smoked salmon) · 200g cream cheese · chilli powder · lemon juice · eight large slices of smoked salmon · watercress
Mix the crabmeat and cream cheese with a pinch of chilli, a squeeze of lemon juice and seasoning to taste. (If you're using smoked trout or salmon as the filling, whizz it to a rough paste in a food processor first.) For a fairly formal look, you could line small ramekins with smoked salmon, put in the filling and fold the salmon over to make a tidy parcel – otherwise just spread the filling on the smoked salmon and wrap it up like a rug. Serve with a handful of watercress and some thinly sliced brown bread and butter.

potted shrimps

A starter that's as simple as kiss your hand, although there are two pitfalls. The first is serving the shrimps straight from the fridge, the second is heating them up too much. Served ice-cold, the butter in which the shrimps are potted doesn't spread, it fractures – and you can neither taste the shrimps nor the butter. Served boiling hot, the butter turns into an oily puddle and the texture of the shrimps is ruined. For perfect potted shrimps, simply take the shrimps out of the fridge a good hour before you want to serve them (assuming your kitchen is warm). They will then slide out of their pots in a soft but coherent mound. Potted shrimps are quintessentially English and, spread mouthful by mouthful on warm shards of white or brown farmhouse toast, they are quite divine.

One more note of caution: make sure the pots definitely contain brown shrimps. I haven't forgotten the unfortunate time when Young's – normally good potters of shrimp – had to use pink prawns because they couldn't get the real thing. Last but not least, cut the bread for the toast quite thickly – don't even think of using pre-sliced stuff – and trim off the crusts.

eight little tubs of potted shrimps · cornichons (tiny gherkins) or quartered lemons · watercress
Turn the shrimps on to the plates, as described above. Put a little pile of cornichons (or a lemon quarter) alongside, a clump of watercress and triangles of hot toast. Tuck any extra toast into a cloth-lined basket, to keep it warm.

feta, watermelon and toasted almond salad

This is still one of my all-time favourite starters. The flavours are sharp, fresh, cool, and just challenging enough: texture-wise, the crumbly, dryish cheese is lifted by the crisp, juicy chunks of melon and the nuts add a marvellous 'meatiness'. As ever, the secret lies in the excellence of the ingredients, which means using in-season melon and authentic Greek feta. (Despite an EU ruling that feta should have protected geographical status, Denmark continues to demand it be allowed to produce its own lack-lustre version. What hasn't helped the Greeks' cause is that quite recently Danish customs intercepted a consignment of feta, supposedly produced in Greece but actually made in Bulgaria. Red faces all round.) I've suggested using salted, toasted almonds but you could happily use macadamia nuts instead. Best of all are habas fritas: you can find these dried, deep-fried, salted broad beans in any Middle Eastern grocers.

a small ripe watermelon · about 500g Greek feta · a small ripe watermelon · a handful of salted almonds · extra-virgin olive oil

Cover each plate with chunks of melon (as seed-free as reasonably possible), scatter with a handful of roughly cubed feta, then strew with the nuts. Dribble sparingly with olive oil and serve immediately. You can prepare the separate ingredients a good few hours ahead but don't combine them until the last minute as the melon juices will stain the feta.

anchovy, caper and onion bruschetta

I don't think it's my imagination that the sad and inexplicable distaste for anchovies and olives so often demonstrated by the Brits is on the wane. At the Crown and Castle, we used to be frequently asked to 'hold' these salty, sophisticated ingredients, but it's quite a rare request nowadays. Maybe it has something to do with the vastly improved quality... anyway, this is just a pared-down version of that Mediterranean classic, pissaladière. It requires a little cooking but that can be done up to 2 days ahead – just remember to heat the onion mixture up before serving it. The flavours are bold and brash, so it's no surprise that I love them.

two Spanish onions · three or four garlic cloves · olive oil · two tins of anchovies · a handful of black olives · slices of ciabatta cut on a slight angle · chopped flat-leaf parsley

Slice the onions finely and chop the garlic. Heat a generous amount of olive oil in a frying pan over a low flame, then very slowly fry the onions and garlic for 20-25 minutes, or until the onions are really tender and golden. Stir in one and a half tins of anchovies, including the oil from both tins, and most of the black olives, cut in half (and stoned, of course). Put a slice of well-toasted or griddled ciabatta on each plate and then pile on the warm (not hot) onion mixture. Straddle with the remaining anchovies, a few olives and a scattering of parsley.

baked gnocchi with cream, sage and ham

A muddle-it-all-together-and-bung-it-in-the-oven kind of starter, and one you shouldn't begin to consider serving unless the rest of the meal is light. It's not a bit fashionable but, like so many trad dishes, it's sublimely comforting and makes people happy. A simpler dish, gnocchi tossed in a little melted butter and grated parmesan, would make a perfect accompaniment to one of the dark meat stews, such as venison or Catalan beef.

about 1kg fresh gnocchi (from the chilled cabinet) · a (284ml) carton of double cream · 250g mascarpone · two or three fresh sage leaves · about 140g parma ham · finely grated parmesan
Put the gnocchi into boiling salted water, then drain them as soon as the water comes back to the boil. Beat the cream and mascarpone together and stir in the finely chopped sage. Smear a little bit on the bottom of eight gratin dishes, add the gnocchi in a single layer, season with plenty of black pepper and tuck in the chopped ham. Coat with the rest of the cream mixture. The dishes can be put aside in a cool place for a few hours. Shroud the gnocchi with a thick layer of parmesan and bake in a very hot oven for 10-15 minutes, or until the cream is bubbling and patched with colour.

other things to do with gnocchi:
– combine just-cooked gnocchi with enough double cream to coat, then stir in a couple of handfuls of (thawed) frozen peas, a handful of chopped ham and a little chopped tarragon. Cover with finely grated parmesan and bake as above
– do as above, but replace the peas with (thawed) frozen baby broad beans, the ham with roughly chopped gorgonzola, and the tarragon with chopped dill, then bake
– toss fully cooked gnocchi with olive oil, a little finely chopped fresh chilli and strips of wood-roasted red peppers, then strew with finely grated parmesan

parma ham with melon

A classic combination that's always good to eat as long as the melon is really ripe and sweet. Of course, you could also use honeydew, piel de sapo, or charentais melons but I'd avoid the perennially disappointing galia and ogen melons, if I were you – and watermelon simply isn't right for this.

two ripe cantaloupe melons · about 500g very thinly sliced parma ham (or other air-cured ham, such as jambon de bayonne or serrano or san daniele)
It's essential to keep the melon and parma ham apart for as long as possible as slimy ham is horrible (which is why I think ham and tomato sandwiches are an abomination). The melon must be peeled and de-seeded, then either sliced fairly thinly or cut into chunks. Grind black pepper over both melon and ham just before serving.

other things that go with parma ham (or other air-cured hams):

– serve slabs of beautiful, cold, unsalted butter with the ham. Encourage your guests to take a small snip of the butter with each mouthful of ham – it sounds utterly weird but it's how the Italians eat their parma ham and tastes quite wonderful

– peeled and sliced fresh mango or papaya – both fruits are particularly good with the stronger flavoured, smoky, Black Forest ham

– serve a couple of fresh, squishy figs (a cross slashed in the tops, and gently squeezed open) with each plate of ham

pickled herrings with sour cream and apple

I'm not a great fan of pickled herrings but then I'm not the greatest meat-eater in the world, either. If there's one thing being a restaurateur teaches you, it's the ability (and sense) to put things on the menu that other people like eating even if you, yourself, don't. Otherwise, the Crown and Castle would have a menu stuffed full of fish, shellfish and risotto, and not much else. It's my husband, David, who is the herring maven. He is pretty fussy about what constitutes a good herring though, and what goes with them is just as important: this assemblage finds favour.

a (284ml) carton of sour cream · thick Greek yoghurt · fresh dill · sugar · two sharp dessert apples · one shallot · 16-24 pickled herring fillets (depending on size, and any style except creamy)
Mix the sour cream with a little yoghurt (to thicken, rather than flavour), a tablespoon or two of chopped dill, and sugar to taste. Peel and cut the apples into small dice, slice the shallot very finely, then stir both into the sour cream. Serve a dollop with the herring fillets.

pickled herrings with beetroot and horseradish relish

Whatever they do to the cooked, vac-packed beetroot you can buy in every supermarket, I don't like it. The texture becomes as soft and spineless as a motherless jellyfish. I recognise it's useful in an emergency, but if you can bring yourself to spend all of five minutes tucking up some raw, well-washed beetroot in a baggy, cooking foil package, and bunging it in a hot oven for about an hour (depending on the size of the beets), then so much the better. The roots need a quick peel once they've cooled down, but that's it – not so very arduous, eh?

about 600g cooked beetroot · grated horseradish (or horseradish cream) · crème fraîche · 16-24 pickled herring fillets (depending on size)
Grate the beetroot as finely as you can. Combine the horseradish with a few spoonfuls of crème fraîche and add seasoning, to taste. Stir in the beetroot just before serving. The relish should not be too creamy, and you only need to serve a tablespoon or so per person with the herrings.

dressed crab with cress 'soldiers'

Even in the summer, when they are at their best, you won't find dressed crabs in many supermarkets – and you probably wouldn't want to eat them, even if you could. I find most supermarket fish counters pretty disappointing. A giveaway to the freshness of the fish is in the instruction that it must be eaten on the same day as purchase. Given that a piece of genuinely fresh cod will still be fine (if not magnificent) at least four days after it has been caught, this is pretty damning. The way I get round any piscatorial purchasing problems is by shopping online: the fish and shellfish arrives when I want it, and in spanking-fresh condition.

eight medium-sized dressed crabs · mayonnaise · soft green herbs · thinly sliced brown bread · hot mustard and cress (or watercress)

If the 'dressing' of the crab only runs to it having been opened up and cleaned, then put the white meat to one side, and scoop the brown meat into a liquidiser or food processor. Whizz it into a soft mash, with a spoonful or two of mayonnaise – just enough to bind. Pile it back into the shells, then put the white meat back on top. (If you like, you could mix it with a handful of soft herbs, such as fresh tarragon, dill, chervil and/or parsley, first.)

Make eight cress sandwiches using thinly sliced brown bread (this is one occasion when pre-sliced bread is not just permissible but desirable), cut off the crusts, and cut each sandwich into 'soldiers'. Serve the crabs with a small pot (or a big tablespoon) of good quality (home-made? whoa!) mayonnaise alongside, and a few cress 'soldiers'.

sort-of burrata

Burrata is a very soft cow's milk cheese made in Puglia by filling a balloon-shaped lining of curd with more curd and cream. It's incredibly fragile, and must be eaten immediately, which is why you will seldom find it here. I found a recipe for a bastardised version of burrata, using mozzarella and crème fraîche, in the second River Café cook book. Having experimented a little, I've decided it's even better with a mixture of crème fraîche and cream. With a slightly yoghurty, herb flavour, it's fabulous spooned on to garlic-rubbed bruschetta. Buffalo mozzarella tends to come in bigger balls (anything up to 250g) than cow's milk mozzarella.

about 750g buffalo mozzarella · extra-virgin olive oil · fresh mint, basil and oregano leaves · 200ml crème fraîche · 200ml double cream · ciabatta · one or two garlic cloves · bitter salad leaves

Drain the mozzarella, then tear it into large shards. Gently toss with olive oil, seasoning, and a big handful of chopped mixed herbs (going easy on the oregano). Mix the crème fraîche and cream together, pour it over the mozzarella, then leave to marinate in the fridge for 6 to 12 hours.

Just before serving, toast eight slices of ciabatta fairly fiercely then rub one side with the garlic. Pile on the creamy burrata and serve with a clump of bitter salad leaves.

buffalo mozzarella and crushed artichoke crostini

There's a world of difference between the cow's milk mozzarella packed in plastic pouches and buffalo mozzarella sold loose in its own whey (or, even at worst, immersed in its own whey in a waxed paper packet). Most cows' milk mozzarella is as tasteless as macaroni cheese, without the cheese. Buffalo mozzarella has an addictive yoghurt-like flavour that's engagingly assertive, yet cordial enough to be eaten on a regular basis. I say that with some conviction, because whenever we are in the south of Italy we have mozzarella di bufala every single day for breakfast – with and without fresh figs.

about 300g griddled artichoke hearts · salted capers · extra-virgin olive oil · ciabatta · about 750g buffalo mozzarella · wild rocket

Put the artichokes, a tablespoon or two of (rinsed) capers and a slosh of olive oil in a food processor and whizz to a smooth paste. Put a slice of well-toasted or griddled ciabatta on each plate and dowse generously with olive oil. Smear the crostini with the artichoke paste in a casual fashion. Rip the mozzarella into large, shaggy shards, pile it on and around the ciabatta, season well and dress with a little more oil. Finish each plate with a posy of wild rocket.

buffalo mozzarella and comice pear

I can't understand why this oh-so-simple combination is not more popular: for me it beats the usual mozzarella/tomato/basil trio into a cocked hat. It won't work with just any old pears though. Doyenné du Comice (to give this king of pears its formal title) is so very much more seductive than a run-of-the-mill pear, such as Conference. As pears are always picked under-ripe you'll have to be prepared to keep them for a couple of days. A perfect Comice will be deeply fragrant, with madly juicy, tooth-sinkingly soft flesh. The marriage between pear, mozzarella and extra-virgin olive oil is sublime.

about 750g buffalo mozzarella · six ripe Comice pears · wild rocket · mild-flavoured extra-virgin olive oil

Tear the mozzarella into large rags. Quarter, peel and core the pears. Casually stack three wedges of pear on each plate, toss on some mozzarella, add a small heap of rocket and swish the whole lot with olive oil. Season the mozzarella and pear generously with black pepper.

other things to eat with mozzarella:
– replace the artichoke paste (above) with cooked broad beans whizzed to a rough paste with tarragon, roast garlic, extra-virgin olive oil and seasoning
– serve with very ripe, fresh figs, slashed with a deep cross and gently squeezed so they open out like faded tulips
– drape fine slices of parma or san daniele ham next to the torn mozzarella

deli-griddled vegetables with hummus

It's simple, it's summery – the only caveat is you must steer clear of those griddled vegetables that have obviously been 'marked' by a machine to make the lines (rather than genuinely griddled) and which are steeped in cheap vegetable oil, rather than expensive olive oil. A good Italian grocer – physical or virtual – should stock the real thing rather than the industrialised rubbish sold loose on many run-of-the-mill deli counters.

about 300g hummus · a kilo of mixed griddled artichokes, peppers, courgettes, aubergine and 'sun-dried' (in your dreams) tomatoes, all preserved in olive oil · lavash (lasagne-thin flat bread), plain or sesame pitta

All you have to do is put a little mound of hummus on each plate, together with some griddled vegetables, and hand round a basket of warm flat bread.

other things to eat with griddled vegetables:

– crumble Greek feta marinated in extra-virgin olive oil over the vegetables, and add a little chopped chilli and roughly chopped mint leaves

– mix drained labneh (fresh Middle Eastern yoghurt-cheese) with lots of chopped soft herbs, e.g. fresh mint, parsley, chives or coriander, and a little finely chopped (not crushed) garlic and dollop it on the plate with the vegetables

– pistachio, pomegranate and coriander raita (see page 42)

mezé

As Plato advised (oh yes?), a mezé table should offer a wide range of taste, texture and colour, from radishes, olives, cheese and anchovies, to savoury minced meat croquettes and creamy aubergine, chickpea or smoked cod's roe 'salads.' Raid any decent supermarket and/or deli, prepare a few raw vegetables yourself, open up one or two cans or jars, and you should be able to assemble a pretty decent spread. (It helps if you avoid stuffed vine leaves which, in my experience, taste like string vests marinated in battery acid.) Don't forget you'll need fresh herbs, such as parsley and mint, lemon wedges, flat bread or pitta, too.

At least eight dishes of the following: hummus · tabbouleh · tzatziki · taramasalata · barrel-aged feta · olives (black, green, stuffed, plain or marinated) · batons of carrot, cucumber, celery, fennel · lettuce hearts · radishes · baba ghanoush (charred aubergine purée) · griddled artichoke hearts · Greek yoghurt mixed with herbs and garlic · canned marinated seafoods (e.g. sardines, octopus, squid, etc., preferably Spanish, Portuguese or Moroccan) · grilled halloumi · warmed cheese or meat-filled filo pastries · salt cod (or meat) croquettes

Gussy up any shop-bought stuff: e.g. strew chopped flat-leaf parsley over the tabbouleh and serve with wedges of lemon; swirl some olive oil over the hummus and then dust with a little paprika or chilli powder; do the same with the taramasalata; strew chopped chives over the tzatziki.

Right: Mezé

pistachio, pomegranate and coriander raita

You'll see raita listed on most Indian restaurant menus because this cool, fragrant yoghurt is quite sublime with spicy foods. I also love it dolloped on a pilaf and with roast lamb and chicken.

a (500g) tub of real Greek yoghurt · fresh coriander · fresh mint · raw (not salted) pistachios · a pomegranate · (optional) pomegranate molasses

Tip the yoghurt into a bowl and stir in a handful of chopped coriander leaves, a tablespoon of chopped mint leaves, two tablespoons of chopped pistachios and a handful of pomegranate seeds. (I often add a tablespoon of pomegranate molasses, too, because it enhances the flavour: however, it also renders the colour a rather murky café-au-lait, so you may prefer to leave it out.) Add some seasoning to taste, and more herbs or pomegranate seeds, if you like. The raita will keep for at least 2 days in the fridge.

charcuterie

I am always surprised at how many customers at the Crown and Castle order a plate of Spanish or Italian cured meats to start their dinner. When I go out for a meal, I like to order food that I don't eat at home or that's complicated to prepare; on the other hand, we do have marvellous suppliers in the likes of Brindisa and Esperya, and the meats are top-notch. The great thing is that with the proliferation of companies selling excellent food online or by mail order, so does everyone else. To make a good showing, I think you need to serve three or four different types of charcuterie.

First you need to sort out whether you are going to go down the Spanish or Italian route. If you decide on Spain, then I would suggest a selection made from iberico ham or serrano ham (or pata negra, the ham made from free-range, acorn-fed, black-footed pigs that is so divine, and so fiercely expensive, you could happily wear it to Ascot); a spicy cured or semi-cured chorizo (i.e. one that doesn't need cooking); lomo, air-dried pork loin; and salchichón, a salami-like sausage.

Choose Italian cured meats (salume) and the choice is even more extensive. Start with parma or san daniele ham (remembering that prosciutto simply means 'ham' in Italian, not necessarily a supremely good air-cured one) or speck, a punchier smoked ham. Add a distinctive salami, such as fennel seed-flavoured finocchiona; chilli-peppered schiacciata or soppressata; a coarse pork, wild boar or venison salami; or a slice of two of either coppa or capocollo (a big, fat-splotched, ham-like salami).

about 800g assorted cured meats · about 250g good olives or cornichons or baby onions in balsamic vinegar

Arrange the meats, trying to furl or 'wave' at least some of the slices so the effect is not one of pancake-like flatness. Leave a space in the centre of the plate and add a little pile of olives, cornichons or balsamic vinegar-pickled onions – or a mixture of all of them.

bresaola with ricotta

This is another dish where the quality of the ingredient is key to its success. Most people will have bought the type of ricotta packed in 250g plastic tubs. On the tub will be printed a 'use-by' date that is scarily far-distant and means the ricotta has been stabilised to the point where it has lost every scrap of character. Compare it with a crumbling wedge of toothpaste-white ricotta, freshly turned out from its wet paper wrapping and it will instantly show up the pasty, mouth-coating, anodyne stuff to be the foul impostor it is. The whole point of ricotta is that it's a fresh cheese that must be eaten within a few days, not weeks.

Ricotta is usually found in pasta dishes or desserts, but the sweet, mild-flavoured, almost jelly-like consistency is equally gorgeous coupled with the lightly salted, Italian air-cured beef known as bresaola. Just like parma ham, bresaola is a 'protected' product that must come from Valtellina in Lombardy, where they've been salting and naturally ageing their beef for six centuries. Most of the better supermarkets stock bresaola. But, just as with parma ham, it is altogether finer if you can buy it sliced to order rather than pre-sliced in a packet. This is partly to do with flavour but more importantly, texture: the pre-sliced stuff will not be anything like as moist and melting as bresaola cut from a piece. If you can't find bresaola anywhere, then you could replace it with cecina, which is a Spanish, smoked, air-cured beef fillet.

about 500g bresaola (or cecina) · about 500g fresh ricotta · extra-virgin olive oil
Put a few slices of bresaola on each plate, dollop on a spoonful or two of seasoned ricotta, then lace both beef and cheese with a peppery extra-virgin olive oil.

other things to do with bresaola:
– drizzle it with first-rate lemon-infused olive oil (Collona is a great brand) and serve with wild rocket
– serve chunks of ripped buffalo mozzarella sprinkled with a *few* drops of good balsamic vinegar

quails' eggs with celery salt

A starter strictly for those who adore eggs, salt, and brilliant bread and butter, so I'll be first in the queue. Nothing could be simpler, but it's important to know your audience: for many people, the thought of an egg is more repellent than alcopops to a claret drinker. If you come across gulls' eggs (an increasingly rare occurrence) they're even nicer – allow two per person. Don't be tempted to buy ready-peeled quails' eggs, though, as they are quite disgusting.

four or five quails' eggs per person · celery salt · coarse sea salt (e.g. Maldon, Guérande) · mayonnaise · sourdough bread · unsalted butter

Boil the eggs until they are just a tad molten in the middle – that's 100 seconds for the quails' eggs – assuming the eggs are at room temperature to begin with. Afterwards, plunge them straight into ice-cold water so they don't end up with a horrible grey halo round the yolk.

Mix the celery salt with coarse salt crystals and put a little pile on each plate, with a splodge of mayonnaise and the unpeeled eggs. Serve with the best-quality, crackling-crusted, chewy, sourdough bread you can find and cold unsalted butter.

egg mayonnaise

Maybe it's because the rest of the starters on our menu are too exciting to resist, but not as many customers as I'd like order egg mayonnaise when we put it on. Well, I love this simple, classic starter, and I know that Delia does too.

a dozen free-range large eggs · watercress and other English salad leaves · really good mayonnaise · milk · anchovies · cayenne pepper · French bread

Simmer the eggs for eight minutes (if they're straight from the fridge), cool them thoroughly under cold running water, then peel and halve them. Arrange the eggs, yolk side-down, in a three-pointed, Mercedes-badge style, on a not-too-thick bed of salad leaves. Let the mayonnaise down with a little milk to make a good coating consistency, then nap the eggs with it. Criss-cross fine strips of anchovy over each half-egg, then dust with cayenne pepper. Serve with scrunchy French bread.

terrine or pâté with chutney

It's a bit of a restaurant thing, but over the last few years terrines which used to be served with nothing more than a slice of toast and a couple of sad lettuce leaves are now nearly always accompanied by a little pot of chutney, relish or pickles. I think it's a marvellous innovation. I love the way the sharp sweetness of the chutney cuts through the rich fattiness of the terrine, and brings a welcome contrast in texture. The secret is in buying first-rate chutney (sorry, but Branston pickle will not do here), and making an effort to complement the flavours. For example, an onion relish would be great with a coarse pork terrine; courgette pickle with a smooth chicken liver pâté; hot piccalilli (again a good one, like Wendy Brandon's) with a ham hock terrine; or a plum or damson chutney with a duck pâté.

about 750g terrine (or pâté) · good quality, 'home-made' chutney · watercress · hand-cut sourdough or rustic bread
Put a thick slice or chunk of terrine (or pâté) on each plate with a little mound of the chosen chutney, relish or pickle, and some picked-over watercress. Serve with hot, thickly cut toast.

pastrami and celeriac remoulade

As so many starters tend to be fish or vegetable-based, I fall on any decent meaty starter with some fervour, particularly those that aren't just a mini-version of a main course. (Much as I love oxtail and the like, even a small portion strikes me as being too blokey a dish to begin a meal.) You could use salt beef instead of pastrami for this assembly but the stuff they sell in supermarkets is normally a travesty of the real thing, so perhaps that's only a good idea if you live near a good Jewish deli. (As a counsel of perfection, you could blanch the grated celeriac for 10 seconds, refresh, drain and dry it – it's not absolutely necessary but takes off any harshness.)

about 300ml good mayonnaise · grain mustard · lemon juice · double cream · fresh parsley · a head of celeriac · 16-24 slices of pastrami (depending on size)
The remoulade can be made up to 2 days ahead. Mix the mayonnaise with a tablepoon or two of grain mustard, the juice of a lemon, seasoning, and enough cream to thin the mayonnaise to coating consistency. Taste, adjust the balance of mustard and lemon juice if necessary, then stir in a handful of chopped parsley. Peel the celeriac, then grate it coarsely (or put it through the fine julienne blade of a food processor) and immediately stir it into the mayonnaise. Divide the pastrami among the plates and serve with a big spoonful of remoulade.

'Urban peasant food': it sounds really pretentious, but how else to describe dishes that are firmly rooted in a poor, rural culture but nowadays are more likely to be made from ingredients purchased in a supermarket? The wonder is that it's taken barely 50 years for the likes of Italian risotto and Spanish tapas to attain worldwide ubiquity – well, developed world ubiquity, anyway. Personally, I'm all for it. Coming from a sea-faring nation that has long plundered the world for new foods, plants, animals and art (remembering the Elgin marbles, I think I'll skip over the thornier aspects of our history), I am perfectly happy with the idea of eating anything from anywhere, as long as it's honestly wrought.

Genuine peasant food shares a common tenet: the ingredients are, or would have been, indigenous to the area. Pizza is not synonymous with Naples because some nineteenth-century Tesco-types decided to build a huge industrialised pizza plant there (although they undoubtedly have done by now), but because the inhabitants could readily get their hands on very cheap, fabulously flavoured tomatoes, garlic, basil and oregano, and bucket loads of fresh mozzarella. People ate what was locally grown.

urban
peasant food

Unless we live in the countryside or grow our own food, we no longer have the seasonal pleasure of picking, pulling or digging up vegetables and fruits. And, because the same foods are sitting on the same supermarket shelves week after week, it's all too easy to forget that most produce still has a season when it's at its best flavour-wise – and should also be good value, if not dirt cheap. I know the supermarkets do their darnedest to ensure year-round homogeny when it comes to food merchandising but you can easily check the packet, box or shelf-label to see where the produce has come from. It stands to reason that if it's December, and the red pepper you are holding in your hand was grown in Holland, then it wasn't brilliant sunshine that caused it to ripen.

A recent trip to Puglia, in the southern tip of Italy, confirmed that fruit and vegetables which have sprung from ancient earth, and burgeoned under the hot, hot sun, have a saturated flavour and sweetness that would have Ceres herself drooling with delight. The nub of what I am saying is, yes, of course you can use battery-farmed poultry and Oxo cubes to make the chicken and lentil stew in this book: but it only takes a packet-of-fags-more money and a tad of extra thought to make something that's genuinely worth the trouble – and it will be so very much nicer to eat.

The stew can be made up to 3 days ahead. The very easy-to-make dumplings can be whizzed together and plumped on top of the hot stew, to cook, just before you sit down to eat. It seems totally appropriate to start a chapter on peasant food with a recipe that's as stout-hearted and honest as they come. It's also in pride of position because it's so nice to cook something with nary a scrap of chilli or coriander to be seen or tasted: this stew is as quintessentially English as rain on Easter Monday. What's so funny (in both senses; a bit ha-ha and a bit queer) is that with the huge variety of restaurants in this country and the ubiquity of pan-world ready meals in the supermarkets, it's the likes of Thai fish cakes that are now seen as staple fare, while something as simple as this stew has become something of a treat.

I can't deny the herb dumplings do demand last minute attention. If you're really stretched, you could leave them out and just serve the stew with lots of mash instead. But I love the particular texture of dumplings, and the way they sop up the meaty brown gravy with fluffy determination. All in all, I guarantee you'll enjoy this reminder that British food can be jolly good – as long as it's prepared with care.

brown beef stew with dumplings

a very large cast iron casserole, with lid (and enough headroom for the dumplings to swell underneath)

about 75g seasoned flour

a few scrapings of nutmeg

a pinch of dried thyme

about 2kg chuck, top rump or thick rib beef *well-trimmed and cut into large bite-sized cubes*

a large knob of butter

groundnut or vegetable oil

2 Spanish onions *chopped into medium dice*

4 large carrots *scraped and cut into medium dice*

1 stick of celery *de-strung and chopped into medium dice*

3 anchovies

1 bay leaf

about 750ml good beef stock

For the dumplings

450g seasoned self-raising flour

1 teaspoon bicarbonate of soda

a small handful of chopped fresh parsley

1 teaspoon fresh thyme leaves

2 large free-range eggs

250ml full-fat milk

For the stew, put the seasoned flour, nutmeg and thyme into a tray or dish then toss in the beef cubes and coat them. Keep any surplus flour.

Heat the casserole over a medium flame, then put in the butter and enough oil so the combined (melted) fats barely cover the base of the pan. When the fat is very hot (but not smoking) add some of the cubes of beef. Do not crowd the pan or the meat will stew rather than colour – on the other hand, put in enough beef to keep the oil 'occupied' or it will burn. When the cubes have coloured on all sides, remove them with a slotted spoon and put them in a dish. Carry on frying the beef in batches, then leave all the cubes to one side.

If you need more fat to fry the onion, add a little more oil, remembering to heat it up first. Fry the onions over a medium flame for about 5 minutes, stirring occasionally, until they have lightly coloured. Add the carrots and celery and continue frying for a few minutes, still stirring from time to time.

Return the beef cubes to the casserole, stir in any surplus flour, then add the anchovies, bay leaf and enough stock to cover the meat. Give everything a good stir, put the lid on, and bring the contents to a simmer over a medium flame. Reduce the heat and cook the casserole at no more than an idle simmer for about 2 hours, or until the beef is tender and the gravy has thickened.

Continue immediately with making and cooking the dumplings (see below). Or, cool and refrigerate the casserole, then reheat it thoroughly on a low-medium flame before adding the dumplings.

Put the self-raising flour, bicarbarbonate of soda, parsley and thyme in a food processor or electric mixer. Whisk the eggs and milk together. (To save some last-minute faffing about, you can get both these elements ready and waiting a couple of hours in advance.)

Slowly pour the liquid into the flour mixture and whizz into a sticky dough, adding a little more milk or flour, as required. Take out the blade/hook and scrape the dough off it, then roughly fashion eight, roundish dumplings.

With the casserole piping hot, plump the dumplings on top of the gravy, put the lid back on, and cook for about 5 minutes. Flip the dumplings over and carry on cooking for another 5 minutes, or until they are swollen and fluffy. The casserole – and dumplings – can be kept warm for at least 15-20 minutes.

goes well with **buttered cabbage with juniper · the best carrots · jazzy parsnip mash**

The stew can be cooked up to 3 days ahead, but a few extra ingredients need to go in 45 minutes before serving. Catalonia is in the top right hand corner of Spain, as you look at the map. It's rather more famous for 'my name is Manuel and I come from Barcelona' than its beef, as decent grazing land is in short supply. Because of this, there are few recipes for mature beef in the Catalan repertoire, but lots for baby beef, i.e. veal. 'Grown-up' Spanish beef tends to require long, slow cooking, hence this stew. With the addition of bitter chocolate and dry sherry, it's deep, dark and full of flavour – it's also very easy to make.

catalan beef stew

a large cast iron casserole, with lid

about 75g seasoned flour

about 2kg chuck steak *well-trimmed and cut into double bite-sized cubes*

200g cubed pancetta

olive oil

500ml amontillado or dry oloroso sherry

2 large Spanish onions *roughly chopped*

6 garlic cloves *crushed and roughly chopped*

3 sprigs each of fresh thyme, oregano and parsley

2 bay leaves

about 1 litre hot water

1kg pebble-sized potatoes (or larger ones halved or quartered) *scraped or peeled*

55g dark chocolate (at least 70% cocoa solids) *roughly chopped*

1 cinnamon stick

Preheat the oven to 140C fan/gas mark 3

Put the seasoned flour in a large tray or dish then toss in the beef cubes and coat them. Keep any surplus flour.

Put the frying pan over a medium flame, add the pancetta and fry for a few minutes, tossing the bits around until they're lightly gilded. Scoop the pancetta out with a slotted spoon and transfer it to the casserole.

Add enough oil to cover the base of the frying pan, and when it is hot (but not smoking), toss in some of the beef. Do not crowd the pan or the beef will stew rather than colour – on the other hand, put in enough beef to keep the oil 'occupied' or it will burn. When the cubes have coloured on all sides, remove them with a slotted spoon to the casserole. Repeat with the remaining beef.

Turn up the flame, pour in the sherry and bring it to the boil. Deglaze the frying pan for 2-3 minutes, then scrape the contents into the casserole.

Add the onions, garlic, herbs and any surplus flour to the casserole, and enough hot water to cover. Stir thoroughly, cover, and cook in the oven for 90 minutes if you're going to reheat the casserole later on, or about 2 hours if you're serving it straight away. Remove the casserole once or twice to give everything a good stir. On the first occasion, make sure the liquid is merely blipping: if it's doing anything more strenuous, reduce the heat.

Increase the temperature to 160C fan/gas mark 4 and continue with the recipe. Or, cool, refrigerate, then fully reheat before adding the final ingredients.

Carefully stir in the potatoes, chocolate and cinnamon stick and season well. There should be enough liquid to just about cover the potatoes, so add a little more hot water if necessary – remember you want a thick, sumptuous sauce, so don't go mad. Return the casserole, covered, to the oven and cook for 30-40 minutes, or until the potatoes are tender to the point of a small knife. Remove the cinnamon stick and any herb stalks before serving.

goes well with **gnocchi · polenta · spinach with capers**

The brisket can be braised 2 days ahead. There are those who love salt beef, my husband being one of them, and those who take one look at the bright pink, blubbery hulk and suffer an involuntary shudder (me). Brisket is actually breast of beef, and is salt beef before it's been salted. I am pleased to say that when it has been braised really slowly, with lots of herbs, vegetables and red wine, it's a very different kettle of…meat.

This is a sort-of Frenchified braise, but you could use a dark beer, such as Guinness or brown ale, as part or all of the liquid. In this case, omit the garlic and olive oil, and substitute a mixture of vegetable oil and butter for the fat, and add two bay leaves, some thyme and a few sprigs of parsley to the pot.

braised beef brisket

a very large frying pan
a large cast iron
casserole, with lid

200g cubed pancetta *(or unsmoked streaky bacon, chopped)*
olive oil
about 3kg beef brisket *well-trimmed and cut into baby fist-sized chunks*
2 red onions *chopped*
3 garlic cloves *crushed and chopped*

2 sticks of celery *de-strung and cut into medium dice*
3 carrots *cut into medium dice*
1 (75cl) bottle of robust red wine, e.g. shiraz
about 600ml hot beef stock
1 funghi porcini stock cube
a dash of Worcestershire sauce

Preheat the oven to 160C fan/gas mark 4

Heat the frying pan over a medium flame. Add the pancetta and toss it around for a few minutes until it has coloured, then transfer the cubes to the casserole, using a slotted spoon.

Pour in enough oil to cover the base of the pan. When it's hot, add a batch of beef, making sure the pan is not crowded. Colour the chunks on all sides then transfer them to the casserole. Brown the remainder of the beef in the same way and then add it to the casserole.

Add more oil to the frying pan, if necessary, remembering to heat it up. Throw in the onions, garlic and celery, and fry them for about 5 minutes, stirring frequently. Add the carrots and continue to fry for a few more minutes, until all the vegetables have taken on some colour. Transfer everything to the casserole, using a slotted spoon.

Turn up the flame, pour in the wine and deglaze the pan. Let the wine continue to bubble until is has reduced by a good third, then scrape the contents of the pan into the casserole. Add the beef stock, crumble in the stock cube, and add a few shakes of Worcestershire sauce. Season generously with black pepper and lightly with salt.

Put the casserole on the stove, covered, and bring to simmering point. Give the contents a good stir, then transfer the casserole to the oven and cook the beef for about 2 and a half hours. Take the pot out and give everything another stir occasionally. When the brisket is spoonably tender, it's ready.

goes well with **buttery mash (of course)** · **the best carrots** · **buttered cabbage with juniper**

The contents of the pie *must* be prepared at least 8 to 48 hours ahead. The pie can be assembled 24 hours in advance with just an hour's final baking needed.

I was not a bit surprised when Simon Hopkinson's book, *Roast Chicken and Other Stories,* was named by *Waitrose Food Illustrated* as 'the most useful cookbook of all time'. The mystery was why it has not always been so lauded. Idiosyncratic but intelligent, personal but ubiquitous, the recipes and writing are simply about cooking and eating marvellous, unpretentious, honest food. Many years ago, when Simon and I both wrote regularly for Sainsbury's magazine, he gave a wonderful recipe for chicken pie. With some minor (and probably unnecessary) adjustments, I've been serving it to great acclaim ever since.

chicken and mushroom pie

a very large cast iron casserole, with lid
an old-fashioned, enamelled baking tin or a roasting tin, about 37cm x 26.5cm

for the flaky pastry

225g frozen unsalted butter

300g plain flour

about 80ml ice-cold water

1 free-range egg beaten with 2 tablespoons milk

for the chicken

2 leeks *very thickly sliced*

6 shallots *halved*

2 carrots *cut into medium dice*

3 sticks of celery *de-strung and cut into medium dice*

a few sprigs of parsley and tarragon

1 teaspoon black peppercorns

about 1.2kg chicken breasts (with skin and bone)

about 1.2kg chicken thighs (with skin and bone)

about 1.5 litres water

50g dried porcini *soaked in hot water to cover*

about 250g chestnut button mushrooms

80g butter (and/or the fat from the stock)

80g plain flour

400ml full-fat milk

200ml double cream

a small handful of chopped fresh parsley

2 sprigs of tarragon *leaves only chopped*

Preheat the oven to 140C fan/gas mark 3

To make the pastry, use the coarse disc of a food processor to grate the frozen butter then tip it into a bowl with the flour. Using a knife, combine the butter with the flour, then mix in most of the water to make a soft dough, only adding the last splash of water if necessary. Collect the dough into a ball with your hands and keep it refrigerated for up to 24 hours.

Put the leeks, shallots, carrots and celery, herbs and peppercorns into the casserole, then add the chicken in (pretty much) a single layer, and pour in enough cold water to cover. Place the casserole over a medium flame. As soon as the liquid reaches the boil, put the lid on and transfer the casserole to the oven. Cook the chicken for 30-40 minutes, or until it's no longer pink. Remove the chicken and leave it to cool.

Strain the cooking liquid, discarding the vegetables, and pour it into a large saucepan. Add the soaking liquid from the porcini (putting the porcini to one side). Tip in the button mushrooms and bring to a simmer over a medium flame. Cook the mushrooms for a few minutes then scoop them out and put them with the porcini. Bring the stock to a boil over a high flame and bubble furiously, uncovered, for 10-15 minutes, or until there is only about 250ml left. Leave the stock to cool, then refrigerate it so you can skim off any fat and use it to make the sauce later on.

Meanwhile, de-skin and de-bone the chicken, then cut the flesh into large bite-sized chunks. (If the chicken has been refrigerated there should be some lovely jelly – add this to the sauce later on.)

For the sauce, put either the fat from the stock and/or butter into a pan over a low-medium flame. When it starts to bubble, tip in the flour and whisk to a smooth roux. Pour in the milk, whisking furiously, then bring the sauce to the boil, still whisking. Reduce the heat and add the reduced stock, cream, and any chicken jelly there may be. Season and continue to simmer for 5 minutes, whisking occasionally, then stir in the chopped parsley and tarragon. Leave the sauce to cool thoroughly.

Preheat the oven to 180C fan/gas mark 6

Bring the pastry to cool room temperature. Divide it into two lumps, one double the size of the other. Roll out the larger lump on a well-floured surface and use it to line the tin, leaving a thin band of pastry hanging over the edge. Combine the chicken, mushrooms and sauce, and tip the mixture into the tin. Brush the pastry band with the beaten egg and milk wash.

Roll out the remaining pastry to a size just large enough to make a neat-fitting lid, then put it in place. Firmly pinch the lining and lid together. Trim off the excess pastry, using a small knife – blade upwards, and working away from yourself. Pinch the edges together again to ensure a good seal. Brush the pie with the egg wash, then cut out a few leaves from the pastry trimmings to use as decoration. Make four small slashes in the lid, then cook the pie on the middle shelf for 50-60 minutes, or until the pastry is golden brown.

goes well with **buttery mash · purple sprouting broccoli · buttered cabbage (without the juniper)**

The lentils can be cooked up to 3 days ahead. The chicken needs last-minute baking, but the complete dish will then happily wait for a while. Even ardent lentil-loathers have been converted into lentil-lovers with this dish. In fact, part of my remit at the Crown and Castle is to bully reluctant customers into trying them (on the side, of course, and with an assurance that they – the lentils, not the customer – will be instantly replaced, if truly detested). With the spices and coriander giving a sprightly zap to the earthiness of the lentils, and the fondant, wood-roasted peppers adding sweetness, up to date I've had a hundred per cent conversion rate.

Chunks of crisp-skinned, juicy chicken go fabulously well with the lentils – but so do scallops and any meaty white fish, such as cod or halibut. I also love lentils served cold, with soft-boiled eggs and tapenade toasts, but I suspect I'm pushing it a bit now – better stick with the chicken.

chicken and lentil stew

1 very large or 2 large roasting tins
a good-looking, large casserole

for the lentils

olive oil

1 large Spanish onion *finely chopped*

4 garlic cloves *crushed and finely chopped*

1 fresh red chilli *de-seeded and finely chopped*

half a teaspoon ground turmeric

1 cinnamon stick

2 star anise

about 4 green cardamom pods *bashed, husks discarded and seeds crushed*

500g Puy or Umbrian lentils *well rinsed*

1 litre hot chicken or vegetable stock

a large handful of coriander *roughly chopped*

about 100g wood-roasted piquillo peppers *cut into thin strips*

for the chicken

3 tablespoons seasoned plain flour

1 tablespoon smoked (or plain) paprika

6 free-range chicken breasts and 8 boneless thighs (with skin) *cut into double-bite-sized chunks*

olive oil

Heat a large heavy pan over a low-medium flame and when it's hot add enough oil to cover the base. When the oil is hot, tip in the onion, garlic and chilli, and stir thoroughly. Cook gently for about 10 minutes, stirring occasionally, until the onion has softened. Add all the spices and fry for 1 minute, stirring constantly.

Raise the heat, add the lentils and just enough stock to cover them. Bring to the boil, covered, then remove the lid, reduce the flame, and simmer steadily for 15-20 minutes for Puy lentils, or 30-40 minutes for Umbrian lentils. (Only add salt towards the end or the lentils will remain irredeemably gravel-like.) When the lentils are just tender to the bite, remove the pan from the heat – you should be looking at a sloppy, sauce-like mass.

Cool and refrigerate, then reheat when required.

For the chicken, mix the seasoned flour with the paprika: you can have it ready in a large tray or dish several hours before it is needed. Check out in advance, too, whether you're going to need one or two roasting tins, remembering the chicken must bake, not stew.

Preheat the oven to 220C fan/gas mark 9

About 25 minutes before you sit down, start gently reheating the lentils over a low flame in a casserole that's good-looking enough to bring to the table.

Toss the chicken in the seasoned flour. Put in enough oil to cover the base of the roasting tin(s), then heat it in the oven. When the oil is really hot (but not smoking), carefully add the chunks of chicken. Bake for about 15 minutes, turning halfway through, until the chicken is well-coloured but still juicy.

Just before you serve the starter, stir the chunks of chicken into the hot lentils (discarding any fat). Add the coriander and piquillo peppers, then put a lid on the casserole and leave it on a warming plate or in a very low oven for up to 30 minutes.

goes well with **French bean and shallot salad · Belgian chicory salad · leaf salad**

The stew can be cooked a few hours ahead but only add the parsley after the stew has been gently reheated. I love Middle Eastern food. I love the judicious spicing, the gregariousness attached to sharing a myriad dishes, and the all-round, unbuggered-up simplicity of it. Having said all that, I now have to admit this stew would not be recognisable to any Lebanese or Egyptian person. Its wonderful flavours are merely redolent of the Middle East.

The chickens need to be cut into 10 portions – 4 bits of breast on the bone, 2 drumsticks, 2 thighs and 2 wing joints.

chicken, squash and garlic stew

a very large frying pan
a very large cast iron casserole, with lid

about 75g seasoned flour

2 large chickens *each one cut into 10 portions, as above*

a mixture of groundnut and olive oil

1 large Spanish onion *cut into medium dice*

2 heads of garlic *the cloves peeled*

1 fresh red chilli *de-seeded and finely chopped*

2 butternut squash *peeled, de-seeded and cut into double bite-sized chunks*

1 (420ml) can of coconut milk

1 thumb of root ginger *peeled and grated*

2 rosemary sprigs

1 teaspoon cinnamon powder

1 teaspoon ground cumin

about 1 litre hot chicken stock

2 handfuls of chopped fresh parsley

Put the seasoned flour into a large dish or tray and coat the chicken portions in it.

Heat a very large frying pan over a medium flame and add enough oil to cover the base. When the oil is hot, put in a few of the chicken portions, and brown them quickly on all sides. Transfer the chicken to the casserole, then repeat with the remaining chicken, adding more (preheated) oil as necessary.

Using the same pan, fry the onion, garlic cloves and chilli for 4-5 minutes, stirring frequently, until lightly coloured, then add to the chicken. Fry the squash, again without crowding. When the chunks are lightly coloured, add them to the casserole. Stir in the coconut milk, ginger and rosemary.

Now add the cinnamon and cumin to the empty pan and fry for 30 seconds, stirring. Turn up the flame, add a ladle of stock, and deglaze the pan for 1-2 minutes. Scrape the contents into the casserole and add enough stock to barely cover the chicken. Cover the casserole, and bring the contents to a simmer. Gently cook the chicken for about 25 minutes, lowering the flame if necessary, until both chicken and squash are tender. Add the parsley just before serving.

goes well with **chickpea and coriander mash**

The beans can be cooked a day ahead. The casserole can be made a few hours ahead, then gently reheated, and the beans added at the last minute. I am particularly fond of braised or stewed guineafowl, especially in tandem with wintry pulses and root vegetables. It's a nice, honest way of eating fowl. Here I've used meaty Spanish judion beans but you could use butter beans instead.

Ask your butcher to cut each of the birds into 8 portions – 4 bits of breast on the bone, 2 thighs and 2 drumsticks.

braised guineafowl with chorizo and judion beans

a very large cast iron casserole, with lid

500g dried judion beans (or butter beans) *soaked overnight in cold water*

250g chorizo *cut into small dice*

olive oil

3 large guineafowl *each one cut into 8 portions*

1 Spanish onion *roughly chopped*

5 large garlic cloves *crushed and roughly chopped*

3 carrots *peeled and cut into medium dice*

3 leeks *very thickly sliced*

a few sprigs of fresh thyme

1 (75cl) bottle of dry white wine

about 500ml chicken stock

Drain and rinse the soaked beans then bring them to the boil in cold, unsalted water. Cook them for about 30 minutes, or until just tender ('old' beans take much longer to cook), then drain the beans and leave them to one side.

Preheat the oven to 140C fan/gas mark 3

Heat a frying pan over a medium flame, throw in the chorizo and lightly colour it, tossing the pieces frequently. Using a slotted spoon, transfer the chorizo to the casserole. Add enough oil to coat the base of the pan and heat it. Add the guineafowl in batches, frying the pieces just long enough to colour them, then transfer them to the casserole.

Reduce the flame, add the onion and garlic to the pan, and fry for 5-6 minutes, stirring occasionally. Transfer the onion and garlic to the casserole, then fry the carrots and leeks, and add them, too. Tuck in the sprigs of thyme. Turn up the flame under the pan, pour in the wine and bring to a boil. Deglaze the pan for 2-3 minutes, then scrape the contents into the casserole. Add seasoning and enough stock to barely cover the guineafowl, then stir.

Cover the casserole, place it over a medium flame, and bring to a simmer. Put the casserole in the oven and cook it for 60 minutes. Stir in the cooked beans 5 minutes or so before the end.

goes well with **garlic mash** · **purple sprouting broccoli**

The whole dish can be made up to 3 days ahead. The first time we cooked this gutsy stew at the Crown and Castle it was for a dinner accompanied exclusively by different styles of sherry, rather than ordinary table wines. (I make this distinction because although sherry *is* a wine, many people seem to think it's a concoction of olives, brandy and Lucozade – anyway, it has become something of a crusade with us to change public perception.) I should also point out that apart from having the most intense, marvellous flavour, this stew is very dark and dramatic – or so I think. My husband agrees with me about the taste, but not the appearance: he thinks it looks like shit. All I can say is, 'which one of us is the cook in the family?'

Ask your butcher to cut each of the birds into 8 portions – 4 bits of breast, 2 thighs and 2 drumsticks.

guineafowl à la montanesa

a very large frying pan
a very large cast iron
casserole, with lid

about 75g seasoned flour

3 large guineafowl *each one cut into 8 portions*

a mixture of groundnut and olive oil

140g cubed pancetta

8 garlic cloves *crushed and chopped*

500g frozen button onions

500g chestnut button mushrooms *left whole*

1 (75cl) bottle of robust red wine, e.g. shiraz

3 sprigs of rosemary

a few sprigs of fresh thyme

about 1 litre chicken stock

4 tablespoons red wine vinegar

200g vacuum-packed peeled chestnuts

lots of chopped fresh parsley

Put the seasoned flour into a large dish and coat the guineafowl portions in it. Heat a huge frying pan over a medium flame and add enough oil to cover the base fairly generously. When the oil is hot, put in a batch of flour-dusted thighs and drumsticks, and let them colour on all sides. Transfer the pieces to the casserole when they're ready. Lightly brown the breasts, then add them to the casserole, too. If you need to use more oil, remember to heat it first.

In the same pan, fry the pancetta for a few minutes until lightly coloured, then add it to the casserole. In turn, fry the garlic and button onions for a couple of minutes, then the mushrooms, transferring each of them to the casserole with a slotted spoon as they're ready.

Preheat the oven to 180C fan/gas mark 6

Add the wine, herbs and chicken stock to the casserole, then cover it and bring the contents to a simmer on top of the stove. Transfer the casserole to the preheated oven and cook for about 20 minutes, or until the breasts are tender, then remove them and set them aside. Carry on cooking the thighs and drumsticks for another 15-20 minutes, or until the leg bones are decidedly loose.

Remove the thighs and drumsticks from the casserole and put them with the breasts. Pick out the herb stalks and discard them. Bring the juices and vegetables to the boil over a high heat, uncovered, and bubble until the sauce has reduced to a gravy-like consistency.

If you are going to serve the casserole later on, leave the sauce to cool before replacing the guineafowl and stirring in the vinegar and chestnuts. After refrigerating, remove any fat that has come to the surface and then gently reheat the casserole in a moderate oven, stirring the contents occasionally.

Put the guineafowl portions back into the hot sauce and let them warm through over a low flame. Stir in the vinegar and chestnuts – the latter don't need any cooking, just heating up – and, finally, strew with the chopped parsley.

goes well with **buttery mash · spinach with capers · purple sprouting broccoli**

The lamb must be marinated for 2 days. Once cooked the braised shanks will keep for up to 3 days. Putting in a regular winter appearance at the Crown and Castle, it's noticeable that this kind of very English, old-fashioned, club-land food appeals mightily to the chaps and older persons. (In a little mental game that affords me some small pleasure, I like betting on what people are going to order before they order it. More often than not I'm right, although sometimes the odd Ghost-clad nymphet will catch me out by ordering slow-roast pork belly with a sizeable hillock of parsnip mash and gravy.)

Back to business: you must know that even the smallest lamb shank is pretty beefy (duh!) so unless you've got a really big pan – I mean something the size of a preserving pan – then you're not going to able to make this. But, if ever there was a reason to buy a large pan, this stupidly tender, utterly savoury dish is it. It's also stupidly easy to make, so go and buy a monster pan now.

braised lamb shanks

a really big non-reactive dish (for the marination)
a monster roasting tin
a monster pan

1 (75cl) bottle of robust red wine, e.g. shiraz

a few sprigs of fresh thyme

3 sprigs of rosemary

3 bay leaves

1 teaspoon black peppercorns

2 Spanish onions *roughly chopped*

3 medium carrots *roughly chopped*

1 whole head of garlic *broken up and very roughly chopped, skin-and-all*

2 sticks of celery *de-strung and roughly chopped*

8 small lamb shanks

groundnut or vegetable oil

about 1 litre lamb or chicken stock

Mix all the ingredients, except the lamb shanks, groundnut oil and stock, in a deep non-reactive dish, then put in the shanks. If there is not enough marinade to cover them, top it up with some cold water. Refrigerate for 2 days, turning the shanks from time to time.

Preheat the oven to 140C fan/gas mark 3

Take the shanks out of the marinade. Heat a very large frying pan. When it's hot, pour in enough oil to barely cover the base. When the oil is hot, brown the shanks (two or three at a time), turning them so they colour on all sides. Transfer the shanks to a large, deep roasting tin. Pour the marinade over them, add the stock and cover the tin with cooking foil, then cook gently for 3 to 5 hours, or until the meat is spoonably tender. (The huge difference in time depends entirely on how big the shanks are.)

Remove the shanks from the cooking liquid then strain it through a sieve into the monster pan. Discard the vegetables. Bring the liquid to the boil, uncovered, then reduce the flame and simmer gently for about 45 minutes, or until the juices have thickened a bit. (The reason for simmering is that the juices will go cloudy if you boil them.) Put the lamb shanks back into the juices and gently reheat.

If you are cooking the shanks in advance, cool the juices and refrigerate them. Put each shank into a plastic bag, force out as much air as possible, seal and refrigerate. To reheat, put the lamb shanks back into the monster pan with the juices, cover with cooking foil, and reheat over a low flame.

goes well with **chickpea and coriander mash · butter bean and rosemary mash**

The creamy sauce *must* be made a few hours in advance and cooled completely before going on top of the moussaka. The complete dish can be made up to a day ahead. Yes, you're right – this is moussaka, a fine dish that has been damned because of its association with Greek package holidays and impecunious students. The secret is to use very lean lamb (or be prepared to drain off any excess fat); blanch the aubergines rather than fry them; and employ a judicious amount of spicing. My husband adores moussaka, which leads me to believe they hadn't heard of it in St. Andrews during the Sixties – either that, or he's even more open-minded than I give him credit for.

For a vegetarian version, omit the meat (adding some chopped carrot, mushrooms and celery in place of it), use vegetable stock, and double the amount of tomatoes.

Greek shepherd's pie

a very large, deep ovenproof dish or roasting tin

100g butter

100g plain flour

1 litre full-fat milk

a few scrapings of whole nutmeg

100g finely grated parmesan

2 whole eggs and 4 large free-range egg yolks *beaten*

6-8 large sweet potatoes *peeled and thinly sliced*

4 large aubergines *thickly sliced*

olive oil

3 Spanish onions *halved and thinly sliced*

3 garlic cloves *crushed and finely chopped*

2 teaspoons ground cinnamon

1 teaspoon ground allspice

1kg lean, minced lamb

400ml hot lamb or chicken stock

200ml robust red wine, e.g. shiraz

a few sprigs of fresh thyme, oregano or marjoram

1 (400g) can of plum tomatoes *drained, cores removed and roughly chopped*

a handful of chopped fresh parsley

To make the sauce, melt the butter in a pan set over a low-medium flame, then whisk in the flour, and cook for 1 minute, whisking occasionally. Pour in the milk and whisk furiously, getting right into the corners of pan. Raise the heat, and continue to whisk until the sauce has thickened.

Reduce the heat, season, and grate in about a quarter of a small nutmeg. Simmer the sauce for 15 minutes, stirring frequently, then tip in the parmesan and stir until it has melted. Remove the pan from the heat and leave the sauce to cool, stirring occasionally. When it is tepid whisk in the eggs and leave the sauce to get cold, stirring from time to time.

Cook the sweet potatoes in boiling salted water for 5 minutes, then drain and leave them to cool. Blanch the aubergine slices by plunging them, a batch at a time, into a very large pan of boiling salted water for 30 seconds. Take the slices out with tongs and drain them on kitchen paper or tea towels. (Do not refresh them in cold water, as you would normally when blanching.)

Heat a very large frying pan over a low-medium flame and then add enough oil to barely cover the base. When the oil is hot, fry the onions and garlic for about 15 minutes, stirring occasionally, until they have softened and are lightly coloured. Stir in the cinnamon and allspice, and cook for 1 minute.

Put the minced lamb into the pan and fry it for about 10 minutes, or until it's no longer pink, stirring frequently to break it up. Add all the remaining ingredients and some seasoning, then stir well. Reduce the heat and leave the mince to simmer gently for 45 minutes, stirring occasionally. Remove the pan from the heat and leave the contents to cool.

Preheat the oven to 160C fan/gas mark 4

To assemble the moussaka, put a single (i.e. not overlapping) layer of aubergine in the bottom of the dish, then a layer of minced meat, then a single layer of potatoes. Repeat the layers until everything is used up then cover with a thick layer of the sauce. Bake the moussaka for 45-50 minutes, or until the top is golden and set.

goes well with **charred tomatoes · leaf salad**

The lamb can't be cooked in advance but as it needs to browse away for ages, with nary a scrap of human interference, it's not such a big deal. Only the easy gravy needs a little last-minute attention. This is another of those deeply satisfactory recipes where the lamb is reduced to a near-fondant tenderness. I love lamb either like this, or frazzled to a black-edged crisp on a barbecue. I must admit it doesn't look too pretty but the pronounced flavour more than makes up for its died-and-dug-up, Steptoe-ish appearance.

It will pay to get a butcher involved in the preparation of the lamb: ask him to cut off the skinny shank (knuckle) end of the leg, so the joint will fit more easily into the casserole. If he'll also remove the skin and fat, that's a bonus, but it's not so difficult to do yourself. It's very important as an excess of fat will spoil the sauce.

well-buggered lamb

a very large cast iron casserole, with lid

3 **whole heads of garlic** *broken into cloves*

a **little olive oil**

1 **large leg of British lamb (about 3.25kg)** *trimmed of the skin and as much fat as possible*

30g **unsalted butter**

2 **leeks** *finely sliced*

1 **large Spanish onion** *cut into small dice*

2 **sticks of celery** *de-strung and cut into small dice*

2 **carrots** *cut into small dice*

500ml **dry white wine, e.g. sauvignon**

1 **bay leaf**

a **few sprigs of fresh thyme**

about 1 **litre lamb or chicken stock**

Preheat the oven to 130C fan/gas mark 2

To help the skins peel off more easily, put the garlic cloves into a heatproof bowl and cover them with boiling water. After 1 minute, drain the garlic and run cold water over it. Peel the cloves, then leave them to one side.

Heat the casserole over a medium-high flame. Add enough oil to barely cover the base and, when it's hot, brown the lamb thoroughly on all sides, turning it with stout-limbed tongs. Remove the lamb and put it to one side.

Tip out the lamb fat from the casserole and discard it. Add the butter and, when it's hot, reduce the flame to low-medium and tip in the leeks and onion. Fry them for 6-8 minutes, stirring occasionally, then add the celery and carrots. Continue to cook for another 5 minutes, then turn the flame up high. Pour in the wine and deglaze the pan for about 5 minutes, or until the volume of wine has substantially reduced.

Put the lamb back in the casserole, add the bay leaf, thyme and garlic cloves. Pour over enough stock to half-cover the lamb, at least. Put the lid on the casserole and braise the lamb for about 3 hours. **Reduce the temperature to 120C fan/gas mark 1** and braise for a further 2 hours. Turn the lamb over every hour or so.

When the lamb is forkably tender and looks really well-buggered, transfer it to a heated dish placed in a warm place, and drape it loosely with cooking foil. It will keep warm for at least 45 minutes.

Strain the cooking juices into a large pan, reserving the vegetables. Bring the liquid to the boil over a very high heat. Bubble madly for about 15 minutes or until the liquid has reduced by about half. Meanwhile, tip the squishy vegetables (discarding the bay leaf and thyme stalks) into a food processor and whizz to a smooth, thick purée. Whisk this purée into the reduced liquid to make a sauce. Check the seasoning (it will probably need some ground black pepper), then keep the sauce warm until you are ready to serve it.

goes well with **garlic mash · the best carrots · spinach and capers**

The casserole can be made up to 2 days ahead, with the breadcrumb crust needing just a few minutes' grilling before the casserole is served. I think we'd all agree that it's perfectly normal to roast lamb French-style, with garlic, rosemary and, maybe, some anchovies. All I've done here is combine the same ingredients with some white beans and red wine to make a robust stew. And, guess what? It tastes good.

If the casserole won't fit under your grill, you can leave out the breadcrumb crust – it won't be quite as good without it, but neither will it be a disaster.

lamb, garlic and haricot bean casserole

a large earthenware or cast iron casserole, with a lid – one that will slide under the grill later on

2 whole heads of garlic *broken into cloves*

olive oil

2 large Spanish onions *cut into medium dice*

250g unsalted pork belly or pancetta *cut into small dice*

about 2.5kg leg of lamb (boned-out weight) *well-trimmed and cut into large bite-sized cubes*

1 (75cl) bottle of gutsy red wine, e.g. shiraz

50g anchovy fillets *drained*

250g dried haricot beans (or cannellini) *soaked overnight, rinsed and drained*

300ml lamb (or chicken) stock

1 ciabatta *turned into coarse breadcrumbs*

To help the skins peel off more easily, put the garlic cloves into a heatproof bowl and cover them with boiling water. After 1 minute, drain the garlic and run cold water over it. Peel the cloves, then leave them to one side.

Heat a large frying pan over a medium flame and, when it's hot, add enough oil to cover the base. When the oil is hot throw in the onions and fry them for about 10 minutes, stirring frequently. Add the garlic cloves and fry for a further 5 minutes. Using a slotted spoon transfer the onions and garlic to the casserole, draining off as much oil as possible.

Add the pork belly or pancetta to the pan and fry for a few minutes, until the bits have coloured, then add them to the casserole.

Preheat the oven to 140C fan/gas mark 3

Season the lamb generously. Turn up the flame to medium-high and, if necessary, add more oil to the pan and heat it up. Fry the lamb, in two or three batches, turning the cubes so they colour on all sides. Remove each batch to the casserole as it's ready.

Pour the wine into the frying pan and deglaze it over a high flame for about 3 minutes, then tip the contents of the pan into the casserole. Stir in the anchovies, beans and stock, then cover the casserole and put it in the oven. Cook for about 2 hours, or until the lamb is completely tender, giving the contents a good stir halfway through. **You can take the casserole to this point and leave it to cool. Reheat it gently but thoroughly before proceeding with the breadcrumb crust (see below).**

Cover the contents of the casserole with a thick layer of breadcrumbs, then liberally splash them with olive oil. Put the casserole (without the lid) under a preheated medium-high grill, about a hand's length from the elements, and leave it there until a golden crust has formed.

goes well with **garlic mash · fennel and black olive gratin**

The ragoo can be cooked up to 2 days ahead. Reheat it before adding the last few ingredients (which can all be prepared a few hours in advance). I've been a restaurateur for over 20 years and lamb has never ceased to be the best-selling main course – hence the proliferation of lamb dishes in this book. I also have it on good authority that lamb tagine is currently de rigueur at Suffolk dinner parties: rather like the year of Delia's chocolate truffle torte, every hostess from Sudbury to Snape is dishing up this good-tempered Middle Eastern stew in the fuddled belief that it's somehow exotic. Okay, that sounds very snobby but we've been combining meat and fruits in Britain for centuries, so really tagine is not so very new. Anyway, by way of a backlash, I am giving this rendition of the late, great Michael Smith's very English recipe for a 'ragoo', as it was called in the eighteenth century – and there's nary a hint of fruit in sight.

English lamb ragoo

a very large cast iron casserole

about 75g plain flour

a pinch of cayenne pepper (or chilli powder)

a 2.5kg leg of lamb (boned-out weight) *well-trimmed and cut into large bite-sized cubes*

a knob of butter

groundnut oil

the zest of 1 lemon *grated*

3 garlic cloves *crushed and finely chopped*

1 or 2 sprigs of rosemary

4 large carrots *cut into medium dice*

4 sticks of celery *de-strung and cut into medium dice*

about 1 litre lamb (or chicken) stock

2 bunches of slim spring onions *trimmed and cut into three at an angle*

2 teaspoons white sugar

6 largish tomatoes *blanched, peeled, de-seeded and diced*

a handful of chopped fresh parsley

Preheat the oven to 160C fan/gas mark 4

Put the flour into a tray or large dish, add seasoning and the cayenne pepper, then toss in the cubes of lamb and coat them. Keep any surplus flour.

Heat a large frying pan over a medium flame, then put in the butter and enough oil so that the combined (melted) fats barely cover the base of the pan. When the fat is hot (but not smoking), add some of the lamb. Do not crowd the pan or the lamb will stew rather than colour – on the other hand, add enough to keep the oil 'occupied' or it will burn. When the cubes have coloured on all sides, remove them with a slotted spoon to the casserole. Colour the remaining lamb and add it, too. Finally, stir any surplus flour and the lemon zest, garlic and rosemary into the casserole.

Using the same pan, add and heat more oil if necessary. Put in the carrots and celery (in two batches if necessary), and fry for a couple of minutes, tossing the bits so they colour a little. Add them to the casserole, using a slotted spoon.

Pour in enough stock to barely cover the lamb, add seasoning, and give the pot a good stir. Bring the casserole to a simmer on top of the stove, then put the lid on and transfer it to the oven. Cook the ragoo for about 90 minutes, or until the lamb is tender. **You can take the recipe to this point, then cool and refrigerate it. Before reheating the ragoo, first remove any fat that may have risen to the top, and be prepared to add a little more stock.**

Heat a medium frying pan over a medium flame and throw in another knob of butter. When the frothiness starts to subside, toss in the spring onions and sugar. Fry the spring onions for a few minutes, tossing them frequently, until they're well-coloured. Remove them from the pan, blot with kitchen paper and leave to one side. (You can sort out the tomatoes now, if you haven't already done so.) Just before you're ready to serve the ragoo, stir in the spring onions and diced tomatoes, giving them a few minutes to heat through. Add the parsley at the very last moment.

goes well with **tray-baked potatoes · buttered cabbage with juniper · purple sprouting broccoli**

Most of the preparation can be done earlier in the day, with the actual cooking taking about 2 hours. It will then keep warm for up to an hour. A northern Italian dish that translates as 'empty bones', ossobuco is a gentle, rich braise of veal shin bones that should be anything but hollow: it's the marrow inside that helps create the sumptuous sauce. Ossobuco is normally served with risotto alla Milanese. Unfortunately, this saffron-tinted risotto requires as much last minute attention as any other risotto. It's also traditionally finished with a scattering of gremolata – a handful of parsley leaves, a little lemon zest and a clove of garlic chopped together very finely. It certainly gives the dish a clout round the ear, but if you don't want to indulge in a spot of bovine GBH, it really won't matter if you omit it.

Ask the butcher for hind-quarter bones cut from high up as they will be meatier and more tender than the front leg bones – I say 'the butcher' as there isn't a cat in hell's chance you'll find shin of veal in the average supermarket, unless you live in Milano. (And, not true: I've just found some in Waitrose.)

ossobuco

a very large cast iron casserole

8 thick, marrow-filled veal shin bones

about 75g seasoned flour

a few scrapings of whole nutmeg

85g unsalted butter

olive oil

2 carrots *peeled and cut into medium dice*

2 stalks of celery *de-strung and cut into medium dice*

300ml dry white wine, e.g. chardonnay

1 (400g) can of tomatoes *drained, cores removed and roughly chopped*

about 800ml hot chicken or beef stock

Do not remove the membrane that holds the meat together around the perimeter, but trim off any obvious fat or lumpy bits. Mix the flour with a little grated nutmeg then dust the fleshy part of the bones with it.

Heat a very large cast iron casserole over a medium-high flame. When it's hot add the butter and oil. As soon as the sizzling has subsided, put in the veal bones and fry them for 2-3 minutes each side, until lightly browned. Transfer the meat to a plate.

Reduce the flame to low-medium, tip in the carrots and celery, and gently fry for 5 minutes, or until the vegetables have slightly softened. Raise the heat and pour in the wine. Bubble it furiously for 2 minutes then remove the casserole from the heat. Arrange the veal in a single layer in the casserole, then pour in the chopped tomatoes and hot stock.

The dish can be taken to this point a good few hours in advance.

Cover the casserole and put it over a medium flame. As soon as the liquid starts to reach the boil, reduce the heat and simmer very gently for 2 hours, or until the meat is almost falling off the bone. The liquid should reduce down to a fairly thickish sauce. If it looks too thin, carefully scoop out the meat, cover it with cooking foil and keep it warm. Raise the heat, bring the sauce to a boil and cook it, uncovered, until it has thickened a bit. Reacquaint the ossobuco with its sauce and serve.

goes well with **polenta** · **pearl barley and pea ragout** · **spinach with capers**

The dried fruits need to marinate for at least 6 hours. The finished dish will keep for up to 3 days. This rich and aromatic stew is based on the nineteenth-century, Pennsylvania-Dutch style of cooking (although I doubt those clean-living folks would have used any alcohol). Eminently suitable for Christmas when the store cupboard would have been full of dried fruits and spices, it still makes sense to cook this in the winter months. If you can find dried fruit that has not been soaked, sweetened or sulphured, the stew will taste a whole lot better. I wish most of the so-called dried fruit sold by supermarkets to hell – try a health food shop for something approaching the real, chewy, sun-dried truth.

homestead pork and dried fruit stew

a large earthenware or cast iron casserole

150g of mixed dried prunes, apples and apricots

125ml amontillado sherry (or tawny port)

250ml dry red wine, e.g. merlot or pinot noir

groundnut or vegetable oil

about 75g seasoned plain flour

2 teaspoons ground cinnamon

2 teaspoons ground cumin

2 teaspoons ground coriander

half a teaspoon ground mace (or nutmeg)

about 1.7kg lean pork, e.g. pork loin or leg

well-trimmed and cut into large bite-sized cubes

4 large shallots *finely sliced*

2 sprigs of fresh thyme or oregano

2 bay leaves

about 1 litre hot chicken stock

the zest and juice of 1 lemon

Put the dried prunes, apples and apricots in a pan with the sherry and red wine and heat to just below simmering point over a low flame. Remove and leave to marinate for 6-8 hours, or overnight.

Preheat the oven to 140C fan/gas mark 3

Combine the seasoned flour and all the ground spices in a large dish. Toss in the cubes of pork to coat them. Keep any surplus flour.

Heat a large frying pan over a medium flame then pour in enough oil to barely cover the base. When the oil is hot, throw in the shallots and fry them for about 5 minutes, or until they have lightly coloured. Transfer them to the casserole using a slotted spoon.

Reheat the pan over a medium-high flame, adding more oil if necessary. When the oil is hot (but not smoking), toss in some of the pork. Do not crowd the pan or the meat will stew rather than colour – on the other hand, put in enough cubes to keep the oil 'occupied' or it will burn. Once the chunks of pork are coloured on all sides, remove them with a slotted spoon to the casserole, and carry on browning the remainder. Put the pan to one side for a moment.

Scoop out the dried fruits from the marinade (reserving it), and add them to the casserole with the herbs. Tip in any of the remaining seasoned flour and give the pot a good stir.

Return the frying pan to a high flame and pour in the reserved marinade. Bring to the boil and deglaze the pan for 2 minutes. Add the hot stock, bring everything back to the boil, then scrape the contents of the pan into the casserole.

Cover the casserole and put it in the oven to cook for 2 hours, stirring it halfway through. When the meat is tender and the sauce is shiny and thick, it's ready. Just before serving, stir in the lemon zest and juice.

goes well with **honourable European slaw (on the side) · horseradish-stuffed potatoes · Trinity red cabbage**

This is a very easy-going casserole that can be made several days ahead. As if venison weren't robust enough already, here I have coupled it with meaty porcini and chestnuts. Unusually, I am not going to eulogise about this stew because I'd as soon eat roast mole as venomson (sic). But I recognise there are people out there with decent palates who love the stuff. So, if you remained dry-eyed when Bambi's mummy was killed, this very popular casserole (with guests at the C&C) is for you.

venison, chestnut and mushroom stew

a very large frying pan
a large cast iron casserole

olive oil

2 Spanish onions *cut into large dice*

4 garlic cloves *crushed and roughly chopped*

about 75g well-seasoned flour

a few scrapings of whole nutmeg

about 1.8kg trimmed haunch of venison *well-trimmed and cut into large bite-sized chunks*

about 100ml brandy or port

about 1.2 litres beef stock

about 30g dried porcini *soaked in just enough hot water to cover*

1 (340g) jar of redcurrant jelly

250g chestnut mushrooms *wiped and quartered*

1 bay leaf

about 500g vacuum-packed peeled chestnuts

Heat a very large frying pan over a low-medium flame, then add enough olive oil to cover the base. Toss in the onions and garlic and fry them for about 10 minutes, stirring occasionally, until lightly coloured. Transfer them both to the casserole. Put the (unwashed) frying pan to one side.

Combine the flour with a little grated nutmeg in a large dish or tray. Toss in the venison chunks and coat them. Keep any surplus flour. Reheat the frying pan over a medium-high flame, adding more oil if necessary. When the oil is hot (but not smoking), toss in some of the venison. Do not crowd the pan or the meat will stew rather than colour – on the other hand, put in enough cubes to keep the oil 'occupied' or it will burn. Quickly colour the venison on all sides then transfer the chunks to the casserole, using a slotted spoon. Repeat with the rest of the venison.

Return the frying pan to a high heat, and carefully pour in the brandy (it can flare up), plus a cupful of stock and all the porcini soaking liquid. Boil rapidly for a couple of minutes to deglaze the pan. Reduce the heat and add the redcurrant jelly. Stir to dissolve the jelly, then pour the contents of the pan into the casserole, add any surplus flour and enough stock to cover, then stir again. Add the porcini, chestnut mushrooms and bay leaf to the casserole and stir them in.

Cover the casserole and place it over a medium-high flame. As soon as the liquid comes to the boil, reduce the flame and very gently simmer the casserole for 1 hour. Stir in the chestnuts and continue cooking for a further 30 minutes.

goes well with **gnocchi · jazzy parsnip mash · the best carrots**

However partial we are to food from other cultures – and we are – it's highly unlikely there'll come a time when the Sunday roast doesn't represent the acme of gastronomic pleasure to the vast majority of Brits. Even teenagers – mad for pizza, Chinese takeaway and cheese burgers – will eschew the 'foreign muck' they're so otherwise fond of, and willingly acquiesce to joining the family for a 'roast dinner' – even though the 'dinner' is as likely to be a carvery lunch at the local pub as it is a noontime meal at home. It seems the need to consume trencherman slabs of roast meat on Sunday is as firmly embedded in our genetic make-up as buying a poke of chips on a Friday night.

Interestingly, beef consumption has shown a steady increase over the past 10 years but pork has done even better, probably because it appears the best value of the mainstream meats. The consumption of both pork and beef are double that of lamb, which has stayed pretty consistently at about 7kg per head per year. I find this fairly modest intake quite strange as lamb has always been the best selling main course in all three restaurants we've owned over the last 22 years. Of course, we do sell a lot of steak, and it's only recently that pork (particularly belly) has been deemed stylish enough to put on a restaurant menu at all, but it still seems a slightly unconvincing statistic to me. Perhaps it's skewed by domestic rather than restaurant sales: lamb is relatively expensive with fewer cheap cuts available, compared to beef and pork.

big roasts

In any case, poultry sales far outstrip any other meat. Where we consume 17kg of beef per person per year (surprised? don't forget hamburgers…) we get through a fairly staggering 29kg of chicken. According to the Red Meat Industry Forum (aka the Red Mean Industry Forum, thanks to a possibly apt misspelling on its website), this increase can be attributed to the perception that chicken is healthy (avian flu?) and the prevalence of chicken-based ready meals – and who am I to argue with the Red Meanies?

Enough of the statistics, although they do show that despite the burgeoning number of vegetarians, deep down in our collective soul we remain implacable carnivores. The French, after all, still refer to us as *rosbifs* and, according to the Commission for Racial Equality, when British people of varying ethnicity were asked to define the concept of 'Britishness', roast beef, Yorkshire pudding and Sunday lunch were oft mooted (along with cucumber sandwiches and curry, it must be said).

Pedantic though it may be, I'd like to make the point that most food described as 'roast' is actually baked. All those gastropub blackboards advertising roast cod or roast butternut squash are telling porkies: true roasting requires hot air to circulate freely around the food, as in a spit-roast, whereas that roast cod they're touting will start off being browned in a frying pan on the hob and then transferred to the oven, where it's *baked*, not roasted. Similarly, as soon as you put a chicken in a roasting tin, with a large proportion of the surface area in contact with the metal, you've prevented true roasting from occurring: wrap a sheet of cooking foil around it and the chicken is closer to being braised. No bad thing, I hasten to add, but roast chicken it is not.

Over the last couple of centuries, there has also been a great deal of research, argument, discussion, theorising, dissertation and comment as to whether it's a good or bad thing to brown a joint at high temperature before reducing the heat. While we now know for a fact that this initial browning does not seal the juices in, as was once thought, it certainly contributes to the flavour. To quote from *On Food and Cooking*, written by the estimable Harold McGee, '…Searing does not seal, but it does brown: it won't prevent flavour from escaping, but it *creates* flavour via the complex browning reactions.'

There is currently a fashion (an intelligent fashion, when in the hands of someone like Heston Blumenthal) for cooking meat at very low temperature for a very long period. Carefully controlled, and using large cuts of meat, this works well and the meat will definitely be the juicier for it. Personally, I am loathe to depart from the searing process, because of the colour and flavour, but I am all for keeping the meat moist and tender.

The best way for the home cook to achieve this is by respecting the 'resting' period that all roast meats, poultry and game require. To quote Harold McGee again, 'A roast that is cut when fresh from the oven will leak much more juice than it would if it were first allowed to sit for 15 minutes…the water-holding capacity of the tissue increases as the temperature evens out and begins to drop.' Another advantage is that as long as the joint is put in a warm place to rest, you can leave it for a lot longer than 15 minutes. I left my 6kg Christmas turkey crown on the warming plate of the Aga for a good 45 minutes, with a thick, clean, oven cloth draped over it, and the turkey was still warm and very tender when I came to carve it. Talking of which, it's really important to use a sharp knife as a blunt one will compress the tissues, once again promoting the flow of juice on to the carving board. Okay, you can pour the juices into the gravy, so they won't be wasted, but it will be to the detriment of the meat itself.

With all this chat about how to achieve the perfect roast, I've yet to mention what is possibly the most important criterion: the quality of the meat (or poultry) must not only be excellent to begin with, it must also be a suitable cut for roasting. All the loving preparation in the world will not transform a frozen Taiwanese chicken into a bird of beauty, and you can buy a piece of brisket with the finest Scottish provenance but if you attempt to roast rather than braise it, the result will still be crap. 'Horses for courses' is particularly apt when describing how to choose the right cut of meat for the right method of cooking (especially if you live in Belgium where I was once duped into eating horse meat: actually it's all right, if a bit sweet). It also explains why the meat in most carveries is so appalling and so cheap: top rump looks fine and is marvellous stewed, but it's rubbish when it's roasted – or baked, if we also apply the correct terminology.

For the perfect roast you should buy your meat from a good butcher; choose a cut that's meant to be roasted; bring the joint to cool room temperature before putting it in the oven; let it rest properly after it comes out; and use a sharp knife to carve it. Easy.

The chicken can be prepared up to 12 hours ahead. Start the cooking about 45 minutes before serving, and finish the pan juices just before you sit down. This recipe is such a cliché, I am almost embarrassed to put it on paper – but obviously not quite embarrassed enough. The truth is it does taste darned good. All you have to do is stuff a good dollop of cream cheese and herbs between the flesh and the skin of some chicken breast quarters, pat them with crushed coriander seeds, then bake them in a hot oven until the skin turns wonderfully crispy, sticky and golden, while the breast remains moist and juicy.

baked herbed chicken

a very large, sturdy roasting tin that will also go on top of the stove

3 garlic cloves *crushed and finely chopped*
a mixed handful of chopped fresh chives, parsley and tarragon
2 good pinches of fresh thyme leaves
about 300g cream cheese
8 chicken breast quarters, on the bone

olive oil
3 teaspoons coriander seeds *well-pounded*
about 200ml of whichever white wine you're serving with the meal *you are serving wine??!!*
1 (568ml) carton of double cream

Mix the garlic and herbs with the cream cheese until well blended. Gently open up the gap between the skin and the flesh of each chicken quarter and push in a good dollop of the mixture, easing it down towards the wing joint.

Oil and season the chicken, then pat the crushed coriander seeds evenly over the skin.

Preheat the oven to 200C fan/gas mark 7

Put the chicken in the roasting tin, skin-side down, and bake for 25 minutes. Turn the quarters and cook them for another 20-25 minutes, or until they are golden brown and the juices run clear if you jab the thickest part with a small, sharp knife. Take the chicken out of the tin and leave it to rest in a warm place for 15-20 minutes.

Just before you serve the chicken, put the roasting tin over a fairly high flame, pour in the wine and bring it to the boil, scraping up all the bits from the bottom. Add the cream and vigorously boil again. When you have a thickish, toffee-coloured sauce, remove the pan from the heat and season to taste. Divide the chicken among warmed plates and pour a little sauce over each portion.

goes well with **garlic mash · tray-baked potatoes · watercress and orange salad**

Prepare the stuffed crown up to 24 hours ahead. It will need to go in the oven a little over 2 hours before you sit down. Turkey comes in for a lot of flack from sophisticated chefs and food writers who deplore its lack of flavour and general chavness. I think the point they're missing – especially urbanites without a cellar, outhouse or larder – is that any apparent timidity of flavour is because the bird has *not been properly hung*. Regardless of whether it's free-range, organic, black or bronze-feathered, turkey will taste of little more than sliced bread if it hasn't been allowed to get somewhat high. I learnt this one Christmas, many years ago, when I ordered the turkey far too early (I thought). It hung around in the cellar for a good 10 days and I am not going to pretend I wasn't a tad dismayed at the decidedly whiffy smell when it arrived in the kitchen. But the pong disappeared on cooking (as it does with any game), the flesh was juicy and the flavour astoundingly good.

Another thing about turkey is that, on the whole, people prefer the white breast meat. The trouble is, buy a turkey with a big breast and you buy a turkey with socking great legs as well (the first of Jade Goody's many appearances in this book). After the initial enthusiasm for sandwiches and risotto has diminished, you're left with a gradually decaying carcass that takes up far too much room in the fridge and isn't pretty (there she goes again…)

In recent years, we've been offered the solution in the form of the turkey 'crown', which is a good-looking, eminently practical joint, comprising the entire breast. Of course, you cannot hang this as you would a whole bird, but life ain't perfect and you can, at least, buy an organic crown. To help keep it moist and add some flavour, I use this stuffing made from fresh, mild cheese and lots of herbs. If you can't be bothered, then just strew the meat with herbs and stick a couple of cut lemons in the tin – but whatever you do, don't dispense with the butter-soaked muslin cloth because it helps keep the meat juicy.

Most of the cooking times given for turkey are far too long, which is why it's so often dry. The reason is two-fold. First, turkey is mostly cooked on Christmas Day – hundreds of thousands of them, all over the country. The result is a big drop in power over the National Grid (true!) with oven temperatures often severely compromised. Second, the Turkey Information Service has to cover itself in case some eejits have not defrosted their cheap, imported, frozen birds properly and, rather than cooking the turkeys, are gaily incubating salmonella bacteria instead. If the bird is fresh and of sound, accountable provenance, it does not require brutal treatment when it's dead.

herb-stuffed turkey crown

a napkin-sized piece of muslin (or threadbare tea towel)
a large roasting tin with a wire cooling rack that fits inside

250g unsalted butter *softened*

2 leeks *finely chopped*

1 Spanish onion *finely chopped*

1-2 sprigs of mint *leaves finely chopped*

2-3 sprigs of thyme *leaves finely chopped*

3-4 sprigs of tarragon *leaves finely chopped*

about 100g cream cheese

50g finely grated parmesan

50g fresh white breadcrumbs

the grated zest of 1 lemon

about 12 thin slices of parma ham

a 3kg turkey crown (boned-out weight)

Melt a knob of the butter in a large frying pan placed over a low flame and fry the leeks and onion for 8-10 minutes, stirring frequently, until they've softened but are still blonde. Leave to cool.

Put the herbs in a food processor and add 50g butter, the leeks and onion, cream cheese, parmesan, breadcrumbs and lemon zest. Add seasoning, then pulse until the mixture forms a rough, sticky, dough-like mass.

Lay a large piece of cling film on the work surface. Place just-overlapping slices of parma ham on it, to form a large rectangular shape big enough to wrap round the crown. Put the crown skin-side down in the middle of the ham, then wedge the stuffing between the breasts. (Jade, stay out of this…) Fold the turkey round the stuffing, then use the cling film to roll the crown back up, with the parma ham binding the joint together. **You can refrigerate the prepared crown for up to 24 hours, then bring it to cool room temperature before roasting it.**

Preheat the oven to 200C fan/gas mark 7

Remove the cling film, then put the turkey on the rack in the roasting tin and season it generously. Melt the remaining butter in a saucepan over a low flame. Take the pan off the heat and put in the muslin. Squidge it around until it has mopped up every drop of butter, then drape it over the turkey.

Roast the turkey for 30 minutes, then **reduce the temperature to 160C fan/gas mark 4** and cook it for another 60 minutes. Whip off the muslin and continue to roast for 40 minutes, then thrust a skewer into the thickest part (avoiding the stuffing). If the juices run clear, rather than pink, it's ready – otherwise, try again in 10-15 minutes. Leave the crown to rest in a warm place, with a piece of cooking foil or a thick oven cloth draped over it, for up to 30 minutes.

goes well with **roasties · Yorkshire pudding · leeks in tarragon cream sauce**

Start roasting the goose about 3 and half hours before you want to serve it. The pears can be made 2 weeks ahead. I don't know why I used to be so suspicious about goose. Even when I was quite happily tucking into grouse and pheasant, I still had deep reservations about goosey-gander. Anyway, I was wrong: once I'd made the first move, goose repaid my trust handsomely with its sumptuous flavour and reverse-of-dry texture. (I don't want to describe it as 'fatty', or you might end up behaving as irrationally as I once did.) With some good gravy and these spiced pears, roast goose is truly delectable.

Save the goose fat and use it to roast potatoes; strain it to filter out the bits, then store the fat in a sealed container in the fridge, where it will keep for a few months. The best pears, flavour wise, are Comice but for this recipe Williams, Rocha or Packham would be fine, although you may need a couple more if you're using the pert but pretty Rocha.

roast goose with spiced pears

a very large roasting tin with a wire cooling rack that fits inside

450ml cider (or white wine) vinegar

a splash of balsamic or sherry vinegar

the juice and whole zest of 1 lemon

450g golden caster sugar

3 whole cloves

1 teaspoon ground coriander

1 teaspoon ground allspice

1 teaspoon ground cinnamon

1 small thumb of root ginger *peeled and grated*

6 firm but not rock-hard pears *peeled, quartered and cored*

a large goose (about 5kg dressed weight) *wiped with a damp cloth and dried with kitchen paper*

Put the vinegars, lemon juice and zest, sugar, spices, and ginger into a heavy saucepan over a low flame. Stir until the sugar crystals have completely dissolved then raise the heat and bring to the boil. Add the pears, reduce the heat and leave them to simmer for 5-10 minutes, or until they're just tender. Leave them to cool in the poaching liquor: they can be refrigerated, still in the marinade, for a couple of weeks, although they can also be used immediately.

Preheat the oven to 220C fan/gas mark 9

Prick the goose all over with a darning-type needle, especially the fatty parts along the sides, neck and vent. Season it well, then tuck some foil around each leg to prevent unsightly scorching. Before starting the cooking, bear in mind that you will need to siphon off the fat (with a baster, preferably) at least once, and probably twice. **Be very careful when removing this extremely hot excess fat.**

Lay the goose breast-side down on the rack in the roasting pan, and put it in the oven for 40 minutes. **Reduce the temperature to 170C fan/gas mark 5** and continue to roast for 100 minutes. **Raise the temperature to 200C fan/gas mark 7,** turn the goose breast-side up and cook it for a further 45 minutes. Remove it from the oven and leave it to rest in a warm place for 25-45 minutes, with a piece of foil draped over it. Carve, and serve with the pears.

goes well with **'toast rack' potatoes** · **horseradish-stuffed potatoes** · **Trinity red cabbage**

Most of the sauce preparation can be done up to 2 days ahead. The duck takes an easy 40 minutes, and the sauce can be quickly finished while it's resting. It is a truth universally acknowledged that even a large duck will only feed four people. It is equally veracious that roast duck provides the most delectable eating. The drawback is that carving a duck is a real bugger: by the time the bird has been hacked to pieces and the carver has got over the shock of seeing the small amount of meat that has been recovered, everything else is stone cold. My solution is to buy duck quarters, and let everybody get on with their own hacking.

Partly because there are no cavities to stuff, and partly because I loathe putting stuffing into cavities (where I have a mental picture of it festering away, all warm and greasy, while the bacteria multiply to plague-like proportions) I've taken those traditional helpmeets, sage and onion, and made them into a sauce instead. And jolly good it is, too. Just one word of warning: use ordinary onions, not Spanish ones, otherwise the sauce will end up tasting far too sweet. This is not just because the handsome Spanish onions are particularly mild, but because the sauce is made with marsala. Although marsala can be dry (like port and sherry), the style most widely available in this country tends to be dark and sticky, with hints of caramel and vanilla. Using Spanish onions in this sauce would make it far too sickly.

roast duck with sage and onion sauce

1 or 2 large metal roasting tins, together with wire cooling racks that fit inside

for the sage and onion sauce
50g unsalted butter
2 tablespoons groundnut or vegetable oil
4 large onions *finely diced*
100ml marsala
400ml really well-flavoured chicken stock

300ml dry white wine
10-12 large fresh sage leaves *finely chopped*
1 (284ml) carton of double cream
for the duck
8 meaty duck quarters *wiped clean, the skins pricked freely, then liberally salted*

To make the sauce, heat the butter and oil in a very large, non-stick frying pan over a low-medium heat, then tip in the onions. Cook them for about 30 minutes, stirring occasionally, until they're meltingly soft and deeply honeyed. Turn the flame up high, pour in the marsala and boil for 3-4 minutes, stirring frequently, until the onions are syrupy and jammy looking. Remove the pan from the heat.

In the meantime, bring the stock to a boil over a high flame and add the wine. Continue boiling furiously for 10 minutes, with the pan uncovered. Scrape in the onion mixture and sage.

You can make the sauce up to this point, then refrigerate it for up to 2 days.

Preheat the oven to 210C fan/gas mark 8

Arrange the duck quarters skin-side up on the rack(s). Roast them for 40 minutes, or until the skin is crisp and dark golden, and the meat is completely cooked – this is not an occasion for pink duck, if there ever is one. You may need to drain off the fat once or twice: very carefully pour it into a heatproof bowl and use it for roasting potatoes. Leave the duck to rest in a warm place for 15-20 minutes before serving it.

Meanwhile, to finish the sauce, bring the stock-and-onion mixture back to the boil, pour in the cream and bubble briskly for 5-8 minutes. The sauce should take on a café-au-lait colour and be of coating consistency. Taste, and adjust the seasoning before serving.

goes well with **roasties · celeriac purée · Trinity red cabbage**

The confit *must* be made at least 2 days, and anything up to several weeks, in advance. Less than 15 minutes' oven-blasting is needed before serving. 'Confit' comes from south-west France, and signifies a process of salting, slow-cooking and preserving meat – often goose, duck or pork – in its own fat. You can buy goose fat in most good supermarkets but if you haven't got quite enough you can use up to thirty per cent lard – no more. With an intense flavour, fondant texture, and crisp skin, this is surely the finest way to eat duck, and a real doddle to cook.

slow-roast duck confit

a very large
roasting tin

for the confit
8 large duck legs
80g coarse sea salt
a few sprigs of thyme or marjoram

a few dried bay leaves *crushed*
10 garlic cloves *crushed*
olive oil
about 1kg duck or goose fat *melted*

Put the duck legs into one or two large, non-reactive dishes that will take them in a single layer. Combine the salt, all the herbs and garlic, then rub the mixture over the legs. Refrigerate the duck for 48 hours, turning the legs once.

Preheat the oven to 120C fan/gas mark 1

Carefully scrape everything off the duck, reserving the herbs and garlic but discarding any liquid. Heat a frying pan over a high flame and when it is hot, pour in enough oil to barely cover the base. When the oil is hot, put in the duck legs, skin-side down. Fry them for 3-4 minutes, or until the skin is golden brown, then turn them and cook for a few more minutes.

Transfer the duck and any fat from the pan to a roasting tin. Arrange the legs skin-side up, scatter on the reserved seasonings, then pour on enough melted fat to barely cover the duck. Roast the legs for about 3 hours, or until the meat is nearly falling off the bone. Allow the legs to cool a bit, then put them into a plastic container. Using a sieve, carefully pour in the still-warm fat, making sure the duck is completely covered. Seal the container and refrigerate the legs for anything up to 4 to 6 weeks.

Preheat the oven to 210C fan/gas mark 8 when you want to finish cooking the duck.

Bring the legs to warm room temperature, scrape off most of the fat, then place them skin-side down in a roasting tin. Roast the legs for 5-6 minutes, then drain off the fat (it can be re-used as long as you filter out any debris), turn the legs and roast for another 5 minutes, or until the duck skin is as dry and crisp as an autumn leaf.

goes well with **chickpea and spinach stew · gently curried peas · watercress and orange salad**

All the preparation can be done up to 3 days ahead, with the final roasting taking a mere 30 minutes or so. We all know that roast pheasant can be as dry as Melba toast, but not if you cook it like this, with the legs slowly baked in plenty of fat and seasoning, and the breasts given a quick blast. Yes, there's some preparation work to be done, but it will pay off in dividends when you find you are actually enjoying eating the tender, toothsome dark meat and juicy, pinkish breast meat. (You can, of course, cook any small game birds the same way.)

roast pheasant, parts I and II

(for the final cooking)
a very large
roasting tin

4 plump hen pheasants *oven-ready*

2 teaspoons juniper berries *crushed*

2 bay leaves *crumbled if dried, finely sliced if fresh*

a big pinch of dried thyme

4 garlic cloves *crushed and roughly chopped*

groundnut or vegetable oil

about 150g pancetta or unsmoked streaky bacon *thinly sliced*

Take a pheasant, fully extend one of its legs, and cut through the skin attaching it to the breast. Note where it's hinged to the carcass and sever between the two joints. Repeat with the other leg. Reveal the wishbone and cut it free, then break away as much of the carcass as you can, leaving just the crown (i.e. the two breasts still on their ribs). Sever the two little joints to free the crown entirely, then trim off any fine ribs, yellow fat, shot-damage or other unlovely bits, to leave a neat joint.

Preheat the oven to 120C fan/gas mark 1 for the legs.

Tidy up the legs, wipe them with damp kitchen paper and then pack them in a snug-fitting ovenproof tin or dish, in a single layer. Strew with all the herbs and garlic, and season well. Pour in enough oil to barely cover the legs, then slow-roast them for at least 2 hours, turning them halfway through, until they're unmistakably tender. Leave the legs to cool in the tin, still immersed in the fat. If you are going to refrigerate them for longer than a day, store the legs in a large plastic bag or tub, packed in the fat.

Preheat the oven to 210C fan/gas mark 8 for the final cooking.

Season the crowns, then drape them with slightly overlapping slices of pancetta to cover them completely. Scrape all the gubbins off the legs and discard it.

Leaving enough room for the legs to go in a bit later, put the crowns in the roasting tin. Roast them for 12 minutes, then add the legs and continue to roast for another 10-15 minutes, depending on the size of the birds and how pink you like your game. Leave the pheasant to rest in a warm place, draped with cooking foil, for 15-20 minutes before serving.

goes well with **celeriac purée · pea and pancetta fricassée · leeks in tarragon cream sauce**

Prepare the saddle a few hours ahead and put it into roast just under 2 hours before it's required. There probably are more expensive cuts of meat, but not many that come readily to mind. The hideous amount of money involved does guarantee an impressive-looking joint of lamb – but, more importantly, a saddle of lamb is beautifully tender and carves like a dream. I'd save this – or beef fillet – not for people you want to impress (a ghastly notion anyway) but for a special occasion when you're surrounded by people who love good food as much as you love them.

Because of the spicy Moroccan-style sausage meat stuffing, this particular saddle of lamb will have unusual attitude. If you want to play it safe, then leave out the merguez and substitute a more benign assuagement (or even sausage meat, preferably lamb).

Ask the butcher to bone out the saddle, freeing up (and reserving) the thin strips of fillet that lie underneath the larger canons, and to leave it untied.

merguez and spinach-stuffed saddle of lamb

a large roasting tin with a wire cooling rack that fits inside

500g leaf spinach

500g merguez sausages *skinned*

a big pinch of ground cinnamon

2 large egg yolks

a little double cream

a 2.2kg saddle of lamb (boned-out weight) *untied*

olive oil

a bunch of dill (or fennel)

Blanch the spinach in boiling water for a few seconds, then drain and squeeze it as dry as you can or the stuffing will be too damp. Chop the spinach coarsely then put it in a large bowl with the skinless sausage meat, cinnamon, egg yolks and enough cream to bind the mixture into a firmish wodge.

Place the saddle skin-side down on the work surface, open it up and put the fillets to one side. Season the lamb, then run the stuffing right down the middle, stopping just short of the ends (it will squish out when you re-tie the saddle otherwise).

Turn your attention to the fillets: you want to reduce the thickness and increase the surface area because they're going to be laid over the stuffing, to act as a protective 'bandage'…so, slit each one lengthways, without cutting all the way through, then open each one out – like a book. Lay these fillets on top of the stuffing, then fold the flaps of the saddle back over and wrap it up in a neat, long roll. Tie the saddle up with string, starting with a loop around the middle, then one at either end, then fill in the gaps, securing the saddle every inch or so.

Preheat the oven to 210C fan/gas mark 8

Rub the saddle with olive oil and season it. Pour a little water into the roasting tin (to help stop the frazzling), put in the rack and strew some fennel on it. Put the lamb on top and roast it for 20 minutes. **Reduce the temperature to 160C fan/gas mark 4** and continue to roast for 65-70 minutes. Take the lamb out, drape a bit of foil or a thick oven cloth over the top, and leave it to rest in a warm place for 20-30 minutes before carving it into thick slices.

goes well with **fennel and black olive gratin · roast red pepper salad · interesting couscous**

Allow up to 36 hours for marination, then start roasting the lamb about 2 hours before you want to serve it. It's undeniable that lambs allowed to scour old-established mountain pasture produce meat with a nuttier, slightly more gamey flavour than lowland lambs. Cook any lamb very rare, though, and all you can taste is wet string. I'd much rather eat knackered lamb but perfection is pleasantly pink.

If you ask your butcher to bone out the leg, carving will be easier than peeling a banana. Needless to say, you won't find this kind of service at the average supermarket where the staff on the butcher's counter wouldn't know a pig's trotter from an oxtail. All the more reason to use a real, traditional butcher.

herb-rubbed leg of lamb

a large metal roasting tin with a wire cooling rack that fits inside

1-2 sprigs of rosemary *leaves finely chopped*
4 bushy sprigs of oregano *leaves chopped*
6 garlic cloves *crushed*
a 2.5kg leg of lamb (boned-out weight) *untied*

extra-virgin olive oil
1 tablespoon fennel seeds
6-8 bushy sprigs of thyme

Combine the rosemary, oregano and garlic and rub the mixture over the flesh side of the lamb. Put the leg back into shape, then tie it up with string to keep everything neatly in place. Pour a spoonful of olive oil into the palm of your hand, rub it all over the leg, then season with ground black pepper and fennel seeds. Leave the lamb to marinate in a cool place for anything from 24 to 36 hours.

Preheat the oven to 160C fan/gas mark 4

Put the wire rack in the roasting tin, strew it with the thyme and place the lamb on top. Roast for 100 minutes (this is allowing 20 minutes per 500g for pink meat, as is probably best – for just-brown meat, allow 25 minutes per 500g). If you want to cook the leg for any longer then you're on your own: I am absolutely not a snob about well-done meat but there's a stage beyond which there's little point in eating the results.

Leave the lamb to rest in a warm place, partly covered with foil or a thick oven cloth, for at least 20 minutes and up to 45 minutes. Untie the string before commencing the (easy) carving.

goes well with **'toast rack' potatoes** · **butter bean and rosemary mash** · **chickpea and spinach stew**

Poach the ham up to 12 hours ahead, then glaze and start to roast it about an hour before you sit down. This is a bit of a cheat in as much as the ham is poached first, to ensure it remains completely succulent: the roasting part comes at the end and is really just to give it a glamorous appearance, and an extra burst of flavour. I think hot ham is one of the unsung glories in the repertoire of British cooking. With a mash of some sort and carrots, this makes a really fine Sunday lunch.

Ham or gammon? Essentially ham is simply a cut from the top half (i.e. the thigh) of a pig's hind leg while a gammon is cut from the ham and then cured and/or smoked. Why the word 'ham' is so much more engaging, I don't know, but it is. Again, it's absolutely essential that you buy good-quality ham from a proper butcher, most of whom will have their own special cure, e.g. Suffolk, Wiltshire or Bradenham. I made the mistake of buying what appeared to be a decent piece of middle-cut gammon from a supermarket once and only discovered on opening up the plastic wrapping that the cheeky buggers had tied various bits and pieces together, to make what looked like a proper cut. Outrageous.

Flavour the stock with whatever roots and herbs you have to hand, bearing in mind to go easy on the carrot as it can make the stock too sweet (and that you'll want to save the stock to make a terrific lentil soup or split pea soup). Give everything a good wash, then cut the veg into chunky pieces.

hot glazed ham

a very large saucepan
(or preserving pan)
a large roasting tin
with a wire cooling
rack that fits inside

a 4kg middle-cut piece of unsmoked gammon
a selection of any or all: 2 leeks, 2 carrots,
3 sticks of celery, 1 large onion (or 4 shallots),
a bulb of fennel, a small bunch of parsley, a
couple of bay leaves, 10-12 peppercorns, a few
juniper berries or cloves

for the glaze
150g smooth Dijon mustard
2 teaspoons ground coriander
1 teaspoon ground cloves
400g golden demerara sugar

Put the gammon (hereafter called ham) in the saucepan, cover it with cold water, and slowly bring it to a boil over a medium flame. As soon as the water starts to look busy, drag the pot off the stove, drain off the water and rinse the ham of any scum.

Start again, with enough cold water to cover, and the pot herbs packed round the ham. Half-cover the pan and bring it to a simmer over a medium heat. Turn down the flame immediately and leave the ham to cook very gently – the water just blipping occasionally – for 2 and a half hours. Take the pan off the heat and leave the ham to cool in the broth, especially if you're going to wait several hours before continuing with the recipe as keeping the ham moist is the name of the game.

Preheat the oven to 200C fan/gas mark 7

Mix the mustard, spices and sugar together. Take the ham out of the broth and cut away the skin and enough fat to leave it pleasingly fringed. Cross-hatch the fat with a sharp knife, then smear it with the mustard mixture. Put the ham on the wire rack in the roasting tin and pour in about a litre of stock (to save the pan from an unholy, stuck-on mess later on). Cook the ham for 40 minutes (if the ham is still warm) or 60 minutes (if the ham has been allowed to get quite cold). Bake until the glaze looks suitably shiny, and the meat is hot. Leave the joint to rest for 15-30 minutes before serving – or you can let it cool completely, of course.

goes well with **butter bean and rosemary mash · red-hot sweet potato gratin**

the Bawden family's roast ham

I ate the best ham of my life last Christmas. Rob bought a half-ham on the bone, weighing about 6 kilograms from his local Suffolk butcher, Rolfe's in Walsham-le-Willows. He then poached it (using almost exactly the same roots and herbs as described opposite), allowing about 20 minutes to the pound. But halfway through the cooking time, he took it out of the broth and started roasting it.

He put the joint on a baking tray, covered it tightly with foil, and sat the tray in the Aga, on the floor of the top right-hand oven (i.e. at high temperature). He left it there to roast for the remainder of the cooking time, less the final 30 minutes. At this point he took out the ham, poured off the cooking juices, and then cut off the skin with a sharp knife, leaving a good band of fat behind. (He's also in the habit of cutting the skin into strips, putting it on a tray, returning it to the hot oven to crisp up – and then eating it when no-one else is looking, but that's doctors for you...)

Rob then scored the fat and plastered on a thick poultice of soft brown muscovado sugar (about 150g) mixed with English mustard powder (2 tablespoons). The ham was put back in the oven for 30 minutes, until the glaze was almost burnt. The triumphant resulting of all this pork-pandering was the most succulent, essence-of-pork ham, each slice edged with a wonderfully crunchy, savoury crust. Quite marvellous. (He also made a sauce with the juices, redcurrant jelly and cream; it was very good but rather upstaged by his youngest son's gratin dauphinois, which was perfect.)

The marination takes from 12 to 24 hours. The pork goes in the oven about 6 hours before you sit down to eat and needs no attention. A recipe along the same lines of the Asian-style pork belly recipe that follows overleaf, here a boneless pork shoulder is first marinated, the treated to a long swelter in a low oven. The result is the tenderest, richly flavoured meat – with little work on the cook's part.

ultra-slow roast pork shoulder

a large roasting tin

5-6 garlic cloves *crushed and chopped*

2 big thumbs of root ginger *peeled and grated*

the juice and zest of 2 limes

2 teaspoons coriander seeds

2 teaspoons ground black pepper

3-4 tablespoons olive oil

3.5kg rolled pork shoulder (boned-out weight)

Put all the ingredients, except the pork, in a food processor and pulse into a sludge. Slather this mixture over the flesh side of the pork and leave the shoulder to marinate in a non-reactive dish for 12 to 24 hours.

Preheat the oven to 210C fan/gas mark 8

Put the joint in a large roasting tin, rub the skin with olive oil then dash it with fine sea salt (to help the crackling crackle). Roast the pork for 30 minutes, then **reduce the temperature to 120C fan/gas mark 1** and continue to cook for 4-5 hours, or until the juices run clear when you shove a fine skewer into the middle.

Let the pork rest in a warm place for 20-30 minutes, with a piece of cooking foil or a thick oven cloth draped over it.

goes well with **red-hot sweet potato gratin · chickpea and coriander mash · gently curried peas**

The fillets can be prepared and even browned a few hours ahead, leaving just 25 minutes or so for the final baking. As far as the cooking is concerned, this is a walk in the park. The only faintly arduous part is ensuring the pork tastes of something. Try one of the traditional breeds, such as Tamworth or Gloucester Old Spot: it will have been lovingly reared and you'll be astounded at the depth of flavour compared to most 'ordinary' pork.

Pork fillet is also known as tenderloin and is the porcine equivalent of fillet steak. Depending on the size, you will get two or three portions from each loin.

pancetta-wrapped pork fillet

a large roasting tin with a wire cooling rack that fits inside

about 2kg pork fillet *trimmed of any sinew and fat*

a few handfuls of mixed soft green herbs, e.g. fresh parsley, tarragon, chives *leaves chopped*

about 20 very thin slices of pancetta

groundnut or vegetable oil

Fold the tail end of each fillet back over itself to make a uniform barrel-shape. Season the fillets, then cut each of them into individual (about 200g) portions, making sure you keep the folded-over piece intact. Roll each little barrel in the herbs so they're pretty well covered.

Make a line of overlapping slices of pancetta, then place a barrel of pork crossways on top and wrap it up, smoothing the joins with your hands – the fat will hold everything in place.

Take a heavy frying pan and heat it over a medium flame. Add a little oil and when it's very hot, fry the barrels, in one or two batches, turning to colour them on all sides and seal the pancetta wrapper. Transfer the barrels to the wire rack set in the roasting tin. **You can take the recipe to this point.**

Preheat the oven to 180C fan/gas mark 6

Roast the pork for 10-12 minutes then turn the barrels and cook them for a further 10-12 minutes. Leave them to rest for 5-10 minutes. Just before serving, cut each barrel in half at a wide angle.

goes well with celeriac purée · red-hot sweet potato gratin · pea and pancetta fricassée

You need to start this recipe at least 3 days in advance. After the initial cooking the belly will keep for up to 4 days and just needs a quick blast in a very hot oven before serving. The pork-savvy Chinese have long been fans of the belly cut; they steam, smoke, stir-fry and simmer it. We turn it into streaky bacon, and that's about it. However, the last few years have seen pork belly take up residency on almost every restaurant menu, from Esher to Edinburgh. The joy for us restaurateurs is that it's not only immensely flavoursome, it's also bloody cheap… well, we need some comfort (and a bit of margin) at a time when it costs more to buy a single cod than a DVD player.

I've allowed a generous amount of pork belly for eight, but it makes slicing through the ribs far easier when it's in a big piece. Anyway, the belly is very good cold, or you can cut any leftovers into strips and use them in a stir-fry.

Asian-style slow-roast pork belly

a big metal roasting tin with a wire cooling rack that fits inside

for the marinade

10 red chillies *de-seeded and roughly chopped*

3-4 thumbs of root ginger *peeled and grated*

5 whole heads of garlic *the cloves peeled and roughly chopped*

8 star anise *roughly bashed*

about 12 cardamom pods *roughly bashed*

2 teaspoons Chinese 5-spice powder

about 3.5kg pork belly *cut between the ribs into 2 equal-sized pieces*

1 or 2 handfuls of coarse sea salt

Make a rough 'mash' of all the herbs and spices and plaster it all over the flesh side of the belly: rub the sea salt into the rind side. Sandwich the two pieces of belly together, flesh touching, wrap the bundle tightly in cling film and leave it in the fridge for 3 days.

Preheat the oven to 130C fan/gas mark 2

Pour a little water into the roasting tin, put in the rack and place the bellies on top, skin-side down. Cover the whole tin with cooking foil and cook for 5-6 hours, depending on the thickness of the bellies. To check if the meat is done, pull on one of the thickest bones and it should slide out like a chocolate flake from a '99' ice cream. Remove the bellies from the oven.

Turn up the oven to 230C fan/gas mark 9.5

While the oven is heating up, take out all the rib bones, using tongs if necessary. Scrape off as much marinade as possible. Put back the bellies (still on the racks, but uncovered and skin-side up) and cook for 15-20 minutes, or until the crackling has crackled.

Take the bellies out of the oven, peel off the crackling (being careful!), scrape off the layer of fat underneath, and leave everything to cool. Refrigerate for up to 4 days, with belly and crackling separately wrapped in cling film. Bring to room temperature before continuing.

Preheat the oven to 230C fan/gas mark 9.5 to finish cooking the bellies.

Put the pieces of belly, fat-side down, in a roasting tin and cook them for about 15 minutes, turning them halfway through so the meat is well-coloured. Cook the crackling for about 10 minutes on a separate baking sheet until it's snappily hot.

goes well with **honourable Asian-style slaw · Asian-spiced potatoes and onions**

Trinity-style slow-roast pork belly

I love this righteous, simple way of cooking pork belly. We had it for dinner just the other night and every single person wiped their plates clean. Prepare and cook the belly in exactly the same way as opposite, including the salting, but mash up the ingredients below to make a very different marinade.

5 whole heads of garlic *the cloves peeled and roughly chopped*

about 50g fresh rosemary *roughly torn*

about 50g fresh thyme *roughly torn*

5-8 fresh bay leaves *roughly torn*

1 heaped tablespoon black peppercorns *roughly crushed*

goes well with **tray-baked potatoes · buttery mash · pea and pancetta fricassée**

The pork needs to marinate for 12 to 24 hours. Start roasting the joint about 2 hours before you sit down. Pork can be very disappointing, but not if you buy rare breed pork, i.e. old-fashioned animals, bred to be fat and luscious-tasting, then brought up – and despatched – with kindness and care. Cooked relatively slowly, with a good larding of appropriate flavourings, and finished with a lacquering of honey, this is roast pork at its simple best.

Ask the butcher to bone out the loin but leave the rind on (rind that he then enthusiastically scores) and to leave the joint untied.

honey and herb-roast loin of pork

a metal roasting tin with a wire cooling rack that fits inside

4-6 garlic cloves *crushed and finely chopped*

2-3 bushy sprigs of fresh thyme *leaves chopped*

1 sprig of fresh sage *leaves chopped*

2 sprigs of rosemary *leaves chopped*

olive oil

2 pinches of ground cloves

about 2.5kg pork loin (boned-out weight)

5-6 tablespoons runny honey

500ml dry apple juice or medium-dry cider

Combine the garlic and herbs. Working on the flesh side, lightly oil the meat, dust it sparingly with the ground cloves and then season it with ground black pepper. Spread the herb mixture over the meat, using your hands to help distribute the flavourings. Roll the meat up loosely, then leave it to marinate in the fridge for 12 to 24 hours.

Preheat the oven to 210C fan/gas mark 8

Curl the loin into a fat sausage shape, and tie it up with fine string: start with a loop round the middle, drawing it tight and knotting it, then move to each end, then fill in the spaces, making a knotted loop every inch or so. Make sure the rind is absolutely dry, smooth it with oil, then rub in plenty of fine sea salt (all of which helps the crackling).

Put the joint on the rack in the roasting tin and cook it for 30 minutes. **Reduce the temperature to 160C fan/gas mark 4** and continue to cook for another 40 minutes. Remove the pork and brush it with the honey. Continue to cook the joint for another 45 minutes, pouring the apple juice or cider into the pan halfway through.

Leave the pork to rest in a warm place, draped with a piece of foil or a thick oven cloth, for 15-30 minutes. (If the crackling needs any crisping up, cut it off in one piece, put it on a tray and bung it in a very hot oven or under the grill.)

goes well with **apple sauce · roasties or horseradish-stuffed potatoes · the best carrots**

The beef can go in the oven about 2 hours before you sit down to eat (and the Yorkshires can cook while the beef is resting). There is something truly magnificent about a great, glistening stand of roast beef: it's impressive, evocative and, for a few minutes at least, all seems right with this stumbling country of ours. Truth to tell, though, I actually prefer all the gubbins that goes with the beef, especially Yorkshire pudding and cauliflower cheese.

Most people regard sirloin as the quintessential joint, but wing rib can also be very good: ask your butcher to chine the sirloin and cut out the thick sinew as it will make carving very much easier.

roast sirloin of beef

a large roasting tin

about 4kg sirloin of beef (on the bone)

dry mustard powder

Preheat the oven to 210C fan/gas mark 8

Season the beef well and dust it with a little mustard powder. Put the sirloin in the roasting tin, the backbone standing vertically, and cook it for 30 minutes. **Reduce the temperature to 140C fan/gas mark 3** and continue to roast it for about 80 minutes for medium-rare beef, which is a good, democratic level of doneness – anyone who likes it well done can have the ends.

Remove the sirloin from the oven, drape it with cooking foil or a thick oven cloth, and leave it to rest in a warm place for about 30 minutes. This is hugely important, not just because the beef will be infinitely more tender for being allowed some relaxation time, but because you can whack up the oven and cook the Yorkshire puddings at the temperature they like (which is not 140 degrees).

(do I need to tell you the beef) goes well with **roasties · cauliflower cheese · the best carrots**

The beef must be cooked 4 to 48 hours ahead. The dressing should be made no more than a day in advance. The idea of doing a lot of cooking on a bright summer's day is not only anathema to any sensible cook, the guests can end up suffering as well. In any case, cold roast beef that has been cooked with the express purpose of being served cold is very different from leftover meat.

Normally beef fillet is sold with the chain attached: this is the strip of meat that runs alongside the main barrel of the meat. Remove as much fat and sinew as you can, without detaching the chain entirely, then tie the fillet back into shape using fine kitchen string. Depending on size, you may need two fillets.

cold fillet of beef with sauce ravigote

a metal roasting tin with a wire cooling rack that fits inside

about 1.8kg beef fillet *well trimmed, as above*

olive oil

dry mustard powder

for the sauce ravigote

a dab of Dijon mustard

the juice of 1 lemon

about 200ml groundnut or sunflower oil

2 large vine tomatoes *blanched, peeled, de-seeded and chopped*

a handful of fresh parsley *leaves finely chopped*

1 bushy sprig of mint *leaves finely chopped*

1-2 bushy sprigs of tarragon *leaves chopped*

a small handful of watercress *leaves fairly finely chopped*

1 shallot *finely chopped*

2-3 anchovy fillets *chopped*

1 tablespoon capers (preferably salted) *rinsed and chopped*

1 small gherkin (or 2 cornichons) *chopped*

Preheat the oven to 220C fan/gas mark 9

Lightly smear the beef fillet(s) with olive oil and a little mustard powder, then season well.

Heat a large, heavy frying pan over a very high flame for 2-3 minutes. When it's almost smoking hot, put in the beef and colour it well on all sides, including the ends. Transfer the beef to the rack set in a roasting tin and cook it for 20 minutes. This will produce very rosy beef: for medium-rare carry on cooking for another 5-6 minutes. Remove the beef and leave it to cool completely.

To make the dressing, whisk the mustard, a little lemon juice and some seasoning together, then whisk in the groundnut oil. Taste, and add more lemon juice or seasoning, as required. Mix the other ravigote ingredients together, and stir them into the dressing to make a thick, sludgy sauce. Serve the sauce in a bowl and hand it around for everyone to help themselves.

goes well with **charred tomatoes · Belgian chicory salad · leaf salad · French bean and shallot salad**

The beef needs to marinate for about 24 hours: cooking takes a mere 20 minutes or so. I have a wretched memory, but I am pretty sure this recipe originated a zillion years ago at Hintlesham Hall – not when we were there but in Robert Carrier's glittering reign. I think it's something I gleaned from his cookery school – a critical success only surpassed by its commercial failure. Whatever, this is a stunningly good way to cook a fillet of beef. My husband actually bothered to ascertain whether I was going to include it, and if you knew how extraordinary that level of interest is, well…

Normally beef fillet is sold with the chain attached: this is the strip of meat that runs alongside the main barrel of the meat. Remove as much fat and sinew as you can, without detaching the chain entirely (unless you're very extravagant), then tie the fillet back into shape using fine kitchen string. Depending on size, you may need two fillets.

One more thing: don't attempt this recipe if you only like well-done beef as the absence of fat will render it dry and tasteless. It's best cooked no more than the rare side of medium-rare.

Japanese-style fillet of beef

a large metal roasting tin with a wire cooling rack that fits inside

about 1.8kg beef fillet *well trimmed, as above*
6 tablespoons sake (or fino sherry)
6 tablespoons Japanese soy sauce
6 tablespoons mirin
6 tablespoons cold water

1 heaped tablespoon caster sugar
2-3 garlic cloves *crushed and finely chopped*
1 thumb of root ginger *peeled and grated*
groundnut or vegetable oil

Put the beef into a snug-fitting, non-reactive dish. (I am not going to keep acknowledging that you may be dealing with two fillets: take it as read.)

Whisk all the other ingredients together, except for the groundnut oil. Pour this marinade over the beef and massage it in a bit. Cling film the dish and marinate the beef for about 24 hours, turning the fillet every few hours… or when you remember, which is not always the same thing.

Preheat the oven to 220C fan/gas mark 9

Remove the beef from the marinade, pat it as dry as you can with kitchen paper and then smear it with a little oil.

Put a large frying pan over a high flame. When the pan is blazing hot, put in the fillet and quickly brown it on all sides, including the ends, using a pair of stout tongs.

Transfer the fillet to the rack in the roasting tin and cook it for about 20 minutes, depending on the thickness/size of the fillet. Leave the beef to rest in a warm place for 10-15 minutes before carving it.

goes well with **honourable Asian-style slaw · purple sprouting broccoli · red-hot sweet potato gratin**

All the preparation should be done a few hours ahead. Put the beef in the oven about an hour before you want to serve it (and, unusually, straight from the fridge). Do I need to apologise for including such a trad recipe? I don't think so, as long as the beef stays juicy and pink. The pastry-wrapped, mushroom-clad beef fillet would look even more spectacular if you stuck a price tag in it: fillet of beef doesn't come cheap. But if you are looking for a swishy dish that's a guaranteed winner, I think you've found it.

Part of the expense is in the fact that you can't use the tail end of the fillet for this recipe: the barrel of meat needs to be a uniform size. If you can't buy a middle-cut piece of fillet weighing as much as you'll need to feed eight, you will have to buy two pieces. The ingredients list is sufficient for the total quantity of beef, whether you are using one or two fillets. However, I am only giving the method to prepare one fillet, as it will over-complicate the recipe if I try to cover both permutations. With your superior brainpower, you won't find it difficult to divide the ingredients and repeat the procedure.

The only real problem with cooking beef Wellington successfully is that the mushroom duxelles can make the pastry soggy. Some food writers suggest a protective lining of finely made pancakes or pancetta or parma ham: I think the bresaola I've used here offers a more apt – and flavoursome – solution. Don't use ready-rolled puff pastry here as the size may not be big enough; use a block of pastry instead. Oh, and with this quantity of mushrooms (which looks huge, but cooks down), I'd use a food processor to chop them.

beef Wellington

a very large frying pan
a large non-stick
baking sheet

groundnut or vegetable oil

1.8kg beef fillet *very well trimmed*

dry mustard powder

85g unsalted butter

3 shallots *finely chopped*

800g flat chestnut mushrooms *wiped and fairly finely chopped*

the juice of 1 lemon

2 bushy sprigs of thyme *leaves finely chopped*

100ml amontillado sherry

150ml double cream

about 200g finely sliced bresaola

a 400-500g block of puff pastry

1 small egg *whisked with a little cold water*

Heat the frying pan over a medium-high flame, add enough oil to cover the base meanly, and let it get very hot. Season the beef then put it in the pan and color it quickly on all sides. Remove the fillet, let it cool completely, then dust it scantily with mustard powder. Leave it to one side.

To make the duxelles, heat the frying pan over a low-medium flame and then add the butter. When it stops frothing, add the shallots and fry them gently for 2-3 minutes, stirring frequently. Add the chopped mushrooms, lemon juice and thyme, and fry for 10-15 minutes, stirring occasionally, until the mushrooms look decidedly soft.

Turn up the heat, add the sherry, give the pan a good stir, then let it bubble away until the liquid has disappeared. Add the cream and do the same thing: you should now be gazing happily at a thick, dryish, chunky purée (which is oxymoronic but so is Freddy Starr and he still makes me laugh). Remove the pan, season to taste, then leave the duxelles to cool completely.

Tear off a large piece of cling film (or baking parchment) and lay it on the work surface. Arrange barely overlapping slices of bresaola in the centre of the cling film, enough to cover the beef completely. Spread the duxelles over the bresaola, then put the beef fillet in the middle. Using the edge of the cling film to help the procedure, wrap the bresaola and mushrooms round the beef as tightly as possible – like a Swiss roll. Put the cling-filmed beef in the fridge for 30 minutes, or up to several hours.

On a well-floured work surface, roll out a sheet of pastry in a rectangular shape (no thicker than the cover of a hard-back book) large enough to enclose the fillet. Brush the edges with the egg wash. Carefully unwrap the beef from the cling film and put the fillet in the centre of the pastry. Wrap it round, sealing the join firmly, and trimming any excess pastry from the ends so they're not too wodgy. (Pity the poor sod who gets the end piece, otherwise.) Turn the parcel so the join is on the bottom, then refrigerate it on the baking sheet for at least 30 minutes, or for several hours.

Preheat the oven to 160C fan/gas mark 4

Brush the parcel with the egg wash, then bake the Wellington for 30 minutes. **Turn the heat up to 200C fan/gas mark 7** and continue cooking for another 5-10 minutes, or until the pastry is golden and puffy. Leave the beef to rest in a warm place for 15-20 minutes before carving.

goes well with **'toast rack' potatoes** · **celeriac purée** · **spinach with capers**

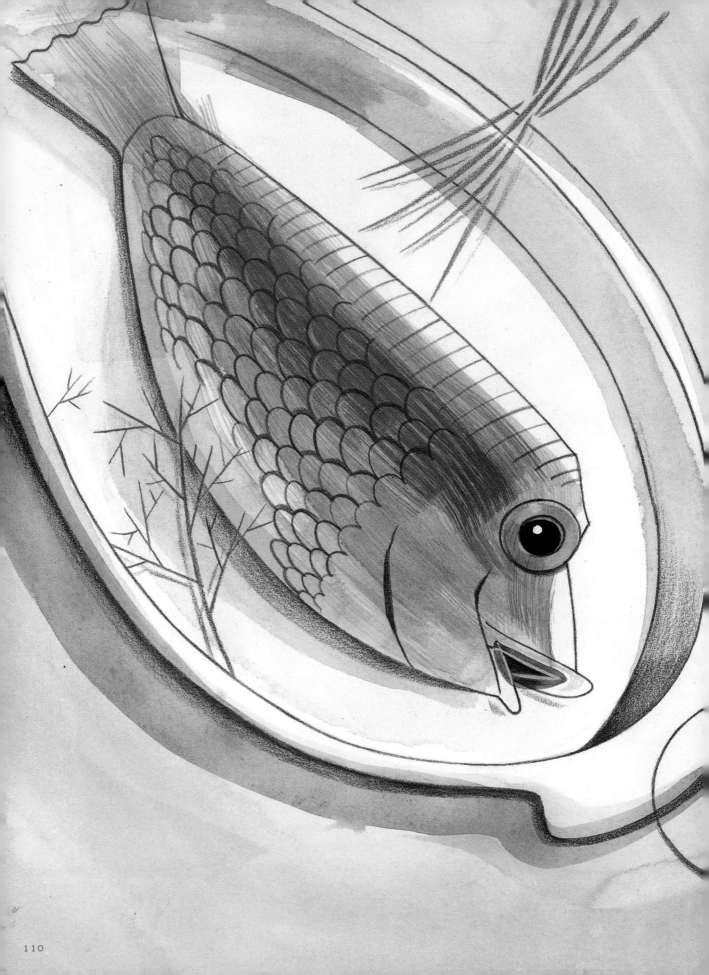

The whole song and dance about vegetarians and vegetarian food has become so boring. Too many vegetarians make a fuss about their dietary needs and then end up ordering fish or even chicken. (At the Crown and Castle, we cooked a special New Year's Eve meat, fish and dairy-free meal for a self-advertised vegan who then chose to end her meal with cheese…grrrr.) On the other hand, too many omnivores think they're being cheated in some way if they don't have a slab of meat every time they sit down to eat. As anyone who loves food will know, footless food can be the best in the world – just think taglierini with white truffles – but I can't bring myself to believe we weren't designed to be omnivores. Each to his own, and let's all shut up on the subject, including me.

In this chapter, there are some obvious stand-alone vegetarian main courses. Of rather more interest, I think, are the dishes which can either be served as a main course or as a side dish. Or, perhaps more pertinently, that can be served as a side dish for the majority of your guests, but will happily convert to a main course for the odd veggie. You will also find a few piscatorial dishes – I wish there were more but, on the whole, fish doesn't lend itself to the kind of pre-preparation necessary to fit in with the spirit of this book. That doesn't mean the dishes that follow aren't jolly good, because they are.

footless food

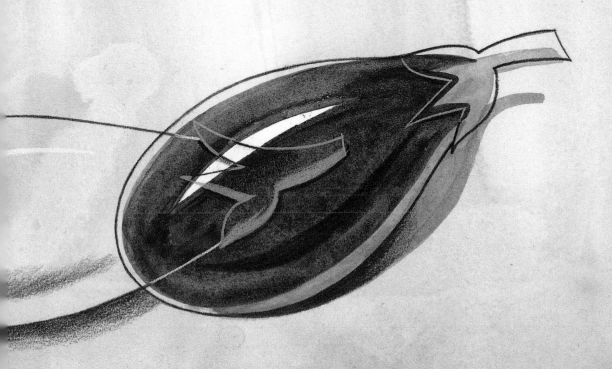

The lasagne can be prepared and assembled the day before it's needed, then baked to order. Yes, it's classic – corny even – but that doesn't stop everyone loving this slinky-creamy lasagne to bits whether they're vegetarian or not.

mozzarella, ricotta and spinach lasagne

a very large ovenproof baking dish, buttered

about 600g leaf spinach *trimmed, rinsed and drained*

a knob of unsalted butter

a few scrapings of whole nutmeg

115g grated parmesan

4 tablespoons double cream

500g ricotta

olive oil

1 small onion *finely chopped*

3 garlic cloves *crushed and finely chopped*

1 green chilli *de-seeded and finely chopped*

about 700g sugocasa (or passata)

1 teaspoon caster sugar

a handful of fresh basil leaves *roughly chopped*

8-10 sheets dried lasagne *cooked and drained*

2 balls of cow's milk mozzarella *drained and thinly sliced*

Heat a large wok over a high flame then toss in a big handful of spinach leaves. Working quickly, toss the leaves continuously until they have just wilted then put them in a colander while you cook the remaining leaves. Squeeze out any excess moisture with your hands.

Melt the butter in a frying pan over a medium heat and put in the drained, cooked spinach. Season lavishly with black pepper and grated nutmeg, and salt to taste. Add half the parmesan and all the cream, and cook for about 2 minutes, stirring frequently. Remove the pan from the heat and leave the mixture to cool.

Briefly whizz the ricotta in a food processor with the remaining parmesan, then add the spinach mixture and pulse for a few seconds until roughly blended. Leave to one side.

Make the tomato sauce. Heat a medium frying pan over a low-medium flame, then add a slug of oil to barely cover the base. When the oil is hot, throw in the onion, garlic and chilli and gently fry for 10-15 minutes. Add the sugocasa, sugar and basil, stir, and simmer gently for about 30 minutes, stirring occasionally. Remove the pan from the heat.

Preheat the oven to 170C fan/gas mark 5 for the final baking.

Assemble the dish starting with a layer of the spinach mixture, then a layer of lasagne, then tomato sauce (spread sparingly). Repeat the layers, finishing with a layer of mozzarella. Bake the lasagne for about 20 minutes if it's freshly assembled, or for about 40 minutes if it has been previously refrigerated. Either way it should end up bubbling and golden.

This can be cooked up to 2 days in advance but the spinach should only be added after the stew has been reheated. There are some really useful dishes that are good to have in the repertoire, and this is one of them. It goes very well with dryish meats, such as duck confit, roast game or lamb, or even sausages. Bear in mind that it could easily be a vegetarian main course, if you leave out the pancetta. In this case, I would grill two thick slices of ready-cooked, oil-brushed polenta (with or without a sprinkling of cheese), and serve this stew with it.

chickpea and spinach stew

about 200g cubed pancetta (or chorizo)

olive oil

2 Spanish onions *cut into small dice*

3 or 4 garlic cloves *crushed and finely chopped*

2 sticks of celery *de-strung and cut into small dice*

3 carrots *cut into small dice*

1 (400g) can of tomatoes *drained, roughly chopped, and cores discarded*

1 tablespoon Marigold vegetable powder

3 (400g) cans of chickpeas *drained and rinsed*

about 200g leaf spinach *trimmed, rinsed and drained*

Heat a large saucepan over a low-medium flame, then throw in the pancetta. Fry for a few minutes, until the cubes have coloured, then add enough oil to barely cover the base. When the oil is hot, add the onions, garlic, celery and carrots. Fry them gently for 10-15 minutes, stirring frequently, until they have softened a little.

Add the tomatoes and their juice, the Marigold powder and enough water to cover. Turn up the heat and bring the contents to a boil, then reduce the flame and simmer for 10-15 minutes. Add the chickpeas to the pan and let them heat through, adding a little more water if the sauce is too thick, then add seasoning to taste. Just before serving, tamp the spinach into the hot stew and cook uncovered for a few minutes, or until the leaves have barely wilted.

The aubergines can be prepared up to 24 hours ahead, then given a final 25-minute baking. This rich aubergine dish is as good playing second fiddle to roast lamb as it is in a starring role. The recipe below caters for eight as a side order and you'll need to double it up if it's going to be served as a main course. You may notice the ingredients list is quite vague in places. That's because it really doesn't matter if either the stuffing or the topping has a bit more or less of one thing or another – it won't ruin the outcome, merely alter it.

aubergines au gratin

a large, ovenproof baking dish, lightly oiled

4 large aubergines

6 large plum tomatoes *blanched, peeled, de-seeded and roughly chopped*

olive oil

1 large Spanish onion *chopped into medium dice*

3 garlic cloves *crushed and finely chopped*

about 120g mushrooms *roughly chopped*

a large handful of fresh parsley *roughly chopped*

1 bushy sprig of oregano *leaves roughly chopped*

about 30g ground almonds

about 30g fresh white breadcrumbs

about 55g grated parmesan

Bring a very large saucepan of water to the boil and blanch the whole aubergines for 5 minutes. (Use the same water to blanch the tomatoes.) Drain and cool the aubergines, then cut them in half lengthways and scoop out the flesh, leaving a centimetre-thick wall. Roughly chop the flesh.

Heat a large frying pan over a low-medium flame and when it's hot add enough olive oil to barely cover the base. When the oil is hot, chuck in the onion and garlic, and fry them gently for 8-10 minutes, stirring occasionally.

Add the mushrooms and fry them for 3-4 minutes, stirring frequently. Stir in the tomatoes, aubergine flesh, parsley and oregano. Reduce the heat and simmer for 8-10 minutes, stirring occasionally, until the vegetables are tender but not mushy. Remove the pan from the heat, taste the mixture and season accordingly. Arrange the aubergine shells in the baking dish and fill them with the vegetable mixture. **You can take the recipe to this point.**

Preheat the oven to 160C fan/gas mark 4

Combine the ground almonds, breadcrumbs and parmesan, then dredge the mixture over the filled aubergines. Trickle with olive oil, then bake the aubergines for about 25 minutes, or until they've reached that hoary ol' golden-brown stage and are piping hot.

The pearl barley can be cooked, and the vegetables fried, up to 8 hours ahead. The ragout will take about 10 minutes to finish. The traditional accompaniment to ossobuco is a saffron-hued risotto Milanese. The problem is that any risotto worth the name requires constant stirring. This creamy, vegetable-packed ragout makes a good stand-in for risotto and does not require stirring. Something of a boon, I think you would agree.

Another virtue is that the ragout makes a jolly good, stand-alone vegetarian main dish but please note these quantities are for a side dish: you'll need to double the recipe to make eight main course servings.

pearl barley and pea ragout

1 tablespoon Marigold vegetable powder

400g pearl barley

100g unsalted butter

1 banana shallot (or 2 small shallots) *finely chopped*

2 garlic cloves *crushed and finely chopped*

2 sticks of celery *de-strung and finely diced*

100ml dry white vermouth

250g frozen peas *defrosted*

a large handful of grated parmesan

a handful of chopped fresh parsley

Put the Marigold powder into a large saucepan, add 2.5 litres of water, and bring to the boil over a medium-high flame. Tip in the pearl barley, stir well, then gently boil for about 25 minutes, stirring occasionally, until the grains are just tender. Drain, reserving any unsoaked-up stock.

Meanwhile, melt 75g butter in a large frying pan over a low-medium heat. Tip in the shallot, garlic and celery, and fry for about 5 minutes, stirring occasionally, until the vegetables have softened a little. Add the vermouth, turn up the flame, and bubble until the liquid has almost disappeared. Take the pan off the heat, scrape the contents into a large saucepan, and stir in the pearl barley. **You can take the recipe to this point.**

Reheat the pearl barley mixture over a low-medium flame, adding a little bit more stock to help loosen it up, and stirring frequently. When everything is hot, add the peas, parmesan, parsley and the remaining butter and stir gently until the cheese has melted. Taste, add seasoning, and more of the reserved stock, if necessary, to make a soft, creamy ragout.

The tart can be completely prepared up to 24 hours ahead. The final baking takes about 20 minutes. Featuring soft, slightly candied squash and savoury onions, this tarte tatin is every bit as good to eat as the original apple version, and rather more cheerful to look at. It makes an excellent vegetarian main course (especially with the pistachio, pomegranate and coriander raita on page 42) but also goes really well with roast meats as a side order. A cook's dream.

squash and red onion upside-down tart

a very large frying pan
a very large, heavy, baking tray
a commensurately sized chopping board or tray

about 1.2kg mixed squashes, e.g. acorn or crown prince or butternut squash *peeled, de-seeded and cut into large bite-sized chunks*

olive oil

4 large tomatoes *cut in half around their midriffs*

100g butter

4 red onions *cut into sixths through the root*

4-6 garlic cloves *crushed and finely chopped*

1 fresh red chilli *de-seeded and finely chopped*

1 teaspoon ground coriander

1 teaspoon ground cumin

2 teaspoons nigella seeds

2 (375g) packets of ready-rolled puff pastry

1 small egg *whisked with 1 tablespoon cold water*

Preheat the oven to 220C fan/gas mark 9

Throw the squash on to the baking tray, add a little oil and toss the chunks to coat them. Arrange the squash in a single-ish layer, then roast for 10-15 minutes – just long enough for it to colour and soften a bit. About 1-2 minutes before the squash is ready, add the tomatoes cut-side down. Remove the tray from the oven and leave everything to cool down.

Put the frying pan over a medium flame and when it's hot add the butter and a little olive oil. Swirl the fats together and when the butter stops sizzling, add the onions, garlic and chilli and fry them for about 7-8 minutes, stirring frequently, until they have coloured. Stir in the coriander and cumin, then fry for 1 minute, stirring constantly, then stir in the nigella seeds. Remove the pan from the heat.

Scrape out the contents of the frying pan to join the squash and tomatoes on the baking tray. Using plastic spatulas – so you don't squish the squash or the tomatoes – carefully mix everything together, then arrange the ingredients in a single layer. Leave to cool completely.

Roll out the pastry to make two sheets large enough to cover the baking tray when they're butted up together. Lay the pastry sheets over the vegetables, then trim off all the surplus. Refrigerate the entire ensemble for at least 30 minutes, and up to 24 hours.

Preheat the oven to 220C fan/gas mark 9

Brush the pastry with the egg wash, then put the tart in the oven and bake it for about 20 minutes (or 10 minutes longer if it has been in the fridge for a long time), checking halfway through that the pastry isn't browning too quickly. The tart is ready when the juices are bubbling around the edges and the pastry is a dark golden brown.

To serve, have the board ready and an attractive, thick (do I need to say clean? I think not…) cloth. Now, the only slightly tricky bit: stretch the cloth across the baking tray, gripping it firmly at either end, quickly invert the tart and immediately place it on the waiting board for an authentic, rustic, almost peasant-like, Burgundian look – and a candidate for Pseud's Corner, perhaps?

The entire dish can be made up to 48 hours ahead. Reheating it will take about 25 minutes. Cauliflower cheese is one of the greatest comfort foods this side of the Bosphorus. As far I am concerned, it's also mandatory with roast beef – in fact, I'm quite happy to ditch the beef and just go with the cauliflower cheese and Yorkshires (plus the other veg), as will any vegetarians you've invited.

This recipe will feed eight as a side dish, so you'll need to double it up if you want to serve it as a main course for eight.

cauliflower cheese

200g mature cheddar *grated*

100g parmesan *grated*

2 medium cauliflowers *cut into chunky florets*

85g butter

85g plain flour

about 600ml full-fat milk

1 bay leaf

150ml double cream

a dab of Dijon mustard

a few scrapings of whole nutmeg

Combine the cheeses and set them aside. Bring a large saucepan of salted water to the boil and cook the cauliflower for 5-6 minutes, or until the stalks are just tender, then drain well. ('Just tender' may sound like a dismissible instruction, but it's crucial: hard, crunchy cauliflower cheese is as miserable an experience as mushy cauliflower cheese.) Arrange the cauliflower in a buttered ovenproof dish, florets skywards, and season.

To make the sauce, melt the butter in a large saucepan over a low-medium flame then whisk in the flour. Cook for a minute, then whisk in the milk, getting right into the corners of the pan. Raise the heat and bring to the boil, whisking the sauce constantly – there's no need to heat the milk first, as long as you whisk madly. When the sauce demonstrably thickens, reduce the heat, add the bay leaf and simmer the sauce gently for 15-20 minutes, whisking occasionally.

Remove the bay leaf and add the cream and/or more milk to make a good, thick pouring sauce. Leave some cheese aside for sprinkling on top, and stir the remainder into the sauce. Cook only for the few minutes it takes to melt the cheese, then stir in a dab of mustard, a little nutmeg and seasoning to taste. Remove the pan from the heat. Cover the cauliflower with the sauce and strew on the remaining cheese.

Either cool and refrigerate the cauliflower cheese for up 48 hours or put the dish in an oven **preheated to 180C fan/gas mark 6** and bake for 10-15 minutes. It's ready when the top is patched tortoiseshell-brown and the sauce is bubbling round the edges. If you are going to cook the cauliflower cheese straight from the fridge, then it will probably need another 10 minutes, or so.

The eggs, potatoes and beans can be cooked up to 8 hours in advance. The dressing can be made an hour or so before the salad is tossed and served. Most restaurant commentators cite The Eagle in Farringdon Road as being Britain's first gastro pub, so when I met David Eyre recently and he sweetly *offered* the fact that the Fox and Goose had preceded his own venture, I felt a childish vindication. The least I can do in return is to acknowledge that this salad emanates from his repertoire, although I have tweaked it a bit. The salad is best served warmish.

Galicia vegetable salad

7 large free-range eggs *at room temperature*

about 750g small waxy potatoes *peeled (or scraped) and boiled*

2 handfuls of broad beans *cooked and the inner skins then popped off*

about 400g fine French beans *top and tailed, and lightly cooked*

16-24 (bottled in olive oil) artichoke hearts *drained*

a bunch of flat-leaf parsley *roughly chopped*

4 spring onions *trimmed and roughly chopped*

1 red chilli *de-seeded and finely chopped*

2 tablespoons red wine vinegar

a dab of Dijon mustard

2-3 garlic cloves *finely chopped*

8 tablespoons extra-virgin olive oil

Put the eggs into a pan of boiling water and simmer them for exactly 6 minutes. Drain off the water, leaving the eggs in the pan. Turn on the cold tap and let the water run over the eggs for 2 minutes (which will prevent that dirty grey tidemark forming round the yolk). Don't peel them yet.

About an hour before the salad is needed, toss the cooked potatoes, broad beans, French beans and the artichoke hearts together in a large bowl. Throw in half the parsley, the spring onions and chilli, and toss again. Leave to one side, but not in the fridge.

Whisk the vinegar, mustard, garlic and some seasoning together, then whisk in the olive oil to make an emulsion. Peel the eggs, cut 4 of them in half, lengthways, and set them aside. Remove the whites from the other 3 eggs, and turn the yolks (reserving the whites) into the dressing. Whisk thoroughly to incorporate them.

Put the vegetables and dressing into a large bowl and toss everything together, gently but thoroughly. Divide the salad among eight summery, shallow bowls. Chop the 3 reserved egg whites roughly and scatter them over the salad, then finish each bowl with a halved egg and some chopped parsley.

The couscous can be made in part up to 48 hours ahead, then finished just before you sit down to eat. This was originally destined for *side orders*, until I realised it was not only a recipe that needed a more formal layout but one that could be used as a vegetarian main course – although I would then feel the need to crown it with a dollop of the pistachio, pomegranate and coriander raita. But why 'interesting'? Simply because couscous is more boring than a bowl of birdseed normally, but in this rendition it's packed with good flavours.

In case of doubt, the couscous required for this recipe is the dried grain that comes in cardboard packets, not the tubs of ready-made couscous you can buy in the chilled snack section of a supermarket. The quantities here will feed eight as a side dish.

interesting couscous

olive oil

2 banana shallots (or 4 small shallots) *finely chopped*

a pinch each of: ground coriander, turmeric, cumin and ginger

250g couscous

250ml boiling water

55g softened unsalted butter *roughly chopped*

the juice of half a lemon

about 100g black olives *cut in half (and stoned, if necessary)*

4 large tomatoes *blanched, peeled, de-seeded and chopped*

a bunch of flat-leaf parsley *roughly chopped*

2 bushy sprigs of oregano *leaves chopped*

Heat a large saucepan over a low flame, then add oil to cover the base. When the oil is hot add the shallots and fry them very gently for 2-3 minutes. Add the spices and fry them for 1 minute, stirring.

Pull the pan off the flame, tip in the couscous, give everything a good stir and pour in the boiling water. Leave the pan for 5 minutes then add half the butter. Use a large fork to incorporate it and fluff up the grains. Add seasoning and lemon juice, to taste. **The couscous can be made up to this point.**

Just before serving, put the couscous in a microwave-proof bowl, gently stir in the olives, tomatoes and herbs, then dot on the remaining butter. 'Ding' for 1 minute on full power, then gently stir the couscous and serve. Or, for the microwave-less (me), put all the ingredients into a foil-covered dish then reheat in a low oven for about 25 minutes, using a fork to fluff up the couscous once or twice.

Prepare the salmon a few hours ahead and put the fish in the oven about 35 minutes before it's required. The title's a bit of a red herring because the only unusual thing about this salmon is that it won't be all dried up and mealy – as long as you follow the recipe. I don't know what it is about salmon served at weddings and the like, but it's always overcooked. I suppose it's because most people have a dread of undercooked fish and so err on the side of caution. While I share a dislike of rare fish, preferring it either unequivocally raw or cooked until *just* done, this isn't a reason to adopt a nappy-boiling technique.

Wild salmon is almost impossible to get nowadays, but organic or Scottish Quality Assured salmon is pretty good. So you don't end up with an unholy mess when it comes to carving the salmon, ask the fishmonger to scale and fillet it in such a way that you have two whole, bone-free sides (like smoked salmon). If he's nice, he'll take out the pin bones, too. Otherwise arm yourself with some tweezers, run your palm gently over the flesh and you'll soon feel where they are.

unusual salmon

a heavy baking tray, long enough to take a whole fish, lined with a double layer of baking parchment, lightly oiled

a 2.5-3kg whole salmon *filleted as above*
2 whole lemons *sliced thinly and pips removed*
3 tablespoons capers *rinsed, drained and roughly chopped*

3-4 bushy sprigs of tarragon (or chervil or dill) *leaves chopped*
1-2 sprigs of mint *leaves finely chopped*
a bunch of parsley *leaves chopped*
olive oil

Pat the salmon fillets dry with kitchen paper. Arrange half the lemon slices on the lined baking tray, and put one fillet on top of them, skin-side down.

Combine the capers and herbs, then plaster the salmon flesh with the mixture. Lay the rest of the lemon slices on top, season with pepper (not salt), and press the other fillet on top to 're-form' the fish. Put the salmon in the fridge for a few hours, then bring back to room temperature before baking it.

Preheat the oven to 210C fan/gas mark 8

Brush the skin with oil, season the fish, then bake it for 35 minutes. Check to see if it's ready by sliding a small knife between the two fillets at the thickest part. The flesh should be opaque at its thickest part: if it's still translucent continue to cook it for another 5-10 minutes. To serve, don't try to carve the fish by cutting straight through it but remove thin escalopes from each fillet.

goes well with **charred tomatoes · pea and pancetta fricassée · French bean and shallot salad**

The squid can be prepared and cooked a day ahead, then gently reheated and finished off under the grill. The thing about squid is that you either have to cook it for two minutes or for at least 30 minutes – anything in between and the squid will be tough enough to tow a car. But you can do a lot with squid: griddle it, deep-fry it, make a salad with it, braise it, stew it, take it to the races…

You can use a food processor to make the stuffing, but don't go mad – the texture should be like coarse breadcrumbs, not smooth and pasty. It's best to whizz the tentacles, carrots and the chorizo separately, but the shallots, celery and garlic can go into the processing bowl together.

I love cleaning squid but if you're not similarly enamoured, the fishmonger will remove the head and 'beak', the milky innards, and the sheath of transparent cartilage that keeps the live squid from collapsing like an old paper bag.

chorizo-stuffed squid

a lightly oiled ovenproof dish large enough to take the squid in one layer

olive oil

3 medium carrots finely chopped

250g chorizo skinned and finely chopped

2 banana shallots (or 3 normal shallots) finely chopped

2 sticks of celery de-strung and finely chopped

4 garlic cloves crushed

250g baby spinach leaves rinsed, patted dry, and coarsely chopped

150g coarse, dry, white breadcrumbs

a handful of toasted pine nuts coarsely chopped

16 medium, not-too-thick squid hoods cleaned

about 700g sugocasa (or passata)

a few sprigs of thyme

Heat the frying pan over a low-medium flame, then add enough oil to cover the base. When the oil is hot, add the carrots and the chorizo, and fry gently for 5 minutes. Add the shallots, celery and garlic (and chopped squid tentacles, if there were any) and continue to fry for about 10 minutes, or until the ingredients have softened but are only very lightly coloured.

Turn off the heat, but leave the pan on the hob and stir in the spinach, moving it around until it has just wilted, then immediately stir in the breadcrumbs and pine nuts (the mixture must still be hot when you do this). Add seasoning to taste, then allow the contents of the pan to cool.

Preheat the oven to 180C fan/gas mark 6

Open up the squid hoods. Using a teaspoon, fill them with the stuffing mixture, keeping any that's left over. Pour the sugocasa into the baking dish, tuck in the herbs, then arrange the squid on top in a single layer. Scatter any remaining stuffing over the top and swish with oil. Bake the squid in the oven for 30 minutes, turning the hoods halfway through.

You can take the recipe to this point, then cool and refrigerate the stuffed squid. In this case, the squid will need to be brought to room temperature and reheated for about 10 minutes in an oven preheated to 180C fan/gas mark 6 before carrying on with the recipe.

To finish the squid, put the dish under a **high preheated grill** for a couple of minutes.

goes well with **leaf salad**

The aioli can be prepared up to 2 days in advance. Apart from cooking the fish, everything else can be made a day ahead. Bourride differs from bouillabaisse in that it's a blonde rather than auburn fish stew. Traditionally, the glossy aioli (garlicky mayonnaise) is stirred into the broth before it's served but this can complicate things. Far simpler, and just as good, is to dollop some aioli on top: as the bourride gets eaten, it forms a great-tasting liaison.

I've suggested using red gurnard as it's an under-rated and (currently) inexpensive fish. You could, of course, use any other firm-textured white-ish fish.

red gurnard, clam and saffron bourride

a big ceramic pestle
and mortar
two pretty large
saucepans

for the aioli

7-8 garlic cloves *peeled*

1 teaspoon Dijon mustard

4 large free-range egg yolks

150ml fruity extra-virgin olive oil

250ml groundnut oil

the juice of 1 lemon

for the bourride

30g unsalted butter

1 tablespoon olive oil

2 banana (or 4 normal) shallots *finely chopped*

2 leeks *quartered lengthways and finely sliced*

1 small head of celeriac *chopped into small dice*

2 pinches of saffron threads

1 litre hot fish stock (or Marigold vegetable stock)

about 400ml dry white wine, e.g. sauvignon

24-40 fresh clams *well-rinsed*

1.5kg red gurnard (filleted weight) *skinned and cut into large bite-sized chunks*

a large handful of chopped fresh chives

I think there's something rather satisfying about making aioli in a pestle and mortar. (You can echo the same method using a liquidiser but, in that case, use 2 whole eggs and 2 yolks.) Put the garlic and a large pinch of coarse sea salt into a mortar and pound to a rough purée. Add the mustard and egg yolks, and pound again. Mix the two oils in a jug, and dribble them very slowly into the mortar, working the pestle constantly. As the aioli thickens, increase the dribble to a thin stream and change to a sturdy whisk. Adjust the texture and flavour with some seasoning and lemon juice – the aioli should be potent but not savage, and as thick as ointment. Refrigerate until required.

Heat a large pan over a medium flame and when it's hot put in the butter and oil. When the butter stops frothing tip in the shallots, leeks and celeriac. Cook for about 5 minutes, stirring frequently, then add the saffron to the vegetables, and cook for a further minute. Pour in the stock and bring to the boil. Reduce the heat and simmer the broth for 15 minutes, half-covered.

Meanwhile, pour the white wine into another large saucepan and bring to the boil over a high flame. Add the clams, cover, and cook them for 4-5 minutes, shaking the pan once or twice, until the shells gape open. Strain the juices through a fine sieve into the first broth. Leave the clams to one side.

You can prepare the recipe up to this point, then cool and refrigerate both clams and broth.

Bring a small amount of broth to a simmer in a large saucepan set over a low-medium flame. Add the red gurnard and gently poach it for 3-4 minutes. At the same time, pour the rest of the broth into another large pan over a medium flame and add seasoning to taste. Add the clams and gently bring them to just under the boil – don't let the clams actually cook or they'll toughen up.

Divide the clams and broth among the plates and add the chunks of red gurnard (discarding the broth you've poached it in). Finish with a scattering of chives and a big dollop of aioli. Serve the remainder in a separate bowl for people to add more if they want.

goes well with **crunchy baguette**

The curry can be made up to 12 hours ahead and then gently reheated. This is based on a fish curry devised by Manju Malhi, who has done a lot to make Indian food accessible to the British market. As with almost any Asian dish, whether you get the spicing correctly balanced or not, it will almost certainly taste a darned sight better than anything you'll get in the average high street restaurant.

If you have any choice in the matter, buy raw tiger prawns with brick-coloured rather than blue-black shells – they both end up the usual lobster-pink once cooked, but the former have a better flavour. As for any accompaniments, I would be very tempted to buy some pilau rice or naan from Waitrose, which has the best-quality Indian ready meals, to my mind. A good-quality mango chutney, lime chutney, or the pistachio, pomegranate and coriander raita (see page 42), would also lend harmony to the meal.

tiger prawn and aubergine curry

a wide, shallow flameproof casserole or sauté pan

for the marinade

1 teaspoon ground turmeric

2 teaspoons ground cumin

2 teaspoons ground coriander

3 green chillies *de-seeded and roughly chopped*

2 handfuls of fresh coriander leaves *chopped*

2 tablespoons groundnut or vegetable oil

40-48 tiger prawns (depending on size) *shelled but with the tails left on*

for the curry

groundnut oil

3 aubergines *cut into large bite-sized chunks*

half a teaspoon cumin seeds

half a teaspoon mustard seeds

4-5 garlic cloves *crushed and roughly chopped*

2 large onions *diced*

1 thumb of root ginger *peeled and grated*

1 (400g) can of tomatoes *drained, roughly chopped, and cores discarded*

500ml fish stock (or Marigold vegetable stock)

For the marinade, put the spices, chillies, half the coriander leaves and the oil in a food processor and pulse to make a rough paste. Daub the tiger prawns with this marinade and refrigerate them in a non-reactive dish for 2-3 hours.

Heat the casserole or sauté pan over a medium flame and then add enough oil to cover the base fairly generously. When the oil is hot throw in a batch of aubergine chunks (do not crowd the pan), and fry them for a few minutes, turning them so they colour on all sides. Using a slotted spoon, remove the chunks and leave them to drain on kitchen paper while you fry the rest – adding more oil and heating it first, if necessary. Leave the well-blotted chunks to one side.

Tip out any excess oil from the pan then add the cumin and mustard seeds. When they start to pop, reduce the heat, add the garlic, onions and ginger, and give everything a good stir. Fry gently for 4-5 minutes then raise the heat, add the tomatoes and stock, and bring to the boil. Reduce the heat and simmer for 10-15 minutes, or until the sauce has thickened a little. Stir in the aubergines, then leave the sauce on a very idle simmer while you cook the prawns.

Heat a large frying pan over a medium flame. When it's hot add enough oil to barely cover the base. When the oil is hot, toss in a batch of tiger prawns, including the marinade. Fry them for 1 minute on each side. Transfer the prawns to the rest of the curry as soon as they're ready. **You can take the recipe to this point.**

Reheat the curry very gently, stirring frequently and adding a little more stock or water if required. Stir in the remaining coriander leaves just before serving.

goes well with Asian-spiced potatoes and onions

The chowder base can be made up to 2 days in advance, with just the haddock and scallops needing to be added at the last minute. I'm normally fairly ferocious in my criticism of chefs or food writers who bastardise classic recipes: what the food gains in pretension it normally loses in honesty and goodness. So, let me be the first to say this chowder does not really need the addition of scallops to make it taste better. On the other hand, I have never forgotten the comment Gertrude Stein's housekeeper made when Matisse (whom she disliked) invited himself to stay for dinner: 'In that case I will not make an omelette but fry the eggs. It takes the same number of eggs and the same amount of butter but it shows less respect, and he will understand.' So, if smoked haddock chowder seems a tad too casual, the scallops will elevate it – socially, at least.

You can buy decent smoked haddock from most supermarkets but to get fresh, diver-caught scallops you'll probably need to source them from an online fish merchant. Although I like scallop roe (the coral), it doesn't cook at the same rate as the white meat, and the 'band' that keeps it attached to the white meat is stringy. So, I prefer to freeze the corals and use them later in a 'red' fish stock.

smoked haddock and scallop chowder

a very large saucepan

a scrap of unsalted butter

2 Spanish onions *cut into sixths through the root, then each sixth into three*

3 garlic cloves *finely chopped*

1 fresh red chilli *de-seeded and finely chopped*

a good pinch of saffron threads

1 small thumb of root ginger *peeled and grated*

3 large waxy potatoes *peeled and cut into large dice*

about 800ml hot fish stock

1 (284ml) carton of double cream

about 2kg undyed smoked haddock *skinned, pin bones removed and cut into large bite-sized chunks*

16-24 scallops (depending on size) *trimmed, corals removed and halved around their midriffs*

1 and a half bunches of slim spring onions *trimmed and cut at an angle into about 4 pieces*

a large handful of fresh coriander leaves (or parsley) *very roughly chopped*

Gently melt the butter in a very large saucepan over a low flame. Tip in the onions, garlic and chilli, and fry for about 10 minutes, stirring occasionally, until the onions start to soften without colouring. Stir in the saffron and cook for 1 minute, then add the ginger and potatoes. Fry for another 3-4 minutes, stirring frequently. Pour in the hot fish stock and bring to the boil over a medium-high flame. Reduce the heat and simmer, uncovered, for 10-15 minutes, or until the potatoes are just tender.

Continue with the recipe or cool the chowder base and refrigerate it, but bring it to a simmer before carrying on, as below.

Add the cream to the hot chowder base and bring it back to just under the boil over a medium flame. Put in the smoked haddock, reduce the heat, and simmer gently for 3 minutes. Add the scallops and most of the spring onions and coriander. Continue to simmer gently for about 2 minutes, or until both the haddock and scallops are just opaque.

Divide the chowder among warmed, flat soup plates and strew the remaining spring onions and coriander over the top.

goes well with **all you need is good bread**

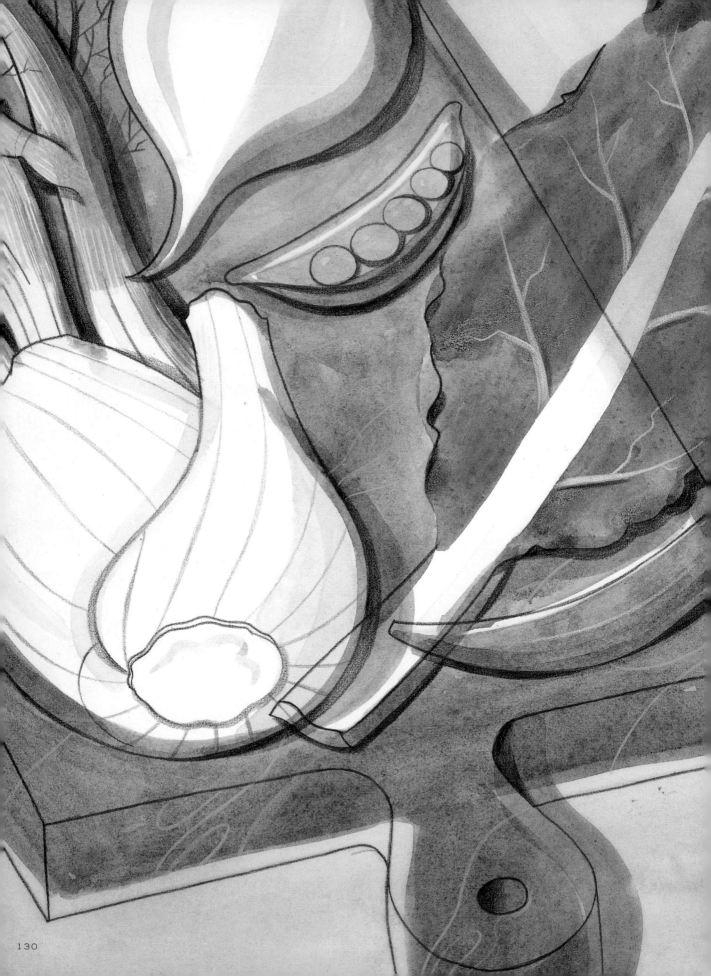

If I've learnt anything about cooking for a mob, it's not to go mad with the vegetables. Unless your guests are farmers, builders or television cameramen, all of whom seem to suffer from ceramaphobia (the fear of empty china), you do not need to provide three veg and potatoes for each and every meal. It took me a long time to wake up to the fact I seemed to be throwing out more veg than I'd cooked and I only wish it had dawned on me a lot sooner.

Obviously the Sunday roast calls for more vegetal support than a Saturday night dinner, on the grounds of tradition and nostalgia, if nothing else. But it's a good idea to engage the brain before embarking on providing a vast array of side dishes. The first point to consider is, are you serving a starter? Personally, I think the first course is normally the best part of the meal, but even I don't think a traditional Sunday lunch needs a first course. If you need to fill the time between guests coming through the door and sitting down, hand round some nibbly stuff with the pre-prandial drinks. This is when the serried ranks of mini-foods lined up on the supermarket shelves come into their own. It's true many of the concoctions are utterly vile, so you'll need to exercise the same caution with these boxes of potentially useful mouthfuls as you would any other ready meal. As ever, keep it simple: I think you'll find more people like warm-from-the-oven cheese straws or really good olives than mini Thai chicken and sweetcorn quiche.

side orders

Don't confuse effort with worth, either. With or without the starter (and a respectful nod to tradition) Sunday lunch won't be any better because you've cooked a myriad vegetables to go with the roast. If you are serving sirloin of beef, your guests will rightfully expect roast potatoes, Yorkshire pudding and gravy to go with it. But that doesn't mean you have to provide another dozen vegetables as well. The core elements are already going to be taxing enough in terms of oven space and timing, so limit the rest of the accompaniments to one root and one green vegetable, maximum.

With other roast meats you can be even more ruthless, especially if there's any stuffing involved. I would choose a potato or farinaceous dish (preferably something that can be baked alongside the roast), and just one other perky-natured vegetable, or even a salad. With cheese and/or pudding to follow, none of your guests are going to leave the table hungry and, just as importantly, you won't be thrumming with anxiety in the run-up to getting the meal on the table. You only have to watch an Italian family having their Sunday lunch (and Italians really do know about good eating) to see the focus is on a beautifully prepared and cooked piece of meat or fish, with perhaps some simply cooked potatoes.

It's no accident that the title of this chapter is called *side orders* because that's what vegetables or salads should be – not a panoply of vegetation to rival the buffet in the Cleveland (Ohio) Hilton. If a 'roast dinner' needs only a modicum of support, a composite dish is even less needy. Take the chicken pie, and it's wonderful amalgamation of friable, buttery pastry; rich, creamy sauce; and gently poached poultry, mushrooms and leeks, as an example. It doesn't need a myriad vegetables to leaven either the texture or flavours: there's enough going on to satisfy the most jaded palate. At the bottom of the recipe, I've suggested that buttery mash, cabbage and purple sprouting broccoli would go with it *but that doesn't mean you have to serve all of them.* I happen to be a carbohydrate fiend, so for me it's mandatory to serve a fluffy pile of mash, not just to help mop up the sauce, but because I adore the combination of pastry and potatoes. (In much the same way, I find it almost impossible to eat pasta without an accompanying hunk of bread – and I wonder why Dumbo is my *nomme de graisse*.)

I also think something intensely green would be a great contrast to the rich suavity of the pie. The ideal vegetable has to be purple sprouting broccoli – or, if it's out of season, then 'normal' or 'tender stem' broccoli, although both of them are rather too 'polite' for my liking. Purple sprouting broccoli really is the bee's knees. I adore its unapologetically 'green' stridency, faint bitterness, and inherently clean, bright flavour. Put this vegetable on to the same plate as the chicken pie and you really do have gustatory perfection.

And that really sums up the whole point of serving vegetables with a main course – to provide a contrapuntal texture and flavour, never mind some much-needed vitamins and fibre. The fact that so many British people think vegetables are there merely to fill up the space on the plate, or to cram their stomachs relatively cheaply, proves that as a country we still have some way to go when it comes to understanding what constitutes good food. (A fact confirmed in my own restaurant last night when, as I passed by her table, a mature female guest thrust her ramekin of vanilla crème brûlée at me in a fairly aggressive manner so she could show me the full horror of the black-speckled sediment that had drifted to the bottom of the dish… I do despair sometimes.)

The trick is to marry the right vegetable with the right main dish. Sloppy dishes do not require soupy vegetables, so don't even think of serving the pea and pancetta fricassée with the chicken, squash and garlic stew. Conversely, the rich, slow-roast duck confit wouldn't gain much from having buttered cabbage with juniper or roast red pepper salad served alongside, but would go down a treat with the gently curried peas both in terms of texture and flavour. Think of the finished plate as a whole, rather than a mass of incidentals, and you should end up with a nicely composed lunch or dinner.

Side orders is also deliberately loose in terms of formal instruction. The quantities are what I would serve for eight people eating a substantial meal but you may want to make a bit more or less, depending on how greedy or hungry you think your guests will be, and whether you're offering a starter and pudding.

In the list of ingredients that preface each recipe, I've only put the specific amount required if I think it's something you may need to go out and buy especially – like a pomegranate – or if the quantity has real significance. When the ingredient comes in a pack size that I know will be more than sufficient for the recipe – such as pine nuts – the amount required is only listed in the method. The same thing goes if the ingredient is butter, or any other staple item you're likely to have in the house.

universal gravy

In an ideal world gravy should be made with the gleanings from the roasting tin but, easy though this may sound, it can be something of a cook's nightmare. Grappling with a hot heavy container that doesn't necessarily want to sit neatly on your stove, while you're simultaneously engaged in bringing all the other components of the meal to a satisfactory climax, can inflame the passions. Personally, I like to get all the gravy making out of the way well beforehand. If any wonderful meat juices are created in the cooking of the joint, I just pour them in at the end.

The secret of good gravy is all in the flavour of the stock. While it's no more difficult to make your own stock than it is to make soup, for some reason it's regarded as something only 'professionals' do, nowadays. (But certainly not when I was young: as I write these words, I can still remember the stench of my mother's weekly stockpot. It permeated the house and made me want to retch. It's only now I wonder what hellish carrion she could have put in the pot to make it smell so evil.) The good thing is that you can now buy liquid stock of reasonable quality from most supermarkets: Waitrose stock (ha!) useful 500ml pouches of 'fresh' lamb, beef and chicken stock, for example.

dripping or vegetable oil · plain flour · red wine · appropriate stock · a funghi porcini stock cube
Heat 50g fat or 2 tablespoons of oil then stir in 50g plain flour and cook for 4-6 minutes over a medium-high heat, stirring frequently. As soon as the roux has coloured, add 350ml red wine and bring to the boil, stirring constantly. When the contents have thickened considerably, pour in about a litre of an appropriate stock (or a pouch plus some water), and a crumbled funghi porcini stock cube. Whisk vigorously until the gravy is lump-free and thickened, then simmer for 10-15 minutes. Season to taste, thinning the gravy down with a little more stock or water, if necessary.

the best and easiest apple sauce

A perfect example of less is more, however trite the expression: this is apple sauce at its purest best.

five or six (depending on size) bramley apples · golden icing sugar
Score the apples fairly deeply round their midriffs, then put them in a baking dish and cook them for about 30-40 minutes at **160C fan/gas mark 4**, or until the insides have collapsed into a tender fluff. Scrape all the flesh out into a bowl and stir in icing sugar to taste, remembering to keep the flavour nice and sharp. The sauce can be made a few days ahead and refrigerated. Bring it to room temperature and put it in a bowl on the table for everyone to help themselves.

Yorkshire pudding

This recipe isn't mine; it comes from *Poor Cook* by Susan Campbell and Caroline Conran. Unlike most recipes I filch (and give credit for, please note), I have never needed to change a single thing as it produces perfect Yorkshires with exactly the right balance of crisp puffiness to spongy pudding. (I am talking about individual puddings here, which I think make far better eating than a big pudding.) Where I think we miss a trick in this country is by serving Yorkshire pudding almost exclusively with roast beef. The fact is they are gorgeous with almost any roast meat, and I've even made them to go with roast turkey at Christmas.

Although the Yorkshires are perfectly edible for many hours after they've been cooked, there is no doubt they are at their most glorious when fresh out of the oven. Cook them while the beef is resting – the furious heat will help any roasties that need extra encouragement, too. The quantities below make about two dozen small puddings (which will all get eaten, I promise). You will need two 12-hole non-stick muffin tins (aka shallow bun tins).

225g plain flour · large free-range eggs · full-fat milk · dripping, groundnut or vegetable oil
Put the flour, a generous amount of seasoning and four lightly whisked eggs in a food processor. With the motor running, gradually pour in a pint of milk. You'll need to stop and scrape down the sides once or twice, but keep whizzing the batter for a couple of minutes until it's completely smooth. Transfer it to an honest pouring jug then refrigerate it for between 1 and 24 hours.

Preheat the oven to 220C fan/gas mark 9. Put a scrap of dripping (or a few drops of oil) in each cup of the muffin tins, then put the tins in the oven and leave until the fat is almost smoking *(almost)*. Carefully remove the tins from the oven and then pour batter into each cup, keeping the level well shy of the top as the puddings rise pretty spectacularly.

Put the tins back in the oven and cook the puddings for 8 minutes, then reduce the oven temperature to **200C fan/gas mark 7** and continue cooking for about 20 minutes, or until the puddings have risen and are toasty-brown around the edges.

roasties

No Sunday lunch is complete without crunchy-edged, fluffy-hearted roast potatoes – or so says my brother-in-law, an expert on all things *Solanum tuberosum*. But if they're going to be good, it's essential to use fairly floury potatoes. And, if you are cooking the potatoes with a joint, the tin must be big enough for them to roast (rather than steam), and the temperature must be high – not easy to achieve, which is why I always cook the potatoes separately, either in the smaller second oven or while the beef is resting (if the roasties are to go with beef, of course).

Then there's the fat…the current mantra is to use duck or goose fat, for the very good reason that it makes beautifully crisp, well-flavoured potatoes. If you haven't just cooked a goose and preserved the bucket-loads of fat that emerge, and if you can't bring yourself to spend a lot of spondoolick on tins of the same, then dripping, groundnut oil or vegetable oil will do instead. In all cases the fat must be hot, hot, hot before the potatoes go in to the tin.

Once they're ready, roast potatoes should not be kept hanging around for too long. The reason why a home-cooked roast lunch is almost invariably better than a restaurant one is because the ingredients are hot out of the oven: the average restaurant roast is all done and dusted by midday, when the first customer comes in. The last customer will get exactly the same food, but two hours older. The beef may withstand some abuse but not the potatoes: the crunchy crust toughens and the fluffy insides turn into a steamy, solid wedge.

eight large King Edward or Maris Piper potatoes · duck or goose fat
Peel, then cut the potatoes into even egg-sized chunks and boil them for about 6 minutes. Drain thoroughly then rough up the surface of each spud with a fork (or shake them vigorously in the pan they were part-boiled in). Put a large roasting tin in an oven preheated to **200C fan/gas mark 7** with enough fat in it to cover the base generously. When the fat is nearly (but not quite) smoking, add the potatoes and roll them around so they're well coated, then season them with salt. Roast the potatoes for 50-60 minutes, turning them halfway through, until they are golden-crusted and tender.

tray-baked potatoes

These butter and stock-enriched, crisp-edged potatoes must be cooked in a tray, or trays, with a really extensive surface area. If you have a modern stove use the oven trays that were supplied with it. The potatoes must be neither too waxy, nor too floury, so something like Marfona or Maris Piper would be better than either King Edward or Desirée. The potatoes can be prepared up to 2 hours ahead, but make sure they are well coated in the stock and butter so they don't discolour.

about 2kg potatoes · softened butter · Marigold vegetable powder

Slice the peeled potatoes using the fine blade of a food processor. Liberally butter the tray(s). **Preheat the oven to 150C fan/gas mark 3.5.**

Put a heaped tablespoon of Marigold vegetable powder into a very large saucepan, add 1.5 litres of water (hot or cold) and bring to the boil over a high flame, whisking to dissolve the powder. Tip in the sliced potatoes, cover the pan and cook for 2 minutes. Take the pan off the heat.

Scoop out the potatoes and transfer them to the tray(s) with a bit of stock to accompany each batch. (Discard the remaining stock, or use it as a soup base.) Spread the potatoes out but don't attempt to overlap the layers in a neat fashion as you would for a gratin: this is a casual, baker's-style dish. Season the potatoes generously then bake them for 30 minutes. Raise the temperature to **200C fan/gas mark 7** and continue to bake for 25-35 minutes, or until the top is golden and crisp. Serve the potatoes straight from the tray, using a fish slice to help lift them out. They won't look too neat but they will taste wonderful.

horseradish-stuffed potatoes

If you don't share the usual British enthusiasm for roast potatoes, these scrunchy skinned potatoes with soft, gravy-lapping insides are fantastic with roast beef – and steak and kidney pie if it comes to that. An added bonus is that they will happily put up with being baked and stuffed a few hours ahead, but keep them cool rather than refrigerated. Use a reasonably floury potato, such as King Edward or Maris Piper. If you can't find jars of grated horseradish, you could use good-quality horseradish cream.

eight large baking potatoes · large free-range eggs · double cream · grated horseradish · lemon juice · salted butter

Preheat the oven to 200C fan/gas mark 7. Bake the potatoes for about an hour, or until the skins are crisp and the potatoes 'give' when you gently squeeze them using a thick, folded oven cloth (steam burns). Keep the oven on.

While the potatoes are cooking, whisk four egg yolks, 175ml double cream, two tablespoons of grated horseradish and a squirt of lemon juice in a large bowl. Cut the baked potatoes in half and scrape the insides into the bowl, reserving the skins. Mash the potato and flavourings together, and add some seasoning. Taste, and add more horseradish, cream or lemon juice, if required.

Pile the mixture back into the skins and dot generously with scraps of butter. Bake the potatoes for 15-20 minutes (or for about 20-25 minutes if they were prepared earlier). They're ready when the top is dappled brown and the insides are piping hot.

'toast rack' potatoes

My sister tells me she first ate these when her Finnish au pair cooked them for the family. As it happens they're Swedish in origin and were named after the restaurant, Hasselbacken (Hazel Hill) where they were 'invented'. I prefer to call them 'toast rack' potatoes because that's what they resemble. Dru still remembers them fondly, so this one is for her.

Choose potatoes with a fairly creamy texture, e.g. Romano, Desirée, Marfona or Maris Peer. A dusting of parmesan mixed with breadcrumbs towards the end of the roasting time will enhance both the scrunch factor and the flavour. You'll need a large kitchen spoon to 'toast rack' the potatoes.

sixteen medium-sized potatoes · butter · olive oil · (optional) finely grated parmesan mixed with fine fresh white breadcrumbs

Peel the potatoes and leave them in cold salted water. Put a potato into the bowl of the spoon and make crossway cuts at 1cm intervals – the rim of the spoon will control the depth of the cut. Repeat with the other potatoes, then blot them dry with kitchen paper.

Preheat the oven to 200C fan/gas mark 7. Heat 55g butter and four tablespoons of oil in a small pan. Put the potatoes, cut-side up, into a roasting tin and brush them generously with the hot fat. Season generously, then roast the potatoes for 45 minutes. Take them out, brush them with more of the fat and sprinkle them – if you like – with a handful of the parmesan breadcrumbs. Continue to roast the potatoes for about 15 minutes if they've got the parmesan breadcrumbs on top, or a bit longer if they're plain. Remove them when they're brown, crusty and tender.

Asian-spiced potatoes and onions

Baking vegetables en masse is a simple way of achieving a variety of flavours and textures without complication. In this recipe, I've suggested adding some subtle spicing to the vegetables. The spices are all available in good supermarkets but you could use ground cumin, cloves or caraway seeds, if you prefer. The vegetables need space around them so, if you have a modern stove, use the oven trays that were supplied with it. Either orange or white-fleshed sweet potatoes would be fine but for the 'normal' potatoes use something not too floury, such as Desirée.

two large Spanish onions · two large sweet potatoes · three large baking potatoes · light soy sauce · sunflower oil · coriander seeds · Sichuan pepper (or black peppercorns) · nigella seeds · whole star anise · (optional) lime juice

Peel the onions and sweet potatoes but not the normal spuds. Cut the onions into sixths through the root end, so the layers stay attached. Cut both types of potato into sixths lengthways, but if the sweet ones are very slim they will only need quartering. Whisk two tablespoons of soy sauce, four tablespoons of cold water and a slurp of oil together in a bowl and leave aside.

Preheat the oven to 200C fan/gas mark 7. Combine a scant teaspoon of the coriander, Sichuan pepper and nigella seeds, plus two star anise in an electric spice grinder or mortar and pulverise into a powder – ignore any coriander husk. Tip the spices into a very large mixing bowl with some seasoning. Add the onion, potatoes and a good slug of oil, then toss thoroughly but gently.

Spread the vegetables out on oven trays and roast them for 25 minutes. Remove the trays and brush the vegetables with the soy mixture, then continue baking for 10-15 minutes, or until the vegetables are slightly charred and tender. Serve immediately, with or without a little squeeze of lime juice – it does add a certain vivacity, but I'm not entirely sure it's necessary.

celeriac oven chips

Practically all root vegetables and tubers make good chips (I haven't tried swede, and hope I never do) but celeriac and parsnips must be the front runners. This recipe will work for both of them but parsnips need much less cooking time. The chips can be cut and, as long as they are blanched and tossed in the curry powder, kept for a few hours in a cool place: raw celeriac will go brown.

three heads of celeriac · groundnut or vegetable oil · curry powder

Peel and cut the celeriac into thumb-thick slices and then into fat chips. Bring a very large saucepan of salted water to the boil and blanch the chips for 2-3 minutes. Drain thoroughly, then throw them back in the warm pan with a dollop of oil, a tablespoon of curry powder and some salt. Toss the chips until they're thoroughly coated, then spread them out on heavy baking sheets. **Preheat the oven to 210C fan/gas mark 8** and bake them for about 25 minutes, or until tender and golden.

red-hot sweet potato gratin

If you're as much a sucker for a voluptuous, creamy gratin as I am you won't need much persuading to try this sweet potato version. It's ludicrously rich so a little goes a long way but (psychologically at least) adding some chilli does help temper the feeling one's arteries are narrowing perceptibly with each mouthful. The gratin looks rather jolly made with different coloured potatoes but don't worry if you can only get a single variety. It will keep, made-up, for a couple of hours before being baked but not much longer.

shallots · garlic cloves · 1kg mixed orange and white-fleshed sweet potatoes · a (568ml) carton of double cream · ground cumin · chilli sauce · butter

Finely chop two shallots and two garlic cloves. Peel the potatoes then put them through the fine slicing blade of a food processor. Tip them into a very large bowl with the shallots and garlic. Add the cream, a teaspoon of ground cumin and a tablespoon of chilli sauce. Use your hands to mix all the ingredients together very thoroughly.

Preheat the oven to 140C fan/gas mark 3. Butter a 26-28cm ovenproof dish. Put a layer of cream-coated potatoes in the bottom of the dish and add seasoning. Add another two layers, seasoning each time. For the final layer, carefully alternate the colours and arrange the slices in a neat concentric design. Pour any remaining cream over the top, dot with butter, then bake the gratin for about 90 minutes. Check to make sure the cream isn't bubbling because if the temperature is too high, the 'sauce' will split. When the potatoes are tender to the point of a small knife, remove the dish and keep the gratin warm for 15-30 minutes – it actually tastes better warm, rather than scalding hot.

buttery mash

I'd rather have mash than chips any day – in fact I envy babies and their delectable, gum-slurping food. Okay, you might not put quite so much milk and butter in a baby's mash, and it's obviously hideously fattening, but who says you have to eat it every day? The potatoes can be cooked and mashed a few hours ahead, then reheated over a low flame, with the milk and butter beaten in as below. (Don't be tempted to mash the potatoes in a food processor as it will simply whizzard them into a horribly gooey mess.)

about 2kg floury potatoes, e.g. King Edward · full-fat milk · softened butter

Cut the peeled potatoes into egg-sized chunks and boil them in a large saucepan of salted water for 15-20 minutes, or until they're completely tender. Drain, then return the spuds to the pan and set it over a very low flame (or on the warming plate of an Aga). Push the potatoes to one side and add about 200ml milk. Let the milk warm for a few minutes, then vigorously mash the potatoes until they are smooth. Add plenty of seasoning, particularly black pepper, then add about 140g butter. Mash again, until the potatoes are silky-fine and absolutely smooth, adding more milk and/or butter, depending on how rich and how soft you want the mash. (In France, pommes purée is almost sauce-like in its consistency.)

garlic mash

There is an unwelcome propensity for throwing everything but the scouring pad into mash nowadays (and into ice cream, too – is peanut butter, cookie dough and pretzel ice cream really an improvement on proper vanilla or coffee ice cream? I think not.) But a straightforward garlic mash is wonderful with stews and, perhaps more unexpectedly, with sautéed cod, halibut and the like. You can make both the potato part of the mash and the garlicky milk a few hours ahead. Reheat them separately in a microwave, or over a low flame (keeping the mash on the move with a wooden spoon), then beat them together.

a whole head of garlic · unsalted butter · full-fat milk · about 2kg floury potatoes, e.g. King Edward · (optional) olive oil

Break up the head of garlic and peel the cloves. (To make this easier, blanch them in boiling water for 2 minutes, drain, run cold water over them, then peel.) Heat 115g butter in a small saucepan over a low flame, then shallow-fry the cloves for 15-20 minutes, or until they're tender. Add 300ml milk, raise the heat, and bring to just below boiling point, uncovered. Pour the garlicky milk into a liquidiser or food processor, then whizz until smooth. Leave to one side if not immediately required.

While the garlic is cooking, cut the peeled potatoes into egg-sized chunks and boil in salted water for about 20 minutes, or until completely tender. Drain, then return the spuds to the pan and set it over a very low flame (or the warming plate of an Aga). Mash the potatoes thoroughly. Pour in the garlicky milk, add seasoning, and beat energetically until the mash is smooth and creamy – you can also add a slurp of olive oil for a more robust flavour and a slicker consistency.

jazzy parsnip mash

A teenaged customer at the C&C, who professed not to like parsnips, lapped up every scrap of this gorgeous mash – such is the power of these sweet root vegetables when they are given a spicy boost. You can make the mash a few hours ahead, then gently reheat it with a drop more milk and a dab of butter, stirring frequently.

about 2kg decorously sized parsnips · butter · ground cumin, chilli and nutmeg · full-fat milk · hazelnut or walnut oil

Peel and cut the parsnips into large, fairly even-sized chunks, discarding any particularly hard cores. Bring a pan of salted water to the boil and put the parsnips in. Cook them, half-covered, for 8-10 minutes, or until they're tender. Drain them well then return them to the pan.

Add about 100g of butter to the pan, with a teaspoon of cumin, a pinch of chilli, a little grated nutmeg and salt, and lots of ground black pepper. Leave over a low flame until the butter has melted, then add 250ml milk and three tablespoons of nut oil. Mash the parsnips and flavourings vigorously until completely smooth – it won't *look* as smooth as potato mash but a quick taste will tell you if there are any lumps left. Adjust the seasonings to taste.

butter bean and rosemary mash

If you think you hate butter beans, and anyone of my age has every right to (I'm thinking of school dinners, gristle-infested stews and bland, overcooked butter beans), this may change your mind. It's particularly good with baked ham. The mash can be made up to 48 hours ahead, and then gently reheated with a little more stock and olive oil.

garlic cloves · shallots · olive oil · the grated zest of an orange · a pinch of finely chopped rosemary · dry white wine · three (400g) cans of butter beans · Marigold vegetable powder

Crush four garlic cloves and roughly chop two shallots. Heat a small frying pan over a low-medium flame, then add enough oil to barely cover the base. When the oil is hot, throw in the garlic and shallots and fry them for 5-6 minutes, stirring frequently. Add the orange zest and a pinch or two of very finely chopped rosemary, stir, and fry for 1 minute. Pour in 100ml white wine, turn the flame up high, and bubble until there's hardly any liquid left.

Scrape the contents of the pan into a food processor then add the drained butter beans and a teaspoon of Marigold vegetable powder. Season generously (butter beans are pretty 'dumb'), then whizz into a smooth mash – I like to leave a *little* texture, but it's up to you. Put the mash back into the pan, set over a low flame, and heat through, stirring frequently. If the mash is too stiff add a little water or olive oil, and adjust the seasoning according to your taste buds' desire.

celeriac purée

Celeriac has a less brutal, more engaging flavour than celery: anyone who doesn't like celery should try it. With the addition of potato, it makes the most wonderful purée (like grown-up baby food), which goes splendidly with duck, goose, game and… well almost any roast meat, actually. You can make the mash up to a day ahead, but bring it to room temperature before gently reheating it – and you'll need to beat in more milk and butter as it will have stiffened up considerably.

garlic cloves · full-fat milk · four heads of celeriac · 1kg floury potatoes, e.g. King Edward or Maris Piper · softened butter · Dijon mustard

Peel and crush three or four garlic cloves, put them in a pan with 300ml milk and bring to just under boiling point over a medium flame. Remove the pan from the heat and leave the milk to infuse.

Peel, and cut both the celeriac and the potatoes into egg-sized chunks, then throw the celeriac into boiling salted water and simmer, half-covered, for 20 minutes. Add the potatoes and cook for a further 15-20 minutes, or until the vegetables are completely tender. Drain them thoroughly, then put them back in the pan. Strain two-thirds of the garlic-infused milk into the pan and mash thoroughly – don't use a food processor because the mash will quickly turn to celery-flavoured grouting. When it's as smooth as vanilla ice cream, beat in 125g softened butter, some seasoning and a dab of mustard, to taste. Depending on how sloppy you want the purée to be, add more of the milk.

chickpea and coriander mash

I love chickpeas but I love gussied-up, blitzed chickpeas even more. This mash is brilliant with griddled squid (by the by), as well as Mediterranean-style stews. You can easily make the mash a few hours ahead, then gently reheat it over a low flame, adding a little more water or olive oil to bring it back to a firm slush (a perfectly logical oxymoron).

garlic cloves · shallots · olive oil · ground cumin · three (400g) cans of chickpeas · Marigold vegetable powder · Greek yoghurt · fresh coriander or parsley

Crush four garlic cloves and roughly chop two shallots. Heat a small pan over a medium flame, then add oil to cover the base. When the oil is hot, fry the garlic and shallots for 5-6 minutes, stirring frequently, until just tinged with colour. Add a teaspoon of cumin, stir, and fry for 1 minute. Scrape everything into a food processor, add the rinsed and drained chickpeas, a heaped teaspoon of Marigold vegetable powder and some seasoning. Whizz to a smoothish mash. Put the mash back into the pan, set over a low flame, and heat through, stirring frequently. If the mash is too stiff add a little water or olive oil, according to taste, then stir in some chopped coriander and a big dollop of yoghurt.

polenta

It's bland and boring, and I love, love, love it. Presumably in an attempt to make polenta more appealing to non-believers, there's a burgeoning trend for stirring cheese, herbs and other flavourings into it but I think this defeats the object as polenta was born to be plain. Its purpose in life is to play a strong supporting role to something more interesting (just like aubergines). My only concession is to stir in a knob of butter and lots of black pepper. To the northern Italians, eating soft polenta with game or chunky sausages is as normal as the British serving roast potatoes with roast beef. Novice polenta-eaters may find grilled polenta more appealing – it's especially good with calves' liver Veneziana or meaty ragouts.

There's no doubt that proper polenta – the sort the cook has to stir for longer than a lifetime, and which demands the wearing of goggles and gauntlet gloves, so viciously does the pot spit – is the best. I know, because I have made it this way myself, and more than once (bravery award in the post). But for all the reasons above, I am not averse to using improper polenta. (I don't mean the slabs or rolls of cooked polenta, which also have their use, but the 'instant' stuff, or 'istantanea', as the excellent De Cecco brand is called).

Even 'instant' polenta requires vigorous attention, so arm yourself with a long, stout wooden spoon and if you can co-opt someone to help with pouring in the grains while you do the stirring, so much the better. Soft polenta has to be served the minute it's ready, but if this doesn't suit you then let it get cold and grill it.

500g instant polenta · butter · olive oil

Bring two litres of water to the boil in a large pan of water. Add some salt, then pour in the polenta very slowly, stirring constantly – the slower it's added to the water the less likelihood of lumps forming. Keep stirring for 5-8 minutes (depending on the brand you use), or until the polenta is softly thick and completely smooth. Stir in a large knob of butter and a good grinding of black pepper, then serve.

For grilled polenta: have an oiled dish or roasting tin ready, and pour the soft polenta into it. Smooth out the surface and leave the polenta to set. It will keep for 48 hours refrigerated. When you want to use it, turn the block out and cut it into slabs – think half a slice of hand-cut toast for size. Brush the slices with olive oil. Heat a griddle and cook the polenta for a few minutes each side, until it's lightly coloured. Or put it under a hot grill and do the same.

courgettes with pine nuts and raisins

A much-used recipe book at the Crown and Castle is *Moro, The Cookbook.* In the vanguard of the fashion for Moorish cooking, it is packed with recipes for delectable-sounding, interesting (but never outlandish) food. We've tinkered with the Moro recipe a bit, adding some saffron and spinach, and halving the enormous amount of courgettes – allowing 200g per person is, I am convinced, a mistake incurred in the translation of the original restaurant recipe to a domestic scale. Anyway, I think it's too much. Except for adding the dill and spinach, the courgettes can be prepared up to 48 hours ahead.

two Spanish onions · 1kg courgettes · raisins · olive oil · saffron threads· toasted pine nuts · 125g young leaf spinach · fresh dill

Halve the onions and slice them finely. Trim the courgettes and cut them at an angle into thick slices. Cover a handful of raisins with warm water, leave them to soak for 30 minutes, then drain them.

Heat a large, wide saucepan over a low-medium flame. Pour in enough oil to cover the base generously, and heat it up. Add the onions, stir thoroughly, then fry them for about 5 minutes. Add a big pinch of saffron and fry for 1 minute, stirring frequently. Add the courgettes, stir thoroughly, and fry them for 6-8 minutes, until they are just tender and lightly coloured. Stir in the drained raisins and a handful of pine nuts, and let them heat through. The recipe can be taken to this point ahead of time, but will need to be gently reheated over a low flame before continuing.

Add the spinach leaves, a small handful of chopped dill and plenty of seasoning. Cook for a couple of minutes, stirring occasionally, until the spinach leaves have just wilted, then serve.

gently curried peas

You don't have to be a huge fan of either curry or peas to enjoy this saucily spiced ragout, which goes particularly well with pork belly and duck confit. Most of the ragout can be made up to 24 hours ahead, then gently reheated, with just the tomato and coriander needing to go in at the last moment. If you can't be bothered to make the tomato concassée, use half a tin of *chair de tomate* instead.

four large tomatoes · a Spanish onion · a red chilli · lime leaves · sunflower oil · mustard seeds · whole star anise · nigella seeds · ground turmeric · ground coriander · ground cumin · 600g peas (shelled weight) · fresh coriander

Blanch, peel, de-seed and roughly chop the tomatoes to make the concassée. Halve the onion and slice it thinly. De-seed and finely chop the chilli. Put three lime leaves in a saucepan with 225ml boiling water, then set the pan aside.

Heat a large, wide saucepan over a low-medium flame, then add enough oil to barely cover the base. When the oil is hot, add one heaped teaspoon of mustard seeds and fry them for about a minute, or until they 'pop'. Add the onion, chilli and two star anise, then fry for 8-10 minutes, stirring, until the onion has softened and is lightly coloured. Add two pinches of nigella seeds and one teaspoon each of ground turmeric, coriander and cumin, and fry for 1-2 minutes, stirring frequently.

If you are using *fresh* peas, add them, and the lime leaves together with the water they have been soaking in. Bring to a boil over a medium heat and simmer until the peas are tender. If you are using *frozen* peas, add only half the soaking liquid from the lime leaves, bring the contents to a boil and then immediately remove the pan from the heat. Season to taste, then remove the star anise before stirring in the coriander and the tomato concassée.

pea and pancetta fricassée

Finding decent quality fresh peas is almost impossible but here any deficiencies in quality are well masked. The fricassée is intentionally sloppy so you'll need to serve it in those big (and now unfashionable) cheffy-style soup plates. Most of the recipe can be made a day or so ahead.

garlic cloves · a large Spanish onion · three carrots · two sticks of celery · three courgettes · vegetable oil · 140g cubed pancetta · about 500ml vegetable or chicken stock · 500g fresh peas (shelled weight) · fresh chervil

Crush two or three cloves of garlic then chop them finely. Cut the trimmed and/or peeled onion, carrots, celery and courgettes into small dice.

Heat a large, wide pan over a low-medium heat and add enough oil to barely cover the base of the pan. When the oil is hot, add the garlic, onion and pancetta and fry gently for about 5 minutes, stirring occasionally. Add the carrots and celery, and fry for another 3-4 minutes, stirring occasionally. Add the courgettes and pour in just enough stock to cover. Bring to a simmer and cook for a few minutes, or until the courgettes are barely tender. Tip in the peas and a small handful of chopped chervil, then cook for 3-4 minutes, or until the vegetables are tender but definitely not mushy.

Right: Pea and pancetta fricassée

trinity red cabbage

It's hard to think of a more accommodating vegetable – once cooked, the spicy red cabbage will keep for a week in the fridge and can then be reheated either in a microwave, or over a low flame. Marvellous. The only problem is I feel the same way about red cabbage as I do venison, in other words I can't stand the stuff. But we get lots of compliments about the way we cook it at the Crown and Castle so what do I know…

a large onion · a red cabbage · duck or goose fat (or dripping) · ground cardamom · ground cinnamon · red wine vinegar · redcurrant jelly · dark muscovado sugar · a bramley apple ·

Cut both the peeled onion and apple into small dice. Cut the cabbage into eight wedges, remove the hard cores, then finely slice the wedges crossways. **Preheat the oven to 120C fan/gas mark 1.**

Heat a non-reactive casserole over a low-medium flame and add a knob of fat. When the fat is hot, fry the onion for 3-4 minutes, stirring occasionally, then stir in a generous pinch of cardamom and a teaspoon of cinnamon, and fry for 1 minute. Raise the heat, add the cabbage, a tablespoon of red wine vinegar, a heaped tablespoon of redcurrant jelly and three tablespoons of muscovado sugar, then stir thoroughly. When the pot starts to bubble, cover the casserole and put it in the oven. Cook for 90 minutes, stirring once in a while. Peel and cut the apple into small dice and stir in when the cabbage is just tender. Carry on cooking for about 20 minutes, then remove the casserole and season the cabbage to taste.

buttered cabbage with juniper

I adore cabbage in all its many guises, except for red cabbage and Brussels sprouts which I dislike more than Jack Straw, Trevor MacDonald and Donald Trump put together (and that's a lot). This cabbage tastes equally good without the juniper (the berries that give gin its idiosyncratic flavour), but do try it this way at least once as it's a jolly good combo, especially with game.

a Savoy cabbage · butter · Marigold vegetable powder · juniper berries

Trim the coarse outer leaves from the cabbage then cut it into eight wedges. Cut out and discard the hard cores, then slice each wedge into ribbons, crossways. Rinse the cabbage in a colander and pile the damp shreds into a very large saucepan. Add two big knobs of butter, two teaspoons of Marigold vegetable powder and a teaspoon of crushed juniper berries. Cook the cabbage over a medium-high flame, covered, for 3 minutes. Remove the lid and start tossing the cabbage with two wooden spoons or salad servers. Continue to cook it like this for about 5 minutes, or until the cabbage is tender but still has a little bite left. Drain off any excess liquid, season to taste, and serve.

spinach with capers

Spinach is a truly beautiful vegetable, whether it's served plain or creamed (but never when it's overcooked and soggy). This nutty, buttery version is really good, but I do know the world divides between those who love capers, and those who would rather talk about African debt relief with Jade Goody (I'm going to regret this JG refrain, I know). By all means, omit the capers, but don't pass on clarifying the butter: it may seem like a chore, but clarified butter doesn't burn easily, and keeps for at least 2 weeks in the fridge. The spinach itself can be prepared up to 24 hours in advance.

unsalted butter · about 2.5kg leaf spinach · grated nutmeg · capers

To clarify the butter, put 125g butter into a small saucepan, heat it over a low-medium flame until it starts to bubble, then pull the pan to one side. Wait until a milky cloud has settled on the bottom, then carefully pour off the clear, golden liquid on top – that's clarified butter. Discard the cloudy sediment.

Using a very large saucepan (so the water stays more or less on the boil), blanch the spinach in batches, 30 seconds at time. Refresh the leaves in ice-cold water, then drain thoroughly. Pile the spinach into the middle of a clean, threadbare tea towel (again in batches, if necessary), twist the ends and squeeze dry.

Heat a very large frying pan over a medium flame, then add the clarified butter and some grated nutmeg. After a few minutes, when the butter is ginger bread-coloured and smells nutty, stir in the spinach and grind in lots of black pepper. Stir again, then add a small handful of rinsed capers. Lower the heat and continue tossing the spinach for a couple of minutes, or until it has warmed through – it doesn't need any cooking as such.

purple sprouting broccoli

I adore the colour, texture and the slightly mineral flavour of purple sprouting broccoli. In fact, I am not sure I wouldn't rather eat it than asparagus. Its normal late-winter appearance seems to come earlier each year, but if you can't find any by all means use normal green calabrese. In this case, you'll have to cut any thick stems lengthways to make flat-sided florets and it will also need blanching for a minute longer. You can prepare the broccoli up to 12 hours before frying it.

garlic cloves · about 700g trimmed purple sprouting broccoli · sunflower oil · toasted sesame oil

Cut five or six garlic cloves into very fine slices. Bring a large saucepan of salted water to the boil and blanch the broccoli for 2 minutes. Drain, refresh in ice-cold water, then drain again and pat dry.

Heat a very large frying pan over a medium flame, then add enough sunflower oil to barely cover the base. When it's hot, throw in the garlic and fry for 2-3 minutes, stirring constantly. As soon as it is a light golden colour (garlic carries on browning very quickly, so beware), add the broccoli and 3 tablespoons of sesame oil. Toss gently but thoroughly, then fry for 2-3 minutes, until the florets are piping hot and imbued with the garlicky oil.

the best carrots

Half the reason why these carrots are so good is down to the way they are cut (as ever, far easier to do than describe), and half to the glossy, sweet glaze. This depends entirely on the ratio of liquid to surface area and heat, so be prepared to ditch some liquid if the carrots are nearly cooked and there's still too much of it sloshing around: listen for the bubbling noise to change to a soft phut-phut, and then a sharp spit-spat as the clear, shiny glaze develops. These carrots go down a storm, so it's worth mastering the technique. You can get everything ready in the pan a few hours ahead (except the herbs and lemon juice).

1.5kg medium carrots · unsalted butter · golden caster sugar · fresh dill or parsley or tarragon · lemon juice

Put a (topped, tailed and peeled) carrot on the board with the thick end pointing left (if you're right-handed). Place a big chopping knife about 4cm up from the thin end of the carrot, the blade at a 45 degree angle, and cut. Roll the carrot a quarter turn towards you, place the blade 4cm up the carrot, and repeat the action. Keep turning and cutting, discarding the last piece if the core is too thick and woody.

Put the carrots, 115g butter and three tablespoons of sugar in a wide, shallowish saucepan, so the carrots are pretty spread out, then add cold water to barely cover. Put the pan on a high flame, covered, until it reaches the boil then take off the lid and keep boiling for 8-12 minutes, or until the carrots are tender. Off the heat, add two or three tablespoons of chopped herbs, seasoning, and a good squeeze of lemon juice, to taste. Toss the carrots to coat them in the glaze, and serve.

charred tomatoes

Tomatoes not only become delightfully jammy when they've been baked slowly, the flavour intensifies too – an admirable thing, especially when the toms are hothouse nonentities. This technique also explains the popularity of 'sunblush' tomatoes – why *do* people have to come up with these appallingly coy descriptions? The tomatoes are best served at either room temperature or warm from the oven – but not fridge-cold.

eight large tomatoes · garlic cloves · olive oil · balsamic vinegar · dark muscovado sugar · fresh basil leaves

Cut the tomatoes in half around their midriffs. Slice three or four garlic cloves into long slivers. **Preheat the oven to 140C fan/gas mark 3.** Put a big griddle over a medium-high flame. Brush the surface of the tomatoes with oil, place them cut-side down on the hot griddle, and cook for 1 minute.

Carefully transfer the tomatoes to a baking tin, cut-side up this time. Brush them again, first with balsamic vinegar and then with more oil. Put two or three slivers of garlic on each one, followed by a pinch or two of muscovado sugar. Bake the tomatoes for 1 hour, or until they are sticky and deeply coloured. Before serving trickle on a drop more oil and scatter the tomatoes with torn basil leaves.

fennel and black olive gratin

This is brilliant with roast lamb. Please don't be tempted to omit the olives as they help create one of the most interesting gratins I've ever made or eaten. The fennel can be prepared and blanched up to 24 hours ahead, but assemble the dish only an hour or so before it needs to go in the oven.

four plump bulbs of fennel · butter · 100g dry-cured olives (preferably with herbs) · a (284ml) carton of double cream · grated parmesan

Trim any discoloured or coarse outer layers from the fennel. Peel off the layers, one by one, cutting off the root part as you go. (Fennel peelings are great in a shellfish stock). Cut the layers into tulip petal-sized pieces, always slicing along the grain. Bring a pan of salted water to the boil, throw in the fennel and boil, uncovered, for 5 minutes. Drain thoroughly.

Preheat the oven to 200C fan/gas mark 7. Lightly butter an ovenproof dish and arrange half the fennel in the bottom. Roughly chop the olives and scatter them on top. Cover with the remaining fennel, season, and pour over the cream. Strew with a thick layer of grated parmesan. Bake the gratin for about 20 minutes, or until the cream is bubbling and the fennel is tender. Leave to cool for 5-10 minutes before serving – the gratin is better warm than roasting hot.

creamed mushrooms

This is simply a good-tasting mess of creamy mushrooms that never fails to please. The mushrooms can be cooked a few hours ahead, then gently reheated.

two red onions · garlic cloves · 750g flat mushrooms · olive oil · unsalted butter · grated nutmeg · mascarpone · grated parmesan · fresh parsley · (optional) lemon juice

Roughly chop the onions. Crush and finely chop four garlic cloves. Wipe the mushrooms and *very* roughly chop them, trimmed stalks and all.

Heat a very large frying pan or wide, shallow saucepan over a low-medium flame. Add two tablespoons of oil and a big knob of butter and when the fat is hot, add the onions and garlic. Fry for 5-6 minutes, stirring occasionally. Add the mushrooms, a little grated nutmeg and seasoning. Toss the mushrooms in the fat, then fry them for 3-4 minutes, stirring frequently, until they have just wilted.

Stir in a dollop or two of mascarpone, a handful of grated parmesan and a handful of chopped parsley. Cook for about 2 minutes, or until everything is piping hot and the 'sauce' has thickened. Adjust the seasoning to taste, and add a squeeze of lemon juice if you want to temper the richness.

leeks in tarragon cream sauce

I love this simple but elegant way of serving leeks: tarragon has a marvellous affinity with them. As an added bonus, the dish can be cooked a few hours ahead and gently reheated. You'll need both whole sprigs of tarragon and chopped tarragon leaves, but don't put the latter in until just before serving.

a (568ml) carton of double cream · fresh tarragon · about 1.5kg leeks

Put the cream in a saucepan with a few sprigs of tarragon and bring to the boil over a medium flame, uncovered. Bubble for a few minutes, or until the cream has thickened a little. Take the pan off the heat and leave it to one side.

Slice the leeks in half lengthways, then cut them into centimetre-thick slices. Bring a pan of salted water to the boil, throw in the leeks and boil for 2-3 minutes, or until the leeks are *just* tender. Drain them really thoroughly, blotting up the excess moisture with kitchen paper or a clean tea towel.

Return the leeks to the dry pan, add plenty of seasoning and strain in the infused cream (discarding the sprigs of tarragon). Reheat the leeks over a medium flame, stirring occasionally. Simmer until the cream is thick enough to coat the leeks nicely, then stir in a couple of tablespoons of chopped tarragon just before serving.

watercress and orange salad

Roast duck (or confit) is the obvious thing to eat with this vibrant salad, but it's jolly nice with roast pork or chicken, too. One of my pet hates about any salad is when the leaves aren't broken into forkable, one-bite mouthfuls, and watercress is particular trying in this respect: having a clump of oily greenery slapping round your cheeks, like a seal with a herring, is not a good look. So, do make sure you break the sprigs up. Both the leaves and the dressing can be prepared up to 24 hours ahead (refrigerate the leaves in a plastic bag) but don't dress the salad until the last minute.

four bunches of watercress · two heads of Belgian chicory · three juicy oranges · red wine vinegar · Dijon mustard · extra-virgin olive oil

Trim the watercress assiduously and tear it into attractive, not-too-large sprigs. Trim the chicory and tear off the leaves, breaking them in half. Discard the hard cores. Remove the zest from one orange and chop it finely. Squeeze the juice from this orange. Slice off both peel and pith from the other two oranges, then cut between the membranes to remove 'clean' segments of orange flesh.

To make the dressing, whisk a tablespoon of red wine vinegar with a scant teaspoon of mustard and some seasoning. Add six tablespoons of olive oil and whisk into a thick emulsion. Whisk in the orange zest and about three tablespoons of orange juice. Taste, and adjust the flavours to your liking. Toss the watercress and chicory with the dressing, add the orange segments and gently toss again.

French bean and shallot salad

A classic French dish, and in its simplicity one of the best. Obviously the salad goes very well with cold meats, but I love it with smoked fishes and, as long as it's not fridge-cold, roast chicken. French beans come into their own in the spring, when home-grown greenery has yet to arrive and root veg has started to outstay its welcome. If you buy extra-fine beans you won't have to snap or cut them in half as the length will be okay; fine beans may need to be cut in half. Both beans and dressing can be prepared up to 24 hours ahead. Assemble the salad just before it's needed.

about 600g extra-fine French beans · Dijon mustard · red wine vinegar · lemon juice · groundnut or sunflower oil · double cream · shallot

Bring a pan of salted water to the boil and blanch the beans for 2 minutes, then refresh them in ice-cold water. Drain and pat them completely dry with kitchen paper. Top and tail the beans (I can't stand the current cheffy fad for leaving on the wiggly stalks).

To make the dressing, whisk a teaspoon of Dijon mustard, a tablespoon of red wine vinegar and a tablespoon of lemon juice together with some seasoning. Add 6-8 tablespoons of oil and whisk into a thick emulsion. Add 2 tablespoons of double cream and whisk again.

Toss the beans in the dressing, put them in a serving dish, then scatter them with a little finely chopped shallot – not so much that all you can taste is onion, but enough to add a bit of chutzpah.

honourable Asian-style slaw

Maddening, I know, to tell you how good this is with Asian-style fishcakes and griddled tiger prawns, when there isn't a recipe for any such food in this book (ah, but there is in *Fat Girl Slim* – go purchase). But it's also excellent with Asian-style pork belly and soy-marinated roast beef, and you will find those recipes here. The slaw is a real palate wakener and very popular at the Crown and Castle. Without the bean sprouts, sesame seeds, dressing and herbs (all of which can be added at the last minute), the slaw will keep for up to 48 hours.

a red onion · two courgettes · two carrots · a red pepper · a handful of radishes · 125g bean sprouts · toasted sesame seeds · Thai fish sauce · dark soy sauce · sweet chilli sauce · golden caster sugar · two limes · fresh mint · fresh coriander

Do whatever you have to do to smarten up the veg, whether it's scraping, peeling, de-seeding or topping and tailing. Halve the onion from root end to stem, then slice it finely along the grain. Cut the courgettes and carrots in half to shorten the length, then cut all the veg into fine matchsticks (except the bean sprouts, which already are… sort of). Jumble all the vegetables and the sesame seeds together in a bowl.

To make the dressing, whisk two tablespoons of Thai fish sauce, one tablespoon of dark soy, one tablespoon of sweet chilli sauce, a teaspoon of sugar and the juice of a lime together. Taste, and add more lime juice and sugar if you think the dressing needs further sharpening or sweetening: it should be zingy but not cauterisingly acidic. Pour the dressing over the slaw, add a tablespoon of chopped mint leaves and a big handful of chopped coriander, then toss thoroughly.

honourable European slaw

Am I alone in finding commercial coleslaw utterly loathsome? Every tub I've ever broached (or been served) seems to taste of metal filings soused in battery acid. The worst cook this side of the Humber would have to make coleslaw very badly indeed to rival the repellent qualities of the factory-made stuff. I am pretty sure the secret of a good slaw is in keeping the onion content to a minimum and having a decent dressing, but see what you think… the slaw will keep for at least 48 hours.

a quartered white cabbage · a quartered red cabbage · a shallot · two sticks of celery · three carrots · sherry vinegar · grain mustard · golden caster sugar · sunflower oil · crème fraîche · double cream

Cut each quartered cabbage in half, remove and discard the cores, then finely slice each wedge crossways. Slice the shallot finely. Grate the celery and carrots coarsely. Combine all the vegetables in a large bowl.

To make the dressing, whisk two tablespoons of sherry vinegar, one tablespoon of grain mustard, one teaspoon of sugar and some seasoning together. Add six tablespoons of oil and whisk to a thick emulsion. Add two tablespoons of crème fraîche and five tablespoons of double cream and whisk again. Taste, adjust the seasonings, then pour the dressing over the vegetables and toss thoroughly.

Belgian chicory salad with mustard dressing

A vigorous-tasting salad of pearly-white, bitter chicory leaves, napped in a smooth, sweetish mustard dressing, this is a marvellous side dish with game and roast meats. Both the dressing and the prepared leaves (store the latter in a plastic bag) will keep refrigerated for 48 hours.

six heads of Belgian chicory · a bunch of watercress · fresh chives · Dijon mustard · caster sugar · cider or white wine vinegar · groundnut or sunflower oil · whipping cream

Trim the chicory and tear off the leaves, roughly breaking them in half. Discard the hard core porn – ah, I think I meant to write 'part'. Rummage through the watercress, discarding any hairy or coarse stalks. Combine all the leaves with a small handful of chopped chives.

To make the dressing, whisk a tablespoon each of mustard, sugar and vinegar together with some seasoning. Whisk in three tablespoons of oil, then about 150ml of cream. The dressing should be smooth, thickly pourable and politely piquant, so adjust any of the elements to your taste.

Pile the leaves on to a flattish dish then trickle the dressing over them in a casual but attractive manner. Don't toss the salad, though, as it will end up looking an almighty mess.

roast red pepper salad

There is a world of difference between winter-grown, tasteless, even-sized, hot-house peppers and the ripe, almost claret-coloured, knobbly looking ones grown in the Mediterranean area – and only available in the summer. (There's also a world of difference in the price: in season, peppers cost half as much.) The latter are the sort you need for this simple but sumptuous salad. It can be made and dressed up to 48 hours ahead, but bring the salad to warm room temperature before serving it.

eight ripe red peppers · a tin of anchovies · red wine vinegar · fruity extra-virgin olive oil · (optional) dry-cured black olives

If your stove is gas-fired, balance the peppers over the burners' naked flames and blacken them on all sides, turning the peppers with stout tongs. It makes an unholy mess and takes a good 15 minutes, but there is something rather satisfying about watching them blister and char. (Or, rather more prosaically, you could put the peppers under a very hot grill – but they'll still need turning.) When the peppers are completely black, seal them in a large plastic bag and leave them for about 10 minutes. Scrape off the blistered skin, being careful not to burn yourself on any hot steam that may escape. Halve the peppers, de-seed them and discard the stalks. Cut the petals of flesh into thick strips and trim off the raggedy edges.

To make the dressing, pound two or three strips of anchovy in a mortar, then whisk in a tablespoon of red wine vinegar and some ground black pepper (but not salt). Add 7-8 tablespoons of oil and whisk to a thick emulsion.

Arrange the peppers in a serving dish (earthenware looks good) then cover with the dressing. Gussy up the salad with a handful of stoned olives or a few more strips of anchovy – the latter would be my preference.

guidelines for a fine leaf salad

Making an omelette is often used as a test to determine whether a person can cook. While I agree that turning out a soft pouch of creamily coagulated curds requires particular skill, I think that assembling a good salad requires an even greater deftness of touch – and shows an ability to bring both disparate and similar ingredients together in an harmonious yet exciting whole.

My favourite traiteur/café in London is Ottolenghi (in fact, there are three branches, as I write). The reason is that the food – mostly big, bold salads, genuinely rustic breads, seasonal tarts and cakes – is demonstrably home-made, with commensurate vitality and honesty. But, as demonstration that even the good guys don't always get it right, a salad I ate there recently – comprising beetroot, a chunk of undistinguished apple, olives, anchovies and capers – simply didn't work. It's fairly obvious the aim was to sharpen up the innate sweetness of the beetroot with a salty, sharp stab of flavour from the other ingredients. Unfortunately, it tasted overwhelmingly of saline vinegar: not so much the gentle tinkle of a triangle as the shrill, nasal squawk of the bagpipes.

There are three indisputable secrets to making a good salad. The first is to put together leaves which provide a pleasing contrast of texture and flavour. A salad comprising nothing but bitter leaves, such as radicchio, batavia and chicory is only a good idea if you think it's going to cure you of syphilis or bad breath. Throw in some sweeter leaves, such as Little Gem or romaine (cos lettuce is the same thing, by the way), and the balance becomes much more agreeable; add some peppery leaves, such as wild rocket or watercress, and the salad really starts to sing; finish it with a few tiny sprigs of parsley, chervil, tarragon or chives and you've got an operatic triumph on your table.

What a salad never needs is the addition of a harsh, strident flavour, such as raw onion. Anything wet and soggy, like over-ripe tomatoes or cucumber (or damp lettuce leaves for that matter) does a salad no favours either. And, because so many people hate beetroot (mostly because they've only ever had the disgusting vinegary stuff), there's little point in inviting the disapprobation it will cause by including it. (Unless you're having me round to dinner: one of my favourite salads of all time is rocket with home-roasted beetroot, soft-boiled eggs and anchovy dressing.)

Finally, any self-respecting salad not only needs a good dressing, it needs an *appropriate* dressing. From a textural point of view, it's madness to coat the tender leaves of an old-fashioned, round lettuce with a thick mayonnaise-based dressing because you'll end up with what looks like avocado face pack: delicate leaves need a delicate dressing. In contrast, thick-ribbed, crisp leaves, such as romaine, can easily withstand ointment-thick dressings, viz. Caesar salad. Then there's the flavour to consider: a robust, toasted oil dressing would be great with something like avocado and spinach salad or a ballsy gruyère, chicory and fresh walnut salad, but utterly repulsive with an egg and anchovy salad, I think you'd agree.

The point is you need to exercise the same intelligent thought you'd bring to bear in baking an extravagant cake as in making a simple salad. Salads aren't simple, which is why a good salad is so demonstrably better than an average salad.

salad dressings

A carefully devised dressing is vital in separating a marvellously inviting array of leaves from a bit of vegetation dallying on its way to the compost heap. Choosing the right oil for the dressing, be it olive, walnut, pistachio or sesame oil, and the right dressing for the ingredients, is really important. For example, olive oil doesn't have a uniform taste – extra-virgin is no indication of flavour, just a guarantee that the oil is derived from the first cold pressing. Olive oils all have an individual flavour, perhaps hot and peppery, or green and grassy, and should always be chosen to match the particular character of the salad ingredients. And, while it's fine to keep a dressing for 2 or 3 days, after that period I think most dressings start to get musty, despite still being edible – strictly speaking.

For all dressings, start off by vigorously whisking the acidic part (e.g. vinegar or lemon juice), with ground black pepper and fine sea salt (and mustard, if using), then stream in the oil(s) and carry on whisking until the dressing has emulsified into a thickish liquid.

a strong nutty dressing

1 tablespoon red wine vinegar

a dab of Dijon mustard

3 tablespoons groundnut or sunflower oil

3 tablespoons walnut, pistachio or argan oil

a mild nutty dressing

1 tablespoon red wine vinegar

3 tablespoons groundnut oil or sunflower oil

3 tablespoons hazelnut or almond oil

a sweet-tart dressing

1 garlic clove, very finely chopped

a pinch of sugar

2 tablespoons pomegranate molasses

2 tablespoons extra-virgin olive oil

2 tablespoons groundnut or sunflower oil

a light herb dressing

1 tablespoon tarragon or white wine vinegar

1 garlic clove, very finely chopped

a dab of Dijon mustard

2 tablespoons extra-virgin olive oil

4 tablespoons groundnut oil or sunflower oil

a handful of finely chopped fresh chervil, tarragon, dill, parsley and/or chives

a classic vinaigrette

1 tablespoon red wine vinegar

a dab of Dijon mustard

3 tablespoons extra-virgin olive oil

3 tablespoons groundnut oil or sunflower oil

my 'house' dressing

1 tablespoon sherry vinegar

1 tablespoon red wine vinegar

a dab of Dijon mustard

2 tablespoons pistachio or argan oil

2 tablespoons extra-virgin olive oil

2 tablespoons groundnut oil

Of all the chapters in any family cookery book, the pudding chapter is the one that needs no introduction, no explanatory preface and no cajolement to try something that may be unfamiliar. A sugar-infused finale to the meal is not just desirable but obligatory for most people.

This may come as a something of a surprise given the prevalence of health warnings about fat, sugar and carbohydrates. But, regardless of government proscriptions and the trend towards healthy eating, I can tell you that nothing makes a scrap of difference to the high consumption of desserts – well, certainly not when people are eating out.

The desire to finish lunch or dinner with something sweet is not confined to any particular section of society either. Young or old, fat or thin, oiks or snobs, polite or rude, male or female, it matters not a whit – there is a general passion for puddings. The take-up on our weekend menus proves the point: we offer two courses, with the main course price including either a starter or a pudding, and a third course available for a modest extra charge. Of the customers who only want two courses, at least seventy per cent will opt out of the starter in favour of a pudding, normally with an embarrassed or apologetic explanation as to why. Being someone who wants both a starter and a dessert (hang the main course), I am the last person to cavil. And, it's why the introduction to this collection of delectable tarts, cakes, pies, puddings and pavlovas is little more than an explanation as to why it needs no introduction.

big cakes
and confections

As a cook, I hate it when I'm cruising through a recipe and there's a sudden demand for a litre of custard I haven't got. Of course, the author doesn't entirely abandon the cook: there's always a recipe for custard tucked away somewhere at the back of the book, it's just that you didn't know you had to make any custard, hadn't planned on making any custard, and haven't got the time to make any damned custard. (Okay, okay, I can hear the admonitions that surely I, as a food writer, know you're always meant to read through the recipe first. Well, call me arrogant, call me stupid, but more often than not – like you – I don't bother.)

But… as a cookery writer, I do feel it's nonsense to repeat a recipe time and again that uses the same ingredients and techniques. This is just such a case because you can't make a tart without pastry to hold in the filling. My solution is to put this (standard, basic – call it what you will) recipe at the start of the chapter, and to shout a loud, clear warning at the very beginning of any recipe that requires a baked-blind pastry case.

Oh, and in case you're wondering about the title, there's absolutely no need to make both sweet and savoury shortcrust pastry as the filling will influence how the tart or pie tastes, hence this generic recipe. The pastry is very buttery so must be rolled out in a cool environment or it will fragment – however the amount of butter is also what makes it so good to eat.

universal shortcrust pastry

a heavy baking sheet

225g plain flour

1 teaspoon icing sugar

a pinch of fine sea salt

140g cold unsalted butter *roughly cubed*

1 large free-range egg yolk

3 tablespoons ice-cold water

It is easiest to use a food processor: whizz the flour, icing sugar and salt together for a few seconds, then add the butter. Whizz for another few seconds until the mixture looks like coarse breadcrumbs.

Whisk the egg yolk and water together and pour it into the flour mixture. Process until the pastry has collected in a ball around the spindle. Take it out, press lightly and quickly into a fat disc-shape and then wrap in cling film and leave to rest for at least an hour in the fridge.

Bring the pastry to cool room temperature. On a well-floured surface, and using a well-floured rolling pin, roll the pastry out to book-cover thickness. Line the tin with it, without any pulling or stretching, or it will shrink back when it's baked. Trim off the excess pastry, using a small knife – blade upwards, and working away from yourself. (You can leave an overhang – as many professional chefs do – and trim the excess off after it's baked. I don't, because I worry that it will fracture the case, but the decision is yours: I'm pretty cack-handed, you may be dexterous.) Put the lined tin back in the fridge to chill down for half an hour or so.

Preheat the oven to 180C fan/gas mark 6

Put the baking sheet in the oven to heat up. To blind-bake the pastry case, first protect it with baking parchment (just roughly torn or cut – don't make a meal of it), then tip in dried beans or über-smart ceramic baking beans to weigh it down. Cook the case on the baking sheet for 12-15 minutes, or until the pastry has 'set' and has a dry look about it. Remove the parchment and beans (keeping the latter for later use, of course), then carry on baking the case for another 5 minutes or so. The pastry should be very lightly coloured and without any hint of rawness. You have now got a 'blind-baked' pastry case. Hurrah.

Blind-bake a pastry case, as described at the start of this chapter. The filling can be made 2 days ahead and kept refrigerated. Assemble the pie and bake it no more than 3 or 4 hours before it's needed. There aren't many desserts more popular than lemon meringue pie. It's the combination of silky-textured, mouth-puckering lemon custard and crazily sweet, marshmallow meringue that does it. I'll admit, it's partly to be clever that I've used fragrant passion fruit juice instead of the traditional lemon in this recipe: the mitigating factor is that it tastes so good.

passion fruit meringue pie

a 26-27cm diameter x
4cm deep metal flan
tin with removable
base

about 10 passion fruit (250ml juice needed)

375g golden caster sugar

6 heaped tablespoons cornflour

2 pinches of fine sea salt

450ml cold water

8 large free-range eggs *separated*

175g unsalted butter *roughly cubed*

the juice of 1 lemon

Scrape all the pulp and seeds from the passion fruit into a food processor. Whizz them for about 30 seconds, then push the juice through a sieve and discard the seeds. Leave to one side.

Combine 150g caster sugar, the cornflour and salt in a large saucepan, then gradually whisk in the cold water to make a smooth mixture. Whisk the egg yolks and add them to the pan. Put the pan over a medium-high flame and bring the mixture to the boil, whisking most of the time. As soon as the mixture thickens dramatically, count to 30, then remove the pan from the heat.

Beat in the butter, then put the pan into a sink of ice-cold water and whisk for a minute or two to take the heat out. Add the passion fruit juice, taste, then add a squirt of lemon juice – the lemon really helps to bring out the flavour so be pretty bold with it, but not so courageous that you end up with lemon meringue pie rather than passion fruit pie… leave the filling to cool completely, giving it an occasional whisk to stop a skin forming.

Prepare the pie to this point, refrigerating the filling until it's required.

Put the egg whites and half the remaining sugar into a food mixer, or a very large, grease-free bowl if you are using an electric whisk. Whisk until the mixture is thick and glossy, and stands up in firm peaks, *then* add the rest of the sugar and continue to whisk until the peaks are even stiffer.

Preheat the oven to 170C fan/gas mark 5

To assemble the pie, dollop the filling into the pastry case, making sure it goes right into the corners as it tends to shrink away during baking. Pile the meringue on top and spread it out, taking it right to the edges, then swirl it into flamboyant peaks.

Put the tin on a heavy baking sheet and cook for 8-12 minutes, or until the meringue is a perfect sea of pinky-brown-capped waves. Cool the pie in its tin for at least 45 minutes before transferring it to a flat serving plate, but don't attempt to take it off its metal base. It should be served as soon as possible as the meringue starts to soften and weep as the hours tick by.

Blind-bake a pastry case, as described at the start of this chapter. The tart can be made up to 2 or 3 days ahead, but keep it cool rather than refrigerated.

A Frenchified rendition of that good old staple, Bakewell tart, for which there are more 'authentic' recipes than there are photographs of Elizabeth Hurley turning up to a first-night party – and as many claims that it should really be called Bakewell pudding. To be honest, I couldn't give a damn. All that matters is that the combination of fine buttery pastry, red fruit jam and squishy, almond-flavoured frangipane is very attractive, if fairly prosaic – not at all like Jade Goody, but quite like Elizabeth Hurley.

frangipane tart

a 30-32cm diameter
x 3.5cm metal flan tin
with removable base
a heavy baking sheet

400g unsalted butter *softened*

400g golden caster sugar

8 large free-range eggs *lightly beaten*

3 tablespoons plain flour

400g ground almonds

a few drops of almond essence

about 450g damson jam (or cherry, loganberry, plum, raspberry)

3-4 tablespoons flaked almonds

Preheat the oven to 160C fan/gas mark 4

Cream the butter and sugar in a food mixer until soft, pale and light. Slowly pour in the eggs, alternating them with a tablespoon of flour (to help stop any curdling – although adding the ground almonds will return the mixture to normal, so don't panic). Beat in the ground almonds, and add a few drops of almond essence. Taste the mixture: it should have a definite flavour of almonds, without being too overpowering.

Spread the jam quite thickly in the bottom of the pastry case, but don't go crazy or it will bubble through the frangipane: on the other hand, don't be too mean or you won't see or taste any jam at all.

Pile the almond mixture on top of the jam, smooth out the top and scatter on the flaked almonds. Put the tart on to the baking sheet and then into the oven for 30-40 minutes, or until it's golden brown and firmish to the touch. Leave the tart to cool in the tin before releasing it. Serve with thick cream or custard.

Blind-bake a pastry case, as described at the start of this chapter. Make the syrup up to 48 hours ahead but don't assemble the tart more than 8 hours before it's required. I go a bit soppy when I see a proper strawberry tart, the showy, glazed fruit plumped on top of a thick bed of old-fashioned crème patissière, the pastry a crumbling, buttery shell. Oft as not the eating doesn't quite square with the gorgeous appearance but, heck, that's life.

Here, I've substituted the crème pat. (as we call it in the trade) with a mascarpone base that probably isn't quite as luxurious-tasting as the real thing but perhaps tastes a bit more modern – no flour, you see – and is far easier to make.

raspberry tart

a 30-32cm diameter
x 2.5cm metal flan tin
with removable base

140g golden caster sugar

150ml hot water

3 tablespoons crème de framboise

500g mascarpone

about 800g fresh raspberries

about half a jar of redcurrant jelly

Put the sugar and water in a small, heavy saucepan, place it over a low-medium flame and stir until the crystals have completely dissolved. Turn up the heat and bring to a boil. Bubble furiously, without stirring, for about 5 minutes, or until a thickish golden syrup has formed. Remove the pan from the heat, stir in the liqueur, then leave the syrup to cool completely.

Put the mascarpone into a mixing bowl and beat in the cold syrup. Using a palette knife, spread the mascarpone over the bottom of the pastry case in an even layer. Arrange the raspberries on top, in a closely-packed concentric circle, starting from the outside.

Put the jelly in a small pan and add a couple of tablespoons of cold water. Stir over a low flame until the jelly has melted. Using a pastry brush, coat the raspberries with the jelly so they glisten prettily. Keep the tart cool, preferably not in the fridge, and serve the same day.

Blind-bake a pastry case, as described at the start of this chapter. The tart can be kept cool for about 8 hours but don't glaze it more than an hour or two ahead – after which it must not be refrigerated as the glaze will weep. If ever a recipe *didn't* need any spiel, this lemon tart is it. It's simply one of the sharpest, silkiest lemon tarts I've ever eaten. And is there anything better than lemon tart to finish a meal?

possibly-the-best lemon tart

a 26-27cm diameter x 3.5cm metal flan tin with removable base
a heavy baking sheet
a kitchen blow torch

400ml double cream
7 large free-range eggs
300g golden caster sugar

250ml lemon juice (about 6 lemons)
a few tablespoons icing sugar

Put the cream in large saucepan and slowly bring it to the boil over a low-medium flame. Take the cream off the heat and leave it to one side for a few minutes.

Preheat the oven to 150C fan/gas mark 3.5

Meanwhile, gently whisk the eggs in a large bowl that will be big enough to take all the mixture. Whisk in the sugar, then the lemon juice. (Don't over-whisk or the mixture will become too frothy and you'll end up with lemon Aero tart.)

Slowly pour the hot cream on to the mixture and gently stir it in. Put the empty pastry case on to the baking sheet. Hold a large sieve over the case and pour the custard through it. (This is to trap any eggy bits.) Carefully transfer the baking sheet to the oven.

Bake the tart in the preheated oven for about 25-30 minutes, or until the custard is firm but still has a slight wobble in the middle. Remove the tart from the oven and leave it to cool completely.

Release the tart, but leave it on the metal base. Sift icing sugar evenly and quite liberally over the surface of the tart, then glaze it using a kitchen blow torch set at a low flame: the sugar must be allowed to melt before it caramelises. Serve the tart naked, or with a dollop of crème fraîche.

Blind-bake a pastry case, as described at the start of this chapter. Make the tart up to 48 hours ahead but if you can keep it cool rather than refrigerate it, so much the better. Warm it in the oven or microwave before serving. Oh, oh, oh – I do so love this tart. It has got the most fantastic cakey-squidgy-fondant texture and there are plenty of nuts but not so many it feels like you're licking out tractor tyres. The bourbon also gives it a telling kick. Served warm with vanilla ice cream, it probably accounts for two days' worth of calories. Another problem is the tart is so rich there's probably enough here for about 14 servings…what the hell.

pecan and bourbon tart

a 30-32cm diameter
x 3.5cm metal flan tin
with removable base
a heavy baking sheet

600g shelled pecan nuts

175g unsalted butter *softened*

250g dark muscovado sugar

6 large free-range eggs *lightly beaten*

1 and a half teaspoons fine sea salt

650g golden syrup *warmed in the tin so it flows more easily*

a few drops of vanilla essence

6 tablespoons bourbon

Preheat the oven to 150C fan/gas mark 3.5

Put 500g of the pecan nuts in a food processor and whizz to the texture of coarse breadcrumbs, then leave them to one side.

Put the butter and sugar into a food mixer and beat for a few minutes, until the mixture is soft, pale and lighter in colour. (Or, use electric beaters.) Pour in the eggs very slowly, so the mixture doesn't curdle. Stir in the chopped pecans, salt, golden syrup, vanilla essence and bourbon.

Put the blind-baked pastry case on to a heavy baking sheet, then pour in the mixture. Sprinkle the remaining whole pecan nuts on top.

Bake the tart for about 50-60 minutes, or until firm to the touch and well-browned. Leave it to cool in the tin before releasing it. If you are not serving the tart immediately, it responds very well to a warm-up in the microwave, should you have such a beast. An accompanying scoop of vanilla ice cream is mandatory, as far as I'm concerned.

Blind-bake a pastry case, as described at the start of this chapter. The tart can be made up to 36 hours ahead and kept refrigerated. The nature of a chocolate tart may not be stringently defined, but in practical terms we all know when we are in the presence of the perfect, ur-chocolate tart (boy, do I miss Jonathan Meades' restaurant reviews). Not only should it taste as if it were the embodiment of all bitter chocolate, but the texture must flutter tantalisingly on the border between custard-creaminess, silky-unctuousness and molten-firmness – and, of course, the pastry must be whisper-fine, short and buttery. Here's that recipe.

bitter chocolate tart

a 26-27cm diameter x 3.5cm deep metal flan tin with removable base
a heavy baking sheet

450g dark chocolate (at least 70% cocoa solids) *broken*
200ml full-fat milk

1 (284ml) carton of double cream
4 large free-range eggs

Preheat the oven to 150C fan/gas mark 3.5

Melt the chocolate either in a microwave, or in a saucepan standing on the warming plate of an Aga, or in a bain-marie, the bowl suspended well clear of barely simmering water.

Meanwhile, combine the milk and cream in a large saucepan and heat to just under boiling point over a low-medium flame.

In a large mixing bowl, whisk the eggs just long enough to combine them. Pour the hot milk mixture over the eggs and lightly whisk. Rinse out the pan, pour the embryonic custard back in, and return it to a low-medium flame. Cook the custard, stirring constantly, until it thickens. (To be very safe, you can do this in a bain-marie but, personally, I think life's too short: it is unlikely to curdle as long as you stir it continually, and take the pan from the heat the minute it thickens.)

Pass the custard through a fine sieve on to the melted chocolate and gently beat them together (not too vigorously as you don't want to create bubbles). Put the pastry case on the baking sheet, then pour in the chocolate mixture. Put the tart into the oven and cook it for 5 minutes, then immediately switch the oven off.

Leave the tart to 'set' for about 1 hour, without opening the door. Take the tart out of the oven and leave it to cool completely. Don't release it from the tin until it's quite cold. Serve with a big blob of crème fraîche.

The marzipan crust can be cooked 24 hours in advance. Make the filling and assemble the pie no more than 5 or 6 hours before serving it. I am not sure if I'm astonished or not that the late Michael Smith's seminal recipe book *Fine English Cookery* is 33 years old. His recipes, along with Robert Carrier's and Jane Grigson's, formed the core of my repertoire when I first started cooking. This impossibly rich chocolate pie tipped up on our table rather too often, I suspect.

chocolate pie with toasted marzipan crust

a 25-26m diameter x 4cm deep non-stick metal flan tin with removable base, smeared lightly with a tasteless vegetable oil (or almond oil)

for the crust
250g ground almonds
85g caster sugar
the whites of 2 medium eggs *lightly whisked*
icing sugar

for the filling
350g dark chocolate (at least 65% cocoa solids) *roughly broken*
425ml single cream
(optional) whipped cream and toasted almonds

To make the crust, mix the ground almonds and sugar together, with just enough whisked egg white to form a lump of stiff paste (i.e. marzipan). Leave the paste in the fridge for about an hour.

Preheat the oven to 160C fan/gas mark 4

Dust a work surface with some icing sugar, then roll the paste out as thinly as you can. Lay it in the tin and press it evenly over the base and up the sides. Press, patch and mould as required – it won't come to any harm. Bake the crust for 20-25 minutes, or until it's golden and firm: if it seems to be darkening too quickly, reduce the heat – nuts burn easily!

Allow the crust to cool (and set) for about half an hour or so before gently releasing it. Don't let the crust get completely cold as it may stick – and afterwards don't refrigerate it as it will gradually soften (it tastes like old honeycomb and makes wonderful fridge-pickings the next day). Instead, store it in a cool place, wrapped in cooking foil.

For the filling, put the chocolate into a heatproof bowl. Bring the cream to a boil in a pan set over a medium flame, then pour it over the chocolate. Let the chocolate melt then stir until the cream is completely smooth. Leave it to cool. As the chocolate cream starts to set, start beating it, using electric beaters. Keep a beady eye on what's going on and if you see the cream starting to split, stop beating immediately. When the chocolate cream has puffed up, forms thick ribbons, and has lightened in colour, it's ready. Keep it in a cool place, not the fridge, until you're ready to fill the pie: pile the cream into the case, pushing the mixture right into the corners, then smooth the top.

Depending on your creative skills, you could pipe whipped cream on top and stud the swirls with toasted almonds. Otherwise, just serve the pie with a jug of thick cream.

The cake will keep for 2 days, preferably in a cool place rather than the fridge but, in any case, bring it to room temperature before serving. Back in the days when a dog peeing on Blue Peter constituted sensational television, I used to make Elizabeth David's chocolate and ground almond cake with, perhaps for our guests, monotonous regularity. The reason was quite simply that it was fail-safe (not something that can be said about a lot of ED's recipes, despite the sublime prose). Unsullied by any flour, the texture is beautifully squishy and every molecule tastes unflinchingly of chocolate. Over the years I've fiddled with the original recipe – what insubordination – but I think it may be even better now. A bowl of whipped cream or crème fraîche is all that's needed with this cake.

chocolate cardamom cake

a 24-25cm diameter springform cake tin, well-buttered
a heavy baking sheet

250g dark chocolate (at least 70% cocoa solids) *roughly broken*

170g unsalted butter *softened*

170g ground hazelnuts or ground almonds (or a mixture of both)

170g golden caster sugar

6 large free-range eggs *separated*

2 tablespoons dark rum (or brandy)

3 tablespoons extra-strong coffee

finely ground seeds of 3-4 cardamom pods

Preheat the oven to 130C fan/gas mark 2

Melt the chocolate either in a microwave, or in a saucepan standing on the warming plate of an Aga, or in a bain-marie, the bowl suspended well clear of barely simmering water.

If the chocolate isn't already in a very large bowl or saucepan, scrape it into one now. Beat in the butter, ground nuts and sugar to make a smoothish paste. Add the lightly beaten egg yolks, rum, coffee and ground cardamom seeds, and stir thoroughly.

Whisk the egg whites into soft peaks that just hold their shape. Using a large metal spoon, fold in about a fifth of the egg whites to lighten the chocolate mixture. Carefully fold in the rest of the egg whites, trying to keep everything as light and airy as possible.

Turn the batter into the cake tin, then put the tin on a heavy baking sheet and cook for about 45 minutes, or until the cake has risen and is tender-but-firm when you press it in the middle.

Leave the cake to cool thoroughly in the tin before releasing the sides.

You can make the sponge cake up to 2 days ahead, and the tiramisu 24 hours in advance, then assemble the cake a few hours before serving it. This is seriously sensational: a billowing assembly of feathery sponge cake, cream, mascarpone, more cream, and more mascarpone – oh, and a touch of alcohol, chocolate and coffee besides. Tiramisu translates from the Italian as 'pick-me-up'. Heaven knows why, unless it means, 'Be a darling and gather me up when I collapse in a groaning heap from eating too much of this pudding.' No question, this is a dessert that will be greeted with rather more rapture if it's served after a light meal than a rich one.

tiramisu cake

a 24cm diameter springform cake tin, lightly buttered and the base lined with baking parchment
a wire cooling rack

for the cake

250g plain flour

1 heaped tablespoon baking powder

250g golden caster sugar

250g unsalted butter *softened*

3 large free-range eggs *beaten*

for the tiramisu filling

3 large free-range eggs *separated*

350g mascarpone

1 (568ml) carton of double cream *whipped*

115g golden caster sugar

4 tablespoons extra strong coffee

4 tablespoons dark rum and/or Tia Maria

a little cocoa powder

Preheat the oven to 180C fan/gas mark 6

To make the cake, first sift the flour and baking powder together, then leave it to one side. Put the caster sugar and butter in a food mixer and beat for several minutes until the mixture looks creamy and pale. With the machine still going, add half the eggs, then half the flour, then the rest of the eggs and the flour. The batter should drop lazily from a spoon: if it's too thick, add a drop of milk.

Dollop the mixture into the prepared cake tin and bake it in the preheated oven for about 50 minutes, or until it's golden and springs back when you press the middle. Leave the cake to cool in its tin for 10 minutes, then turn it out on to a wire rack and remove the baking parchment from the base. When the cake is quite cold, wrap it in cling film and store it in an airtight tin.

In a really big bowl (that will take all the ingredients), beat the egg yolks and mascarpone until smooth. Using a large kitchen spoon, fold the whipped double cream into the mascarpone mixture.

Combine the egg whites and sugar and whisk them into soft peaks that just hold their shape. Fold about a fifth of the egg whites into the mascarpone mixture to loosen it, then fold in the remainder. Now stir in the coffee and alcohol, always working to keep the mixture as light and airy as possible.

Using a long-bladed, serrated knife (e.g. a bread knife), carefully cut the cake in half through its midriff, starting at one side and gently sawing your way through to the other side in one sweeping movement – do *not* plunge the point of the knife into the middle of the cake and turn the cake on its axis, as you'll end up with a dispiriting mess.

Turn what was the upper half of the cake, crust-side down, on to a serving plate and cover it with half the tiramisu mixture, then sift a little cocoa powder over it. Gently press the bottom half of the cake on top, crust-side up, and swirl the remaining tiramisu all over it. Finish with another light dusting of sifted cocoa powder. Refrigerate the cake until about half an hour before you want to serve it.

Not only will the cheesecake keep chilled for up to 3 days, I actually think it's best served straight from the fridge. What constitutes a good cheesecake is as difficult to determine as why the same football team, with the same manager, plays with the force of Titans one season, and like a herd of silly Satyrs the next. Personally, I like a cheesecake that has a distinctly home-baked look, the crust cracked and uneven, the texture slightly grainy. This one is much smoother – almost too perfect. It's incredibly popular at the Crown and Castle. (And, it's even nicer made with fresh goat's curd cheese, by the way.)

We serve the cheesecake with a dollop of fruit compote, normally blueberry but sometimes loganberry or blackcurrant: it needs to be a sharp fruit. If you can't be bothered to heat up some berries with sugar so the fruit slumps a little and creates a syrup, buy a bottle of good-quality fruit compote.

New York-style baked vanilla cheesecake

a 22-24cm diameter springform cake tin, lightly oiled, then lined on base and sides with baking parchment
a heavy baking sheet

175g plain digestive biscuits *finely crushed in a plastic bag*

50g unsalted butter *melted*

225g golden caster sugar

3 tablespoons cornflour *sifted*

the seeds of 1 vanilla pod

a few drops of vanilla essence

750g full-fat Philadelphia cream cheese

2 large free-range eggs *lightly beaten*

1 (284ml) carton of double cream

about 2 tablespoons black poppy seeds

Preheat the oven to 180C fan/gas mark 6

Combine the crushed biscuits and melted butter in a bowl, then press the mixture evenly over the base of the lined cake tin. Leave to one side.

Combine the sugar, cornflour and vanilla flavourings in a food mixer. Put the machine on the lowest setting, then add the cream cheese and beat until smooth – it's important not to whisk unwanted air into the mixture. Slowly add the eggs, then the cream – the mixture should now be smooth and thick.

Put the tin on a heavy baking sheet, then pour in the cheesecake mixture. Gaily scatter the top with the poppy seeds. Bake the cheesecake for about 45 minutes. Now crank the oven up very high for 5 minutes, or until the top of the cheesecake has lightly coloured. Remove the cheesecake from the oven and leave it to cool in the tin before refrigerating it.

The cake will keep for at least 2 days refrigerated but bring it back to room temperature before serving it. Not being stupid, we always have some sort of chocolate dessert on our menu at the Crown and Castle. Apart from the odd skirmish with a chocolate pot or tart, the offering alternates between this achingly chocolate cake and a hot bitter chocolate mousse – the latter having become something of our signature dish. The reason the cake is 'sad' is quite simply because there's no flour involved (great for gluten-free bods) so it sinks back after cooking and looks a little depressed (literally). But it tastes utterly divine.

'sad' (but not suicidal) bitter chocolate soufflé cake

a 28cm diameter springform cake tin, lightly buttered, lined on base and sides with baking parchment, buttered again then dusted with cocoa powder

600g dark chocolate (at least 70% cocoa solids) *broken*

420g unsalted butter *roughly chopped*

15 large free-range eggs *separated*

350g golden caster sugar

6 tablespoons cocoa powder *sifted*

Preheat the oven to 180C fan/gas mark 6

Melt the chocolate and butter either in a microwave, or in a saucepan standing on the warming plate of an Aga, or in a bain-marie, the bowl suspended well clear of barely simmering water. Once melted, gently beat the chocolate and butter together.

Meanwhile, lightly whisk the egg yolks in a large bowl. Mix the sugar and cocoa powder together, then add it to the egg yolks and beat well. Combine with the chocolate mixture and stir thoroughly.

Whisk the egg whites to a firmish peak. Fold about a fifth of the egg whites into the chocolate mixture to lighten it. Carefully fold in the remaining egg whites, a quarter at a time, keeping as much air in the mixture as possible. Turn the batter into the prepared cake tin and bake for 30 minutes, or until the cake has risen and the crust is firmish to the touch (it will be softish underneath). Remove the cake from the oven and leave it to cool in the tin for 10 minutes.

Dust the top of the cake with a little sifted cocoa powder then put a small saucer on top, and then a can of baked beans (or some such) to weigh it down. Leave the cake for about 15 minutes then remove the weight and saucer. (Don't leave it any longer or the saucer will become embedded.) Release the cake from the tin only when it is quite cold.

The cake can be made up to 24 hours ahead as long as it's kept cool, rather than refrigerated. A moist and surprisingly delicate cake, despite having a slightly gritty-but-pleasing texture, courtesy of the polenta. Cakes made with this fine cornmeal have become something of a restaurant cliché – then again, it's only because a lot of people find something agreeable that anything becomes a cliché. I think it's delightful, especially served with mascarpone flavoured with grated orange zest or even a dollop of marmalade.

You really do need to have a good read through this recipe before starting to make it. The oranges take an hour to boil and another 15 minutes to cool but you can prepare the rest of the cake in the meantime.

orange and polenta cake

a 24-25cm diameter springform cake tin, buttered, and sparingly coated with polenta grains

3 medium oranges (unwaxed if possible) *washed*
2 tablespoons dark coarse marmalade
200g ground almonds
140g polenta grains

1 scant tablespoon baking powder
7 large free-range eggs plus 2 large egg yolks
350g golden caster sugar

Fill a saucepan with water, bring it to the boil over a high flame and boil the whole oranges for about 1 hour, or until they are squidgy. Drain off the water, leave the oranges until they're cool enough to handle, then cut them in half and remove any pips. Put the oranges in a food processor and whizz them to a smooth purée. Add the marmalade and whizz again, then leave to one side.

While the oranges are cooling, tip the almonds, polenta and baking powder into a bowl and mix them together. Leave to one side.

Preheat the oven to 160C fan/gas mark 4

Put the eggs, egg yolks and sugar into a food mixer and beat for about 5 minutes, or until the mixture looks like a thick, foamy milk shake. Beat in the almond mixture, then the orange purée. Pour the batter into the prepared cake tin, leaving a fingertip's space for the cake to rise. Bake the cake for 15 minutes then **reduce the temperature to 120C fan/gas mark 1** and bake for a further 60-70 minutes.

When the cake is golden brown, risen, and just firm to a gentle press, it's ready – don't worry if it appears too damp and makes a bubble-bath-bursting noise. Leave the cake to cool (and sink a little) in its tin, then run a palette knife around to release it. As the cake is large and fragile, don't attempt to transfer it to a serving plate without using a proper cake lifter. If you haven't got one of these, leave the cake on its metal base and transfer the whole thing to a serving plate.

You can make this good-tempered cake up to 2 days ahead. If it has been refrigerated, it's imperative to bring it to room temperature before serving it. I say 'autumn' pear cake, because I really don't think there is much point in buying or eating pears at any other time of the year. This is a cake best served slightly warm as it's decidedly puddingy, albeit with a sandy-textured top – and perfect with a dollop of mascarpone enlivened with Poire Williams eau de vie (or Calvados), or even real custard. I am passionately fond of Comice pears, which have a particular, chin-drooling juiciness and fragrant flavour. For this cake, by all means use Williams or Rocha, but I wouldn't waste the ingredients on Conference, personally.

autumn pear cake

a 24-25cm diameter springform cake tin, lightly buttered, the base and sides lined with baking parchment and buttered again

250g golden caster sugar

250g unsalted butter *softened*

4 medium free-range eggs *separated*

250g ground almonds

3 tablespoons Poire Williams eau de vie (or Calvados)

6 dessert pears, e.g. Comice, Williams *peeled, quartered, cored and finely sliced lengthways*

for the 'crumble'

75g self-raising flour

50g light muscovado sugar

30g unsalted butter *roughly chopped*

Preheat the oven to 150C fan/gas mark 3.5

To make the cake, put the sugar and butter into a food mixer and beat for a few minutes, until the mixture is soft, pale and light. Lightly beat the egg yolks with a fork. With the machine at slow speed, gently pour them in, alternating with the ground almonds to help stop the mixture from curdling. Add the alcohol, then leave to one side.

Whisk the egg whites into soft peaks that just hold their shape. Using a large kitchen spoon, fold about a fifth of the egg whites into the cake mixture, to lighten it. Carefully fold in the remaining egg whites, trying to retain as much air as possible in the batter. Still working deftly and quickly, fold in the pears, then pile the mixture into the prepared cake tin.

For the crumble, combine the flour and muscovado sugar, then rub in the butter until the mixture is like very coarse breadcrumbs. Scatter the crumble over the top of the cake, then bake it for about 90 minutes, or until it's firm and golden brown. Leave the cake to cool in its tin.

The pie can be assembled up to 8 hours ahead, and baked straight from the fridge about 2 hours before it's needed. Knob-free, because there is nothing complicated about this pie: it's just pure, simple apple pie like wot my ma used to make, with no cinnamon, no cloves, no butter, no lemon juice, nor any other tomfoolery.

If there is any secret to why it's so bloody good, it's partly because of the fabulous pastry, and partly because the apples are piled really high, way past the rim of the dish. Thus they provide a decent amount of filling and support the crust while it cooks, so the pastry ends up with that humpy, home-made, generous look.

I should warn you that what looks like an enormous pie will not seem quite so huge when you come to cut it. I reckon it happily feeds about five adults and two children, but if there are only adults round the table you may want to make two slightly smaller pies instead, increasing all the ingredients by about a third.

knob-free apple pie

a deep, traditional, white-enamelled, blue-rimmed pie dish, measuring 32cm x 24cm *from one edge of the rim to the other – not the base on this occasion!*
a buttered pie raiser

a ball of pastry (see first recipe of the chapter)
8 large Bramley apples (or about 2.5kg) *quartered, cored, peeled and cut into chunky slices*

about **160g golden caster sugar**
1 large free-range egg white *lightly beaten*

Take out the pastry, let it return to cool room temperature, then roll it out – the pie wants a substantial-but-crisp crust, so make it a tad thicker than the chamois-leather thickness used to line a flan tin. Upturn the pie dish on to the centre of the pastry and use it as a template – adding an extra inch all the way round – to cut out the top crust.

From the remnants of the pastry, cut out a two-inch wide strip long enough to go round the dish. Butter the rim of the dish, then arrange this strip so it covers both the rim and a little way down the sides. Press it into place, making joins where necessary. Put the pie raiser in the middle of the dish.

Put a layer of apples into the dish, sprinkle them generously with sugar, then continue layering and sugaring them until they form a big heap around the pie raiser.

Brush the pastry on the rim with cold water, then cover the apples with the top crust. Using both forefingers and thumbs, pinch the pastry rim and top crust together, 'crimping' your way round the pie to make a tight seal. Take a small, sharp kitchen knife and make a few slashes in the top crust, then put the pie in the fridge to rest for at least 30 minutes and up to 8 hours. (Cling film it lightly if refrigerating for any length of time.)

Preheat the oven to 170C fan/gas mark 5

Just before the pie goes in the oven, brush the top crust with the egg white, then sprinkle it fairly thickly with caster sugar. Bake the pie for about 45 minutes, or until the crust is a shimmering, golden brown. It's better served very warm than piping hot so will relish being left in a warm place for anything up to 2 hours.

Crumbles can be reheated but they're never quite the same as when served freshly from the oven: time the cooking so the crumble comes out just as you sit down.

I doubt if there's a British cookery writer alive who hasn't recorded his or her pet crumble recipe somewhere. There's only one reason why I am adding another one and that's because I want to give you what I think is the best recipe – and that happens to be the most basic recipe. Yes, of course you can add oats, muesli, different sugars, nuts, lemon, spices and sundry other flavourings *but it doesn't make the crumble any better to eat!* (I am allowing myself a rare exclamation mark.) We food writers always want to add our own personal signature to recipes (never mind our childish disappointments and granny's laundry list), but some recipes should be left alone – and this is most definitely one of them. Remember, 'keep it simple' (which I should belatedly explain is an Escoffier command – although being French he actually said, 'faites simple').

As with so many fruity puddings, it's the ones that are both sweet and sharp, and 'bleed' profusely, that work the best. Depending on the season, bramley apples, rhubarb, victoria plums, damsons and gooseberries would top my list. Prepare the fruits in the normal way (i.e. wash, peel, core, etc.) and cut them into double bite-sized chunks or slices, as appropriate. Oh, and another pet bugbear – don't mix the fruits. With the honourable exception of blackberry and apple *it doesn't make the crumble any better to eat!*

a classic apple crumble

about 1.5kg bramley apples (or fruits as above)
225g golden caster sugar, plus extra for sweetening the fruit

400g plain flour
300g unsalted butter *roughly chopped*

Preheat the oven to 180C fan/gas mark 4

Thickly slice the peeled apples and tip them into a large ovenproof dish that will provide a good fruit to crumble ratio – the topping should be no more than three-quarters of an inch thick. Sprinkle the fruit with about 6 tablespoons of caster sugar, or to taste. How much, exactly, is a wee bit difficult to gauge until the fruit is cooked, I know, but obviously sharp bramley apples and mouth-puckering damsons will require more than dessert gooseberries and plums.

Traditionally, you should rub the flour and butter together but I find it easier to use a food processor with the pulse button engaged. Either way, rub or whizz the flour and butter so it looks like jumbo porridge oats – don't make it too fine as you want a crumbly, not a sandy topping. Stir in the 225g caster sugar, then strew the mixture over the fruit. Don't be too tidy about it: this is meant to be a homely pudding. (And sorry about all the admonitions.)

Cook for 35-45 minutes, or until the crumble is golden and you can see jammy-looking syrup bubbling up around the edge of the dish. (It's why the fruits must be the type to render up their juices; non-slumping dessert apples just don't work.) But if you've used the right fruit and it's still not happening, or the topping looks too pale, crank up the heat for 10 minutes towards the end.

You can serve crumble with ice cream but, really, you should proffer a big jug of custard.

proper custard

1.2 litres full-fat milk

1 vanilla pod *split lengthways*

1 heaped teaspoon cornflour

225g golden caster sugar

12 large egg yolks

Put the milk and vanilla pod into a saucepan over a low flame and bring to the verge of a simmer. Immediately remove the pan and leave the milk to infuse and cool for about 15 minutes.

Meanwhile, sift the cornflour with the sugar. Put the egg yolks in the bowl of a food mixer, add the sugar and beat until the mixture is pale and thick. (Or use electric beaters.)

Fish out the vanilla pod (wash it and thrust it into a canister of sugar, there to weave its perfumed spell) then pour the milk on to the egg and sugar mixture. Briefly beat or stir to combine.

Rinse out the milk pan and return the custard mixture to it. Place the pan over a medium flame and, stirring or whisking almost continuously, cook until the custard has demonstrably thickened and has just started to bubble. (Faint hearts use a double boiler; impatient souls do as I do, and risk the custard curdling – highly unlikely as the cornflour is there to stabilise it. Anyway, you can always whizz it in a liquidiser, if the worst comes to the worst.) Even if you are intending to serve the custard hot, it's still worth plunging the base of the pan into a sink of ice-cold water to take out some of the heat.

The pudding will keep warm for 2-3 hours but it also loves the microwave. If you own one you can cook the pudding up to 3 days ahead. The whole world and its mother (well, Delia anyway) has made this recipe their own but it really belongs to the late Francis Coulson of Sharrow Bay hotel fame. As the hotel still keeps the recipe under wraps, I am relying on John Tovey's rendition: he worked there before opening up at Miller Howe. The recipe was passed on to me by Nigel Slater, who also worked at Miller Howe when he was a boy.

The marvellous thing about sticky toffee pudding is its enduring popularity, which transcends winter, summer and any amount of health warnings about fat and sugar. (Rather extraordinarily, very few people eat what is already an exceedingly calorific pudding without an additional larding of ice cream, cream or custard.) Personally, I think we Brits are genetically programmed to adore stodge – only global warming and the demise of our species will end the affair.

the original sticky toffee pudding

a 23cm square cake tin (or white-enamelled tin), well-buttered

225g stoned dates *very roughly chopped*
300ml boiling water
2 teaspoons Camp coffee essence *(and bearing in mind this pudding's provenance, how apt is that...)*
225g self-raising flour
1 teaspoon bicarbonate of soda
100g unsalted butter *softened*

175g light muscovado sugar
4 large free-range eggs *lightly whisked*
for the toffee sauce
1 (568ml) carton of double cream
150g dark muscovado sugar
150g unsalted butter

Preheat the oven to 160C fan/gas mark 4

Soak the dates in the boiling water, add the coffee essence and leave to cool. Combine the flour and bicarbonate of soda and set aside.

Put the butter and sugar into a food mixer and beat for about 4 minutes, or until the mixture is soft and pale. Keep the machine on a slow speed and slowly pour in the eggs, alternating with the flour. Add both the dates and the soaking water, and stir – the batter will be pretty runny.

Pour the batter into the tin and cook the pudding for 55-60 minutes, or until it's firm and springy.

To make the sauce, put the cream, sugar and butter into a saucepan over a low heat and stir until the sugar has dissolved. Then turn up the heat and bring the sauce to a boil for a few minutes until it thickens up – be careful, it's bloody hot!

An easy pudding that does need fairly last minute assembly but which will keep warm happily for 2 to 3 hours before being served. There is nothing remarkable about bread and butter pudding but it's a perennial favourite, especially with the more mature person. I pride myself, perhaps wrongly, for inventing the idea of using panettone instead of bread – well, it's a good 16 years that I've been making it this way. The difference is subtle but absolute, with a harmonious, gentle fragrance lacking in the original. If you think you don't like bread and butter pudding, do try this: lashings of double cream in the custard makes another huge difference.

I like to use Carluccio's chocolate and coffee panettone, but if you can only find 'plain' panettone, then you might like to add a shot of sweet PX sherry or a jigger of strong coffee to the custard.

panettone bread and butter pudding

a fairly deep ovenproof dish with a large surface area, buttered

about 80g unsalted butter *softened*
about 250g panettone *cut into 1cm-thick slices (the thick bottom crust discarded)*
750ml full-fat milk

450ml double cream
75g golden caster sugar
9 large free-range eggs *beaten*

Preheat the oven to 140C fan/gas mark 3

Thickly butter the slices of panettone then arrange them in a single layer, butter-side up, in the dish. Tear the slices to patch them in, especially if the dish is oval or round.

Pour the milk and cream into a saucepan, put it over a low-medium flame and gently bring to simmering point, then immediately remove the pan.

Meanwhile, put the sugar and eggs in a food processor and whizz for about 2 minutes, until the mixture is pale and thick. (Or use electric beaters.) Pour in the hot milk and cream, and pulse for a few seconds – just long enough to combine without getting too frothy. (Add the sherry or coffee at this point if you're using either of them.) Pour the custard over the panettone, pressing the slices down so they are completely submerged. Leave them to soak for about 10 minutes.

Put the dish in the oven and bake for 55-60 minutes. When the pudding is ready the top should be pale gold and dry-looking, and the custard should shiver gently when you move the dish. Let the pudding rest in a warm place (I throw a clean oven cloth over the top and leave it on the Aga's warming plate) for at least 30 minutes, and up to 2 hours, before serving it. People who care more about eating than health or weight will like a jug of cold single cream served with it.

Cook the baba no more than 4 to 8 hours before you want to eat it as, like most yeasty things, it's at its most joyous when freshly made. The syrup can be made a week ahead as long as it's reheated before being used. If you've only ever eaten commercial rum baba, then this will be a revelation. Home-made, and eaten the same day, it's light, fragrant and wonderful. I suggest making the baba on a day when you're really keen on being in the kitchen, and have plenty of time, because it is a bit of a fiddle – but one with a very pleasing result. Do make sure you use a ring mould – the type of tin that looks like a circular moat – as it affects the eating quality and cooking times appreciably.

rum baba

a 23cm diameter ring mould of about 1800ml capacity, lightly buttered, then floured
a heavy baking sheet

for the baba
225g strong white bread flour
1 teaspoon fine sea salt
1 tablespoon golden caster sugar
1 sachet of easy-blend dried yeast
150ml full-fat milk *at room temperature*

3 large free-range eggs *well beaten and at room temperature*
85g unsalted butter *softened*

for the syrup
350g granulated sugar
250ml hot water
100ml dark rum (or orange liqueur if you prefer)

Combine the flour, salt, sugar and yeast in the bowl of a food mixer. Pour in the milk and eggs, then beat thoroughly to a thick batter. Remove the beaters, cover the bowl and let the batter rest in a warm place for an hour, or until it has just about doubled in volume and looks bubbly.

Preheat the oven to 160C fan/gas mark 4

Using a wooden spoon, beat the softened butter into the batter for a minute or so – it should thicken a little. Pour the batter into the ring mould, to about two-thirds of the way up – no more. Put the mould on the baking sheet and leave it for about 15 minutes, again in a warm place, until the batter starts to surge up the sides.

Bake the baba for about 35 minutes, or until it is golden and firm to the touch, then leave it to cool in the tin for 10 minutes before turning it out into a deep serving dish.

To make the syrup, put the sugar and hot water into a small saucepan over a low flame. Stir until all the crystals have dissolved and the liquid is translucent. Raise the heat and boil furiously for 10-15 minutes, without stirring this time, until it's decidedly syrupy. Remove the pan and stir in the rum.

While the baba is still warm, prick it enthusiastically with a skewer, then drench it with the syrup. Leave the baba to soak, and every time you pass by spoon up some syrup and pour it back over.

Traditionally rum baba is served with a cloud of whipped cream piled in the centre, but pouring cream is just as acceptable. As I'm not wild about cream, I sometimes make an orange salad as a rather lighter accompaniment.

The pavlova part can be made a day ahead, then wrapped in foil and kept cool (but not refrigerated). The fool can be made 24 hours ahead. Assemble the pavlova a few hours before serving it. As far as I am concerned, the whole point of a fool is to cut docile-natured cream and custard with a fruit that has plenty of acidity and punch: something astringent and assertive, like rhubarb, blackcurrants or gooseberries. It won't have escaped your notice these fruits all need a blast of heat to coax the juices to run. A crunch-crusted, marshmallow-hearted pavlova also needs something sharp to offset the all-penetrating sweetness. So, a creamy, voluptuous rhubarb fool pavlova would seem to tick all the boxes – just like most people filling in a questionnaire on the frequency of their sexual activity.

rhubarb fool pavlova

a 24-25cm diameter springform cake tin, lightly oiled and lined with baking parchment – or draw a 25cm circle on a parchment-lined baking sheet

for the pavlova

1 rounded teaspoon cornflour

200g golden caster sugar

4 large free-range egg whites *separated*

1 tablespoon fruit (or cider) vinegar

for the fool

about 450g rhubarb *cut into little-finger lengths*

icing sugar

675ml double cream

225ml full-fat milk

1 vanilla pod *split lengthways*

90g golden caster sugar

(the 4 egg yolks reserved from the pavlova)

a few drops of vanilla essence

Preheat the oven to 130C fan/gas mark 2

Mix the cornflour and sugar together and set aside. Put the egg whites into a very large, grease-free bowl and whisk into stiff, glossy peaks. Using a large metal kitchen spoon, fold in a fifth of the sugar mixture, then add the rest, a quarter at a time. Whisk in the vinegar.

Pile the meringue into the cake tin and build it up the sides, leaving a depression in the middle (for the filling). Or, spread the meringue over the drawn circle, leaving a 1cm border. Use the back of a large spoon to make a shallow dip in the middle, and build the sides up into swirly peaks.

Bake the pavlova for 20 minutes, then **reduce the temperature to 120C fan oven/gas mark 1**, and continue to bake for 40 minutes. Turn off the oven, leaving the pavlova inside for at least 2 hours, with the door firmly shut. When it's cold, carefully take the parchment off the pavlova before transferring it to a serving plate. (Or carefully wrap it in foil and store it in a cool place until needed.)

Preheat the oven to 200C fan/gas mark 7 for the rhubarb.

Strew the rhubarb in a single layer on stout baking tray(s) and sprinkle liberally with icing sugar. Bake for about 10 minutes, or until the rhubarb is tender but not mushy, then leave it to cool.

Put 225ml of the double cream and all the milk in a large saucepan, and add the split vanilla pod. Put the pan on a low-medium flame and bring to just under boiling point. Remove the pan from the heat and leave the milk-cream to infuse for about 15 minutes.

Meanwhile, put the sugar and the 4 reserved egg yolks in a food mixer and beat for a few minutes, until the mixture is pale and creamy. Strain the milk-cream on to the egg yolk mixture and briefly beat them together. (Rinse, dry and use the vanilla pod to infuse a canister of sugar.)

Rinse out the saucepan, return the custard mixture to it and place the pan over a low-medium heat. Stirring almost constantly, cook the custard until it thickens. Take the pan off the heat immediately, stir in the vanilla essence to taste, and put the pan in a sink filled with ice-cold water. Leave the custard to cool, stirring frequently at first, then occasionally.

Whisk the remaining double cream until it is very thick and floppy, then fold it into the cold custard, then whisk again until the mixture forms soft peaks. Stir the cold rhubarb into the cream mixture – not too thoroughly, but just enough to achieve a pretty rippled effect. (The rhubarb must be really cold or it will curdle the cream.)

Pile the fool into the pavlova with artful-yet-careless abandon. Once assembled the pavlova should be kept chilled, but not for too long as the meringue will deliquesce and lose crispness – actually it's rather nice, but not as it should be.

The meringue layers can be made up to 2 days ahead, then wrapped in foil and kept cool (but not refrigerated). Assemble the cake a few hours before serving it.

Crunchy-edged, marshmallow-soft, gently spiced meringue roughed up with toasted hazelnuts; autumn-fragrant blackberries; soft, billowy cream…what more could you want – except a rather less flowery, over-blown description, perhaps. No matter, this really is one of those oooh-ahh type desserts, and we all love cooking, serving and eating them, don't we?

hazelnut meringue and blackberry cake

Three 24-25cm diameter springform cake tin bases (not the sides), lightly oiled and lined with baking parchment – or draw three 25cm circles on parchment-lined, heavy baking sheets

2 pinches of ground mixed spice

1 heaped teaspoon cornflour

280g golden caster sugar

5 large free-range egg whites

100g hazelnuts *toasted and roughly chopped*

1 (284ml) carton of double or whipping cream

3 tablespoons crème de mûre (blackberry liqueur) or crème de cassis (blackcurrant)

about 500g blackberries

3-4 tablespoons golden icing sugar

Preheat the oven to 120C fan/gas mark 1

To make the meringue, first combine the mixed spice, cornflour and sugar.

Whisk the egg whites in a clean, grease-free bowl until they form stiff peaks, then whisk in a large tablespoon of the sugar mixture. Using a large metal spoon, fold in the rest, about a fifth at a time. Try to retain as much air in the mixture as possible.

Spread each cake tin base with meringue, leaving a little gap around the edge, then sprinkle the hazelnuts over each layer – don't worry if some spill over the edges. Put the meringues into the oven and cook for 60 minutes. Switch off the oven but leave the meringues inside – without opening the door – for at least 2 hours. Take the meringues out and when they are cold, peel off the parchment very carefully. Wrap the layers loosely in cooking foil and store them in a cool place (not the fridge).

Combine the cream with the crème de mûre and whip it into soft peaks anything up to 12 hours ahead, then keep refrigerated.

To assemble the cake, place a meringue layer on to a decorative serving plate or cake stand, nut-side down. Spread with half the whipped cream and a layer of blackberries. Dust with icing sugar to taste – it will depend on how wild or tame the berries are. Place the next layer on top, nut-side down, and spread with the remaining cream and blackberries. Place the final layer on top, this time nut-side up. Press down gently to mold the cake together.

Once assembled the cake will keep for a few hours in a cool place, and longer in the fridge. Just remember that it will take on a much less crisp, more fudgy texture, the longer it's refrigerated.

You can make and freeze the whole kit and caboodle a week ahead, although for *complete* perfection, apply the meringue just a few hours ahead. There are few puddings as thrilling as Baked Alaska, with its craggy peaks of warm meringue sheltering a hidden core of ice cream. The ludicrously sweet confection was invented in the 1870s at New York's famous Delmonico's restaurant (to celebrate America's purchase of Alaska from Russia), but it is still an out-and-out show-stopper. Traditionally, vanilla ice cream is used, but if you fancy mascarpone, dulce de leche, maple walnut, cherry Garcia, or whatever, why not – I think I'd steer clear of Phish Food, though.

For a flaming tableau effect, heat a ladle of orange liqueur, pour it over the top and light it – just as for Christmas pudding. A 1946 American recipe suggests an even better trick whereby you set three clean, empty, half-egg shells in the meringue (prior to cooking). Then, when the Alaska emerges from the oven, you fill them a third-full with the heated liqueur, set light to it, and whoosh – your own flaming oil wells. This, however, is an Italian version, thanks to the panettone.

baked Italian Alaska

a large flat dish that is both ovenproof and freezerproof

1 (500g) panettone

about 150ml orange liqueur, e.g. Cointreau

2 (500ml) tubs of best quality vanilla ice cream *slightly softened*

6 large free-range egg whites

150g golden caster sugar

(optional) empty, cleaned egg shells

about 2 tablespoons flaked almonds

Use a long-bladed, serrated knife to cut a 'lid' from the top of the panettone, then put it to one side. Scoop out the centre of the panettone, leaving a hollow container with fairly robust walls and bottom. (Scoff the remnants.)

Sprinkle the interior of the panettone with a few tablespoons of liqueur, then pack in the ice cream – it should fill it completely. Sprinkle the cut surface of the lid with a little more liqueur before replacing it on top of the ice cream and pressing it firmly into place. Put the panettone on to a flat dish that will take kindly to both the freezer and the oven – and is also pretty enough to go to the table. (If the panettone is being prepared well ahead of time, wrap it up in cling film before freezing.)

To make the meringue, whisk the egg whites until they form stiff, shiny peaks. Using a metal kitchen spoon, fold in about a fifth of the sugar, then fold in the rest a batch at a time.

Working quickly, take the panettone from the freezer and cover it with a thick layer of meringue (including the gap between the dish and the panettone), then flick the meringue into flamboyant peaks. (Bury the egg shells now, if you're using them.) Scatter over the flaked almonds and put the Alaska back in the freezer, if it's not going to be cooked straight away.

Preheat the oven to 200C fan/gas mark 7

Transfer the Alaska straight from the freezer to the oven and bake it for 5-8 minutes, or until the meringue is dappled golden brown.

Meanwhile, gently heat the rest of the orange liqueur in a small saucepan. Either ladle it over the Alaska, or half-fill the egg shells. Set light to the liqueur, turn off the lights and bring the Alaska to the table while the flames are still licking. Cut it into thick slices and serve immediately.

Apart from some last-minute decoration, the trifle can be made up to 48 hours ahead. I've said it before but that won't stop me saying it again…until you've eaten a proper trifle, one made with real custard and without any garishly coloured jelly or neon-hued hundreds-and-thousands, you have not really had trifle. This is the real thing, rich with eggy custard, sozzled with sherry and finished with peaks of softly swirling syllabub.

The bowl you use must be large enough to take the trifle, obviously. But almost as importantly it must have a large surface area so you can appliqué it with the maximum amount of fanciful but stylish decoration. After all, that's what a trifle is all about – decadent frivolity.

sherry syllabub trifle

a large, handsome
glass bowl

12 trifle sponges

half a jar of good apricot jam (or, better still,
quince or medlar jelly)

150g unsulphured dried apricots *roughly*
chopped (and stoned, if necessary)

200ml sweet Oloroso (or cream sherry)

for the custard

600ml full-fat milk

10 large free-range egg yolks

150g golden caster sugar

1 heaped tablespoon cornflour

for the syllabub

the juice of 1 lemon

100g golden caster sugar

300ml sweet Oloroso (or cream sherry)

1 (568ml) carton of double cream

suggested decorations

toasted flaked almonds; angelica;

crystallised violets; crystallised roses;

natural glacé cherries and fruits;

ratafia; amaretti

Cut each block (of 4) sponges in half horizontally, spread one side generously with jam and sandwich them back together. Break them into individual sponges and line the bottom of the bowl, tearing the sponges up to fill any gaps.

Put the apricots into a saucepan with the sherry and bring to the boil. Immediately remove the pan from the heat, leave the apricots to cool, then spoon the contents of the pan evenly over the sponges.

To make the custard, put the milk into a large saucepan and heat it to just under simmering point. Meanwhile, whizz the egg yolks, sugar and cornflour in a food processor for a few minutes, until the mixture is pale and thick. (Or use electric beaters.) Pour the milk on to the egg mixture and pulse just long enough to combine. Rinse out the saucepan and return the custard to it.

Put the saucepan over a medium flame and bring the custard to the boil, whisking constantly. As soon as the first bubbles appear, count to 30, then remove the pan and plunge the base into a sink of cold water. Cool the custard completely, whisking frequently to start, then occasionally. Cover the trifle base with the cold custard and refrigerate for 4 to 48 hours, cling filmed.

To make the syllabub, put the lemon juice, sugar and sherry into a very large, round-bottomed mixing bowl. Whisk for a few seconds to help dissolve the sugar crystals, then pour in the cream and whisk until soft peaks have formed. Spread the syllabub on top of the custard. The trifle can now be refrigerated for up to 48 hours.

Don't decorate the trifle until just a few hours before serving (because the colours of the decorations often 'bleed', and the nuts and ratafia lose their crispness), but then adorn it as extravagantly as your imagination – and taste – allows.

Everyone knows the French don't have to bother making desserts; they just trip round the corner to their local patissier, snaffle up a picture-perfect apple tart and plonk it on the table with nary an explanation or apology. Of course, this easy habit emanates from a period when all French patisserie tasted as good as it looked. Nowadays there's a tendency for it to be all 'show' and precious little 'do'. Still, the habit continues – in much the same way as the French continue to believe we Brits can't cook, couldn't give a damn about food, and don't have a decent restaurant to our name.

I know the majority of our truly excellent restaurants are located in urban areas, and I know there are still a lot of appalling restaurants in the provinces, but the zeitgeist in Britain is definitely one of a burgeoning interest in decent food, whether it's produce bought online from specialist suppliers or eating out in restaurants and gastropubs. Anyway, it's particularly galling having to put up with French arrogance concerning all matters gustatory when those of us who have been visiting France for a number of decades are only too aware that practically every decent, small-town restaurant has withered to a working-time-directive-induced demise – and those that haven't are knocking out food with about as much flair as Pizza Hut.

fudge-it-nicely
puds

Unfortunately, the burgeoning restaurant culture in Britain doesn't extend to our cake and pastry shops (although we do have some jolly decent bakers now). While French patisserie has, in the main, degenerated to industrialised fakery, ours has never really emerged from this sorry state. There have been a few improvements, though. For a start, cakes and pastries filled with real, fresh cream are the norm nowadays, whereas in my childhood they were mostly stuffed with some sort of aerated vegetable fat: proper cream was unusual enough to merit a sky-blue window-sticker, with a cow drawn on it in outline. I'll also never forget being in Ireland, and seeing bakers' windows full of cakes so crudely formed, and so garishly iced, they looked as if a five year-old had made them out of Plasticine.

With or without fresh cream, there's still an absence of craftsmanship or finesse in most British patisserie and I wouldn't dream of serving it to my friends or family. The quiet, personal consumption of a chocolate éclair on the drive home from the supermarket is one thing, but I wish the big boys would wake up to the fact that their standard 18cm diameter cakes (and tarts) look mean and synthetic, with every perfect swirl of cream yelling its

Wembley-factory provenance. Perhaps it would be different if I lived in London, and had Paul's or Ladurée round the corner. Most of the French-owned patissiers who've set up shop in London offer superb quality cakes but, outside London, it's easier to track down a set of frangipane dentures than a good pastry shop.

All of this preamble explains why it's pretty hopeless relying on outside sources to help put a respectable dessert on the table. By definition, a ready-to-serve cake is only going to be as good as the ingredients and the artistry of the producer and I think I've made it fairly clear that obtaining such a cake is not going to be easy. In any case, one of the biggest problems even a good producer faces is the intrinsic fragility of most patisserie and the difficulties of safe transportation – it also explains why the pastry used in supermarket tarts and quiches is building-site burly rather than flower shop-fragile. However, you will find a few excellent online suppliers of more stalwart baked goods, such as chocolate brownies, in the suppliers' list. For the most delicate cakes you'll have to take yourself to the big city, purchase a fanciful confection and carefully cart it home.

Having given you all the negatives, let me reassure you that there are numerous (virtuous) shortcuts that *can* be made when it comes to desserts. This chapter is absolutely not about 'cheating' but about buying good things and assembling them cleverly, or preparing something simple that doesn't require too much skill or time. In most cases, almost all the work can be completed in advance, leaving you untrammelled by any eleventh hour palaver – or crises.

There are some key ingredients which lend themselves most satisfactorily to this short-cut style of cooking, without disgracing either themselves or you, the cook. In no particular order, these include ice cream, alcohol, fruits, dairy produce and chocolate sauce. Serving a dessert with some good biscuits can add a touch of style too. Shortbread, amaretti, macaroons and most of the Jules Destrooper range – from almond thins, butter wafers and crumbles to dentelles and florentines – spring to mind. *Please* don't serve those cantucci biscuits, though: they not only look like building aggregate, but taste like it unless they're dipped *and softened* in the Italian sweet red wine known as vin santo. That's the whole point of cantucci. Just sticking them on the side of a plate with any old dessert is typical, crappy chef behaviour. End of rant.

Have any, all, or some of these items in your fridge or cupboard and you're well on the way… of course, the ice cream must be really good quality, not sweet-as-fudge, American-style gloop (although even Häagen-Dazs is better than the Walls's Golden Vanilla aerated flump of yesteryear) but proper stuff as made by the likes of Hill Station, Roskilly's, Purbeck, Morelli, Marine Ices or Rocombe. (I do have to make an exception for Ben &

Jerry's Cherry Garcia ice cream, though, which I think is scrumptious. If you're on a diet, as I am – permanently – I also strongly recommend the Cherry Garcia yoghurt 'ice cream' which has less than half the calories of the usual stuff.)

It's also a good idea to have mascarpone, crème fraîche or Jersey cream to hand. You can whip up a dessert in no time with fruit and cream – just think of lemon syllabub. Anyway, apart from using these dairy products as the foundation of a pudding, I am always surprised by the propensity that even figure-conscious people have for pouring a big jug of cream over an already rich dessert.

hot dark chocolate sauce

Always useful and always popular, chocolate sauce can lend interest to many a simple dessert.

about 500g dark chocolate (at least 64% cocoa solids) · a (284ml) carton of double or whipping cream · unsalted butter

Roughly break the chocolate (easiest to do while still in its wrapper: simply smash the bar on a hard surface). Put it in a saucepan with the cream and 150g butter and set it over a *very* low flame (or on the warming plate of an Aga; or use a bain-marie, the base of the pan suspended over barely simmering water). When the chocolate and butter have melted, turn up the heat a little and bring the sauce to just below simmering point, stirring frequently. Remove the pan from the heat and keep the sauce warm until it's required.

chocolate, prune and hazelnut slab

This has been in my repertoire since the days of M'sieur Frog, a great neighbourhood bistro in Islington where I used to eat almost every week in the Seventies. This dead-simple chocolate slab has been called all sorts of things over the years, including 'chocolate biscuit cake'. As it bears absolutely no resemblance to cake, it's a description I prefer to eschew. Whatever its name, I like to serve fingers of it with coffee in lieu of a pud – or with a Palo Cortado or rich Oloroso sherry. If you want to serve it as a more formal dessert, whip up some cream with a dash of rum or brandy, to flop on top.

Needless to say, the better the ingredients the better the result, so use Agen prunes if you can; good-quality nuts and chocolate (I like a 50/50 split of fifty per cent cocoa solids and seventy per cent cocoa solids); and natural glacé cherries. The sherry-maceration is not essential but it does give the chocolate slab extra oomph.

Agen prunes · natural glacé cherries · (optional) rich Oloroso sherry · Rich Tea biscuits · toasted hazelnuts · pecan nuts · unsalted butter · 250g dark chocolate · golden syrup

Roughly chop 150g prunes and halve 50g glacé cherries then macerate them for about an hour in a few tablespoons of sherry. Break 150g biscuits to big gravel-sized fragments (I put them in a plastic bag and scrunch them up with my hands). Roughly chop 50g hazelnuts and 50g pecans. Leave everything to one side.

Melt 150g butter and the chocolate in a bain-marie, or microwave, or on the warming plate of an Aga, then stir in two tablespoons of golden syrup. Add all the other ingredients and stir well. Lightly oil a 20cm x 15cm dish with a tasteless (or light nut) oil. Pour in the chocolate mixture, smooth the top then refrigerate until set. Turn the slab out and cut it into thick fingers using a heavy knife dipped in hot water between slices.

chocolate brownies with pears and mascarpone

Use the very best brownies for this rendition of that classic combination, chocolate, pears and cream. The addition of some chocolate sauce, too, may or may not be over-gilding the lily.

chocolate brownies · a (600g) bottle of pears in their own juices · (optional) eau de vie poire Williams · 500g mascarpone · (optional) cocoa powder

For bite-sized brownies, allow two to three chunks per person, depending on what has gone before and the voraciousness of your guests' appetites. Cut the pears into quarters, and give each person three bits. Stir, if liked, some pear-flavoured eau de vie into the mascarpone. Arrange the brownies and pears artfully, and dollop some mascarpone on top. Depending on the level of ponciness required, dust a little cocoa powder over the top (and trickle on some chocolate sauce).

cassata cake

The original cassata Siciliana is not ice cream but this ricotta, candied peel and bitter chocolate-filled cake. If you can find proper fresh ricotta from an Italian deli (the type that comes in a basket-impressed dome) so much the better. The cake requires no cooking, can be made well ahead of time and, as it's only possible to eat a small slice at a time, it will go a long way.

100g dark chocolate · a panettone · 750g ricotta · golden caster sugar · 175g hand-chopped candied peel · vanilla essence · icing sugar or cocoa powder

Line a lightly buttered 20-21cm springform cake tin with cling film, leaving a good overhang – it's not easy, but push the film into the corners as best you can. Grate or chop the chocolate.

Line the bottom and sides of the cake tin with half-inch thick slices of panettone (discarding the thick bottom crust from each piece). Fill any holes with scraps (any patching-up won't show). Whizz the ricotta and 140g sugar in a food processor, then remove the blade and stir in the chopped peel, a few drops of vanilla essence and the chocolate. Pack the mixture into the lined tin, smoothing the surface. Seal the filling in with more close-fitting slices of panettone.

Pull the cling film up around the cake and cover it closely. Place the base from another tart or cake tin over the top and weigh it down with a heavy can. Put the cake in the fridge for at least 8 hours. Then, carefully turn it out so the bottom is on the top and dust with either sifted icing sugar or cocoa powder before serving.

affogato al caffè

It's almost embarrassingly simple but the delight of *gelato di vaniglia affogato al caffè* never palls, for me anyway. The combination of hot espresso and cold, suave ice cream is fabulous, especially as the ice cream starts to melt and a wonderful cappuccino-ish puddle builds up in the bottom of the glass. The word '*affogato*' is Italian, as you've probably gathered, and means 'smothered'.

two (500g) tubs of vanilla ice cream · eight shots of hot espresso coffee
Put scoops of the best vanilla ice cream you can buy into glasses, then pour a shot of really hot espresso over each one. (Really good, strong cafetière coffee made with high-roast Italian-style beans would do.) That's it.

affogato all'amarena

My mother had a passion for what she called 'amarena affogata' (foreign languages not being her strong suit). Back in the Sixties, she often ordered it at Otello's, our local Italian restaurant in Finchley: I still have a clear picture of the glass goblet filled with sultry dark cherries smothered in vanilla ice cream and finished with a small Alp of whipped cream. At Christmas you can easily find bottled fruits in alcohol, but if you can only find cherries in syrup, I'd add a slug of cherry brandy or kirsch.

two (600g) bottles of Morello cherries in syrup or alcohol · two (500g) tubs of vanilla ice cream · a (568ml) carton of double cream (or whipping cream)
Put gently warmed cherries and their juices into the bottom of glass goblets, add a big scoop of vanilla ice cream and finish with a flourish of whipped cream.

amaretti affogato

Another 'smothered' ice cream sundae that's dead easy to concoct.

two (500g) tubs of vanilla ice cream · amaretti biscuits · amaretto liqueur · a (568ml) carton of double cream (or whipping cream) · a handful of toasted flaked almonds
Put scoops of vanilla ice cream in the bottom of small glass dishes, cover with roughly crushed amaretti, pour on a slug of amaretto, then finish with a cloud of whipped cream and a scattering of toasted flaked almonds.

coffee granita with coffee syrup

Iced, softly crunchable shards of sweet, strong coffee and fabulously rich cream that's both velvety or chewy, depending on how close it gets to the frozen granita… it's simply divine, and probably my favourite way to end a good meal. Don't be tempted to make the granita more than a day ahead.

1.7 litres strong coffee · golden caster sugar · instant coffee granules (or Camp coffee) · Tia Maria (or other coffee liqueur) · Jersey cream
The coffee should be hot: if it's of truly good, almost espresso strength, then just add 100g sugar – otherwise, add a tablespoon of coffee granules as well. Leave the coffee to cool, then taste it –

Right: Coffee granita with coffee syrup

the flavour should be very strong with a hint of sweetness. Pour the coffee into a deep plastic container and freeze for an hour or two, or until the edges have iced up. Stir with a fork (do not whisk, whizz or do anything else to it). Continue to freeze, roughing up the granita two or three times as it 'sets' – the finished granita should be a loosely congealed mass of rough, gravelly shards.

To make the sauce, put four tablespoons of coffee granules (or a good slurp of Camp coffee), three tablespoons of sugar and 250ml boiling hot water into a saucepan and stir over a low flame until dissolved. Raise the heat and bring the syrup to a boil, then simmer for 5 minutes. Add five tablespoons of Tia Maria and simmer for another 5 minutes. Leave to cool.

To serve, spoon the granita into wine glasses, pour a little syrup over the top, then cover with a thick layer of Jersey cream.

macaroons with cherry ice cream

Soft, chewy almond macaroons were ubiquitous in bakers' shops when I was young, but they seem to have gone the way of all confection needing teeth. (I really, really, really miss good old-fashioned British chocolates with nutty, chewy centres – even that old stalwart, Black Magic, seems to have a preponderance of soft, rather than teeth-tugging, fillings. Personally, I can't stand praline and simply don't understand its appeal. If you share my dislike of sweet, claggy, oh-so-boring Belgian chocolates, try Rococo's English collection.) Big digression there; back to the macaroons. Why this works so well is because the almond in the biscuits echoes the flavour of the cherries (remember, they both come from the same *prunus* family).

two (500g) tubs of Ben & Jerry's Cherry Garcia ice cream · sixteen macaroons · bottled (or canned) black cherries · (optional) cherry brandy

Sandwich a thick wodge of ice cream between two macaroons (exuberantly, and not too tidily, it's not meant to look like a petrol station sandwich), then spoon over a few cherries and their juice and, if liked, a shot of cherry brandy.

other biscuit and ice cream combinations:

– sandwich those big chocolate chip cookies with cardamom (or cinnamon) ice cream and trickle with dark chocolate sauce

banana and pineapple 'snow'

Fondant bananas provide a sweet, suave base, the pineapple and lime juice add zing and the whisked egg whites turn this sort-of sorbet into a wonderful iced sherbet. (I know the eggs I buy are from a salmonella-free flock but if you have any concerns about eating raw egg, leave them out.) The 'snow' is best eaten within 2 days of being made.

700g prepared pineapple chunks · five very ripe bananas · a lime · palm sugar (or honey) · the separated whites of four large eggs

Tip the pineapple (including any juices), peeled bananas, the juice of a lime and three tablespoons of palm sugar into a blender and whizz until completely smooth. Taste and add more sugar or lime juice, if necessary. (Remember, freezing will dull the flavour.) Pour the mixture into a plastic container, cover it, then put it in the freezer for about 90 minutes, or until the contents are very thick and cold.

Meanwhile, whisk four large egg whites in a large bowl until they just start to hold their shape. Gently add the sludgy pineapple mixture and whisk until just combined – don't overwork it as the idea is to retain as much air as possible. Pour the mixture back into the plastic container and freeze until firmish. For maximum effect, serve the 'snow' in glass dishes rather than china ones.

lemon meringue ice cream sundae

There's nothing to match that citric stab at the end of a rich meal, whether it's a sublime lemon tart or this adult ice cream sundae. At the Crown and Castle, this is a popular summer dessert both with the customers and our rushed-off-their-feet staff, as it's not exactly taxing on the preparation front.

two or three (500g) tubs of lemon ice cream or sorbet · eight meringues · limoncello
Dollop a ball of lemon ice cream (better still, lemon meringue ice cream) or lemon sorbet in the bottom of a tall sundae glass, then add a layer of roughly crushed meringue (bought meringues in your case; home-made in ours): put in another dollop of ice cream, another layer of meringue, then slosh on a shot of limoncello (the lemon liqueur from Sorrento in Italy). If you haven't got any limoncello, you could use vodka, or even lemon vodka. And if you want to add some lemon curd, I'm not going to stop you.

pineapple glacé Laurent

I frequently used to order something similar to this at Hintlesham Hall (in Bob Carrier's day, not ours) and it's light, refreshing and somehow 'right'. Always cut pineapples lengthways, not in rings. This is because pineapples are not as sweet at the leafy end as the stalk end, so cutting them lengthways guarantees everyone their fair share of sucrosity. Both pineapple and oranges can be prepared a good few hours ahead, and kept chilled.

a ripe pineapple · four to six oranges · three limes · a (500g) tub of mango and lime ice cream (or orange sorbet or mango sorbet)
(You'll probably have too much pineapple for this dish, but I don't think there's anyone who would complain about having some lovely prepared fruit sitting in the fridge.) Cut the peel off the pineapple then quarter it lengthways. Cut out and discard the hard core from each quarter (just as you do for a cabbage). Place a wedge of pineapple flat on the work surface and cut it into thin slices, lengthways. Repeat with the other wedges.

Cut off the peel from the oranges, including the pith, and slice between each membrane to remove perfect skinless segments. Cut one lime in half, and the other two limes into eight wedges each. To serve put overlapping slices of pineapple on each plate, then the orange segments arranged like the petals of a flower with a ball of ice cream forming the centre. Squeeze the juice of one lime over the pineapple, then decorate with the remaining wedges of lime.

knickerbocker glory

No time for sophistication here: just go for the most glorious, colourful combination of fruit and ice cream you fancy. I am *never* surprised at how many adults still adore childish desserts. Do stay within the genre of English summer produce, though – and don't fall about muttering, 'what summer'. Use either strawberry, mixed berry, Morello cherry, peach or raspberry purée and strawberry, raspberry or vanilla ice cream – neither tropical fruit purées, nor spiced ice creams should get a look-in. You can have everything ready, then assemble the sundaes while everyone's chattering.

about 600g fruits, e.g. raspberries, strawberries, banana, peaches · a (284ml) carton of whipping cream · eight small meringues (or trifle sponges) · a pouch of Funkin fruit purée · two (500g) tubs of different-flavoured ice cream · chopped toasted hazelnuts or almonds · artificially coloured, i.e. bright red, glacé cherries

Use either one fruit or, better still, a mixture, and chop very roughly. Whip the cream into soft peaks. Spoon some fruit into each glass, add a thin layer of crushed meringue or broken sponge, then a swish of fruit purée, and a ball of ice cream. Repeat, changing the flavour of the ice cream. Finish with a peak of whipped cream, a scattering of nuts and a cherry on the top.

other ice cream sundaes:

Sundaes always look best served in a tall glass – see Nisbet's in the suppliers' list on page 23.
– put some fresh raspberries, strawberries or mango, in the bottom of a glass, nap with a matching purée, add a scoop of matching ice cream, then top with chocolate sauce (see Funkin on page 20)
– crush one or two amaretti and put them in the bottom of a tall glass, dowse with amaretto, add a thick layer of cut-up bottled apricots, then a scoop of mascarpone or clotted cream ice cream. Repeat the layers, then finish with a swirl of whipped cream and some chopped toasted hazelnuts or almonds
– put a layer of roughly chopped marrons glacés in the bottom of a glass, add a slug of brandy or dark rum, then a scoop of chocolate, or cardamom, or fig and orange blossom honey ice cream, then some roughly chopped florentines. Repeat the layers once, then top with whipped cream and a fine trickle of honey or maple syrup.

other things to do with vanilla ice cream:

If you are folding anything into ice cream it will have to be slightly softened first. If you have a microwave, use the the defrost button for 1-2 minutes. Refreeze the ice cream immediately and work *very* cleanly – I don't want the hygiene inspectors bashing at my door.

– stir a few tablespoons of chopped preserved stem ginger into the ice cream, then dowse with rich Oloroso sherry and scatter with roughly chopped toasted almonds

– stir a handful or two of moscatel sherry-soaked raisins (heat the sherry gently first) into the ice cream and scatter on a handful of chopped toasted hazelnuts

– break up three or four Sesame Snaps into rough shards and stir them in

– especially appropriate for Christmas: cut, crumble or chop about a quarter of a panforte into very small chunks, soak them in rum for an hour or so, then fold them into the ice cream. Serve with chocolate sauce and a thin slice of the remaining panforte on the side

– pretty damned obvious, but pour hot chocolate sauce over it. There aren't many people who don't melt (get the pun) at the thought of it

– pour a measure of treacle-rich PX sherry over the ice cream and serve with florentines

– make a hokey-pokey ice cream by folding in about 200g honeycomb shards. Serve with hot chocolate sauce – or not

Eton mess

Invented at Eton college to celebrate King George III's birthday on the Glorious Fourth of June, this unashamedly luxurious and frivolous concoction is also an ideal way to mask the fact that so many strawberries (a plague on Elsanta) are pretty rubbish nowadays, when it comes to flavour. We know Eton Mess as a combination of strawberries, cream and meringue, but it can also include strawberry jam and vanilla ice cream, as it does here. You will need small glass bowls, high-sided rather than shallow, or sundae glasses.

about 600g ripe strawberries · about 400ml whipping cream · eight meringues · Little Scarlet (or similarly good strawberry) jam · vanilla ice cream

Halve the strawberries; whip the cream into very soft peaks; break the meringues into bite-sized shards. Combine all these ingredients in a large bowl and gently fold them together. Chill for a few hours. Before serving, make sure the ice cream is fairly soft. Put a mound of the Mess into the bottom of a bowl, then a big spoonful of ice cream, then a tablespoon of jam, then cover with another mound of the Mess.

apricot and orange flower compote

Finding a fresh apricot that doesn't have the texture of boiled wool *and* tastes of something –
anything, actually – is less likely to happen than Donald Trump getting a crew-cut (or, Jade Goody
learning Latin – how could I possibly overlook that delightful young woman in favour of an appalling
old *******e. Answers not required). You can tell how sincerely disappointed I am with fresh
apricots. On the other hand, dried apricots – as long as they're not those sulphured or ultra-squishy
ones the supermarkets all seem to sell – have great flavour. Once poached, they make a really
excellent little dessert.

**golden caster sugar · 800g dried apricots · orange flower water · mascarpone (or Greek yoghurt) ·
raw (not salted) pistachios**

Put 400g sugar in a pan with 300ml water, set it over a low flame and bring to a simmer, stirring
occasionally to dissolve the crystals. Add the apricots and continue to simmer, uncovered, for about
5 minutes, or until they have plumped up. Remove the pan from the heat, add two tablespoons of
orange flower water and leave to cool. (If the apricots need stoning, do it now.) Serve the apricots in a
glass with some syrup, a spoonful of mascarpone and a good scattering of chopped pistachios.

fig and honey compote

For this classy little recipe, it's really important to use one of the good varietal honeys, not some
bog-standard affair. At the time of writing, Waitrose stock the wholly appropriate ice cream I've
recommended but if it's gawn by the time you read this (more than likely) use another spicy ice
cream instead.

**a (75cl) bottle of red wine · half a jar of good honey · one or two sprigs of rosemary · fennel seeds ·
about 500g dried whole figs · fig and orange blossom honey ice cream · toasted flaked almonds**

Put the wine, honey, rosemary and a teaspoon of fennel seeds into a saucepan and slowly bring to
the boil, over a medium flame, stirring occasionally. Add the figs, reduce the heat to an energetic
simmer and cook for about 25 minutes, or until the figs have plumped up and the juices are syrupy.
Serve warm with the ice cream and a scattering of toasted flaked almonds.

blackberry and apple compote

This is nothing more than blackberry and apple pie without the pastry. It's wonderful with thick cream or mascarpone if you're serving the compote cold, or with ice cream if you prefer to serve it hot.

about 450g dessert apples · golden caster sugar · about 600g blackberries · cinnamon · (optional) crème de mûre

Peel, core and finely slice the apples. Put 150ml hot water and 150g caster sugar in a wide, shallow pan and bring to a simmer over a low heat, stirring to dissolve the crystals. Add the apples and stir. After 2 minutes, add the blackberries and either a stick of cinnamon or a teaspoon of ground cinnamon, and reduce the flame. Toss very gently, then cook for about 5 minutes, or until the apples are tender and the blackberries are softened and weeping, but not a sludge. Remove from the heat and splosh in some crème de mûre.

strawberry compote with shortbread

This is my take on that American classic, strawberry shortcake. Frankly, its favoured status completely baffles me. What's so wonderful about a few whole strawberries sandwiched in between a couple of dry old biscuits, with a bit of whipped cream? This juicy, pepper-stabbed version is far more interesting. Use even-sized, small-to-medium whole strawberries, that don't have to be cut. If all you can find is hulking great brutes, do something else with them.

about 800g even-sized, smallish strawberries · golden caster sugar · green peppercorns · fraise de bois liqueur (or Cointreau) · Jersey cream · all-butter shortbread petticoat tails

Put the strawberries in a wide, shallow saucepan with a little sugar to taste (only you will know how sweet the berries are, and how much they need), a teaspoon of green peppercorns (drained and rinsed if bottled in brine, or rehydrated if dried) and about 150ml water. Place the pan over a low heat and bring to just below simmering point. As soon as the strawberries have started to wilt, remove the pan and add a generous slurp of the strawberry liqueur. Leave to cool, then serve the compote in glass dishes and hand around a bowl of thick Jersey cream and a plate of petticoat tails.

Edinburgh fog

Atholl brose, cranachan and Caledonian fog are all variations on a whipped up mess of cream, sugar, oatmeal, whisky and marmalade. I have to confess that I find the authentic oatmeal version rather dull, and prefer to use muesli. I also like to trickle the 'fog' with maple syrup (after all most of Scotland emigrated to Canada at one point) but anything sweet, such as honey, will do.

The 'fog' can be made up to 8 hours ahead and refrigerated – but bring it to cool room temperature and give it a good whisk before dividing it among small bowls or big glasses.

about 175g muesli · milk · about 700ml double cream · golden caster sugar · whisky · maple syrup (or honey)

Soak the muesli in a little milk for a few minutes, just long enough to soften the roughness of the cereal. Whip the cream until it's thick and floppy (but not peaked), then gently stir in the muesli, a tablespoon or two of sugar to taste, and six tablespoons of whisky – again, to taste. Dribble the maple syrup over only when the 'fog' is in individual glasses and ready to serve.

other things to make the 'fog' foggier:

– gently fold in about 450g raspberries or blackberries or blueberries

grapes with cardamom and armagnac

It wouldn't be very nice to make your guests have to keep spitting out pips, so you'll either need to buy seedless grapes, or seed them yourself. The advantage of the former is as obvious as the disadvantage of the latter. But the downside is that the flavour of seedless grapes is hardly ever as good as 'proper' old-fashioned varieties, like muscat grapes. You decide.

unsalted butter · ground cardamom · light muscovado sugar · a (568ml) carton of whipping cream · about 600g white grapes and 600g red grapes · armagnac (or brandy) · vanilla essence · palmiers

Put 100g unsalted butter, a scant teaspoon of cardamom and 75g muscovado sugar in a wide shallow pan and heat it over a low flame, stirring, until the sugar melts. Add 100ml whipping cream, stir, raise the heat and bring to the boil. Tip the grapes in immediately, toss them gently to coat, and remove the pan from the heat. Leave them to warm for a few minutes.

Meanwhile whip the remaining cream until it just starts to peak, then add a swish of armagnac and a few drops of vanilla essence, to taste. Continue to whip into soft peaks. Serve the warm grapes in glasses with the cream piled on top, and palmiers on the side.

Right: Grapes with cardamon and armagnac

red pears

It may be a Seventies cliché (or is it Eighties?) but poached pears eat far more excitingly than they sound. I'm very fond of the slightly grainy texture of the pears and the spicy syrup, especially served with a dollop of mascarpone. By all means extract a little of the cores, but don't go too mad or the pears will collapse. And, to stop the pears bobbing to the surface while you're poaching them, cut a saucepan-sized circle of baking parchment and put it on top of them. You can cook the pears at least a day ahead, if not longer.

golden caster sugar · a whole star anise · a cinnamon stick · a bay leaf · eight small to medium pears (not too ripe) · half a bottle of Beaujolais or Merlot · mascarpone · ground cinnamon

Put 400g sugar, 300ml water, the star anise, cinnamon stick and bay leaf into a wide, shallow pan. Heat over a low-medium flame for just long enough to dissolve the sugar, stirring occasionally, then remove the pan. Peel the pears, adding them to the poaching liquid as you go (so they don't go brown). Put the pan over a medium flame and bring the pears to a simmer. Cook them for 10 minutes, then pour in the wine, bring back to a simmer and continue to cook for about 15 minutes, or until the pears are just tender.

Scoop the pears out of the liquor and put them in a serving dish. If the poaching liquid is still too thin, raise the heat and boil the juices down to a light syrup. Leave to cool, then pour it over the pears and chill until needed. Serve with mascarpone dusted with ground cinnamon.

passion fruit syllabub

It's hard to think of a pudding which is as easy to make but as sumptuous as a syllabub. There's no hassle, no strange ingredients or equipment, and it's as speedy as a politician passing the buck. I've used ready-prepared passion fruit juice here, but if you prefer to use fresh juice you will need eight, ripe, slightly wrinkled passion fruit. Take a sharp teaspoon, then scrape both pulp and seeds into a food processor, and whizz for 1 minute. Push the juice through a sieve, using a stiff rubber spatula to force every drop through, then discard the seeds.

150ml dry white wine · golden caster sugar · lemon juice · a (284ml) carton of double cream · a pouch of Funkin passion fruit juice · langue de chat biscuits or palmiers

Put the wine, 100g sugar and a squeeze of lemon juice into a big mixing bowl and whisk for about 30 seconds to help dissolve the sugar. Add the cream and whisk the mixture until it starts to balloon into a thick, floppy mass. Add about 150ml passion fruit juice and carry on whisking until the syllabub forms soft clouds that just hold their shape. Taste, and whisk in more juice, sugar or lemon juice, if you think it needs it.

Spoon the syllabub into little glasses (it's very rich, so you don't need much), finishing each one with a cheeky quiff. The syllabub will keep for up to 48 hours chilled. Serve with elegant biscuits, such as langue de chat or palmiers.

lemon curd fool

Even easier than the syllabub and every bit as luxurious.

1 (568ml) carton of double cream · lemon juice · a (320g) jar of lemon curd · shortbread
Whip the double cream to very soft peaks, adding the juice of a lemon to taste, then gently stir in a jar of lemon curd, keeping it all nice and swirly. Serve in small glasses with shortbread on the side.

Italian lemon cream

A nice example of recipe evolution, this is based on a lemon posset that Simon Hopkinson first ate when Lucy Crabb (a former Bibendum chef) cooked it for him. However, I also have a very early Phillipa Davenport recipe which echoes it very closely, albeit her rendition was allied to an article about Amalfi lemons (which are intensely flavoured but not so acidic as 'normal' lemons), and includes roughly crushed amaretti. Here I've combined the two to good effect, I think. You will need eight small, heatproof glasses or ramekins, by the way.

four juicy lemons · two (568ml) cartons of double cream · golden caster sugar · amaretti biscuits
Squeeze the lemons. Bring the cream and 250g sugar to the boil in a large saucepan (the size is important to allow the cream to bubble without boiling over). Boil for exactly 3 minutes then take the pan off the heat and whisk in the lemon juice. Crumble a couple of small, hard amaretti biscuits into the bottom of each of the glasses or ramekins. Strain the lemon cream into a good pouring jug and leave it to cool for 15-20 minutes. Carefully pour it over the amaretti, trying not to disturb the biscuits too much, although one or two will shoot up to the top. Chill the lemon creams for at least 6 hours, or overnight. Serve with more amaretti, perhaps the soft (morbido) ones, this time.

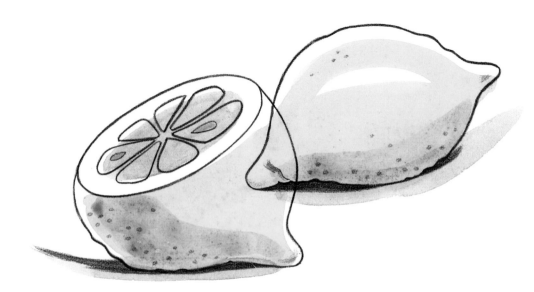

grilled nectarines

So-called tree-ripened, or ripe-and-ready-to-eat fruits are rarely as described – actually, I find it very upsetting that supermarkets persist in this fantastical/fallacious labelling practice – which is why it's often a good idea to cook tree fruits. Here, I've suggested serving the fruits with fresh goat's curd (available from Neal's Yard), but you could use a normal cow's milk curd cheese or really good cream cheese instead. It's a wonderful combination.

eight nectarines (or peaches) · about 250g fresh goat's curd · runny honey (or passion fruit juice)
Turn the grill on high. Halve the nectarines (taking the stones out, of course) and grill them, cut-side up for a few minutes, or until they've coloured and softened. Serve with a tablespoonful of goat's curd on each half, and a trickle of runny honey.

baked peaches with amaretti, chocolate and pine nuts

In Italy the peaches are normally so perfect it seems a travesty to bake them, but bake them they do, often with marsala or amaretti stuffing. In this country, the baking is more to do with mitigating the often woolly texture and lacklustre flavour. The filling can be prepared ahead and kept chilled. Don't stuff the peaches more than an hour before baking them, though.

amaretti biscuits · pine nuts · 100g dark chocolate · vanilla essence · a large egg · four large or eight small peaches (or nectarines) · cocoa powder · crème fraîche
Put 20 small amaretti, two tablespoons of pine nuts and the chocolate, roughly broken, into a food processor and pulse until the mixture is like coarse breadcrumbs. Add a few drops of vanilla essence and a lightly whisked egg. Don't process – just leave to one side for a moment. **Preheat the oven to 140C fan/gas mark 3.**

Halve, then stone the peaches. Dig out a tablespoon of flesh from the centre of each one, using a sharp spoon, and drop the flesh into the food processor. Pulse again, still keeping the mixture coarse. Spoon the filling into the hollowed-out peaches, then put the fruits in a buttered, non-stick baking tin and bake for 20-30 minutes, or until the flesh is tender and the filling lightly browned. Dust the peaches with a little cocoa powder and serve with crème fraîche.

baked fresh figs with mascarpone

I blithely say 'ripe' figs in the ingredients list, knowing darned well that most supermarket figs are as hard as a donkey's hooves. Baking them is one way of solving this problem, the other is for everyone to write to the supermarkets and ask them what on earth is the point of selling fruit that doesn't taste of anything. Wait for September, when the Greek and Cypriot figs come to town – especially the small, green mountain figs – and boy, are they worth eating. These baked figs can be prepared before you sit down, then put in the oven just before they're wanted.

24 ripe green or purple figs · mascarpone · runny honey · Pedro Ximenez sherry (or marsala) · raw (not salted) pistachios

Preheat the oven to 200C fan/gas mark 7. Let's assume the figs are vaguely ripe: cut a deep cross in the pointy end and squeeze the fig, like a baked potato, until it opens up. Put the figs on a heavy baking tray, stuff each one with a big dob of mascarpone and a smaller dob of honey. Splash a little sherry over them, then bake the figs for 5-10 minutes, or until the mascarpone starts to melt, and the figs look warm and squishy. Serve them strewn with chopped raw pistachios.

Now, if the figs are really hard, make the crosses and put them – unstuffed – into the hot oven for about 5 minutes to soften them up. Leave them to cool, then stuff them and proceed with the recipe as before.

figs stuffed with goat's curd and ground almonds

Max, our lovely head chef, says these taste nice. What better recommendation do you need?

about 400g fresh goat's curd (or drained fromage blanc) · 100g ground almonds · golden caster sugar · the grated zest of an orange · 24 ripe green or purple figs · runny honey · flaked almonds

Beat the curd until it's smooth, then mix in the ground almonds, about three tablespoons of sugar and the orange zest. Taste and add more sugar if necessary – the curd should stay tangy, though. **Preheat the oven to 200C fan/gas mark 7.** Cut a cross in the top of the figs, squeeze them open, then stuff in a good spoonful of the mixture. Drizzle them with a bit of honey, add a pinch of flaked almonds, then bake for 5-10 minutes.

lemon curd pancakes

Of course, these rich-but-tangy pancakes would taste even better if you made your own (and home-made pancakes will keep refrigerated for up to 24 hours, if you interleave them with cling film or baking parchment). On the other hand, a thin, delicate crêpe is not the easiest thing to achieve, and it is possible to buy fairly respectable, ready-made pancakes. Personally, I would make as much effort to avoid those revoltingly wodgy ones (that are named in such a way as to suggest some deep-south, American matriarch had a hand in the making) as I would Guantanamo Bay. The genuinely French-style crêpes as sold by Waitrose (in packets of eight) are considerably better, although I am not sure they are quite up to being served plain with lemon and sugar – the best way to eat pancakes, bar none. But gussied up a bit, they'll pass muster.

Make sure the lemon curd is top-notch, too – I tried three leading brands and thought Waitrose's Luxury Lemon Curd was both the smoothest and had the purest, sharpest lemon flavour. You can prepare the pancakes to the point where they're in the dish, and combine the ingredients for the sauce, a few hours ahead – but don't refrigerate either of them.

two (300g) jars of lemon curd · about 300g mascarpone · one or two lemons · eight French-style pancakes · lemon or grapefruit marmalade · light muscovado sugar · whisky · crème fraîche
Mix the lemon curd with the mascarpone, then add the finely grated zest of one lemon, plus enough juice to sharpen the mixture a tad. Spread the filling over the darker, bubbly-side of a pancake, then fold it in half and half again, to make a triangular shape. Repeat with the other pancakes, then arrange them like overlapping tiles in a lightly buttered ovenproof dish.

Preheat the oven to 180C fan/gas mark 6. Put a few spoonfuls of marmalade into a small saucepan and add about 5 tablespoons of hot water, a couple of tablespoons of muscovado sugar and a slurp of whisky. Put the pan over a low-medium heat and bring to a boil, stirring. Pour the sauce over the pancakes, then put the dish in the oven and bake for about 10 minutes, or until everything is piping hot. Serve with crème fraîche.

other things to do with eight French-style pancakes:
Glaze all the pancakes under a hot grill, in a buttered flameproof dish placed a good hand's length away from the elements, so they warm through as well as colour.
– make an apricot filling with a jar (or two) of good apricot jam, a dash of brandy and two tablespoons of roughly chopped hazelnuts, then roll the pancakes up, dust them with icing sugar and glaze. Serve with whipped cream infused with a dash of amaretto liqueur or vanilla ice cream
– roughly chop about 500g strawberries, add a few tablespoons of sugar (to taste) and a dash of balsamic vinegar, and leave to will for a few hours. Fill the pancakes with the mixture, roll them up, dust them with icing sugar and glaze. Serve with whipped cream and toasted flaked almonds
– make Mont Blanc pancakes by mixing a (400g) tin of chestnut purée with a few tablespoons of dark rum, to taste. Spread the purée over the dark side of the pancakes, fold them into triangular shapes and arrange them like overlapping tiles in a dish. Dust them with icing sugar and glaze. Serve with vanilla, cardamom, or coconut and rum ice cream

armagnac-macerated Agen prunes with vanilla ice cream

Agen prunes are the doyenne of dried plums, with a long and respectable history. Sun-dried in south western France, they are made from the Ente plum, which is a cross between a damson and a plum. More to the point, they are wonderfully tender, jammy and intensely flavoured.

24 prunes · armagnac (or brandy) · marzipan · two (500g) tubs of vanilla ice cream · toasted flaked almonds

Leave the prunes immersed in about 200ml armagnac for a few hours, then pick them out, take out the stones and stuff them with a scrap of marzipan. Put a scoop or two of vanilla ice cream in each glass or small bowl, pour over the soaking juices, add the prunes, then scatter with flaked almonds.

caramel toffee fondue

The hint of tautology surrounding the title is because the fondue can either be made from dulce de leche (invented in South America over a century ago and nothing more than milk cooked to buggery) or Ladurée's divine, salted butter caramel. The latter is the cat's Callard & Bowser of exquisite caramels (and all venom to the Suchard group who knocked that quintessentially English brand name on the head), mostly because of the elusive saline edge which tempers the sweetness. The former is now labelled as banoffee toffee (makes me want to throw up, just writing that) and is freely available in supermarkets, good, bad or indifferent.

The current fashion for chocolate fountains has got people dipping fruits (or biscuits and sweets, especially marshmallows) in melted chocolate and here's a variation on the theme. Not all fruits will go the course with caramel, but obvious candidates for this treatment would be bananas, tangerine segments, pears, apricots, apples, figs, dates and grapes, as well as chunks of shortbread, almonds or brazil nuts.

fresh fruits · biscuits · nuts · two (or three) jars of salted butter caramel · double cream

Prepare a plate for each person, with a good mixture of things to be dipped, and a small warmed ramekin. Heat the toffee stuff over a very low flame (really important that it's done gently), then stir in a little cream or milk to make a sauce with a not-too-thick coating consistency. (If you make it too thick, it won't go very far; make it too thin and it won't cling to whatever's being dipped.) Divide the sauce among the ramekins and serve immediately.

cheese

Don't forget that many people, especially wine drinkers (in my experience), prefer to finish their meal with another glass of glorious wine and some cheese. The secret is in offering the best quality cheeses in the best condition. Don't forget the 'keep it simple' mantra. It is far better to offer a single (large) piece of cheese in the peak of perfection, than a motley array of indifferent little wedges. And please don't be so lazy or oblivious to manners and beauty as to offer a board with the cheeses still done up in their plastic wrappings. It's incredibly rude and looks hideous, but perhaps it's only my family who have this habit. (I can hear the howls of outrage already.)

Two of the finest cheese merchants in the country are listed at the front of this book, namely Neal's Yard Dairy and La Fromagerie. Both are run by highly knowledgeable, committed owners (and staff), and offer cheese made with the utmost integrity and care. You can put yourself in their very capable hands with confidence. Undoubtedly they will advise you to offer no more than four varieties, or even one splendid wedge of, say, 3-year old parmesan – as long as you know your guests will love it, too. I usually choose one fresh goat's cheese, such as Tymsboro, Dorstone, Selles sur Cher or Pouligny St Pierre; a blue cheese, perhaps Roquefort (which I adore, especially the Gabriel Coulet one; I find Papillon too salty), Cashel Blue, Strathdon Blue or bleu des Causses; a washed rind cheese, such as Ardrahan, Wigmore, Taleggio or Stinking Bishop; and, either a really soft, white, bloomy-rinded cheese, like Finn or St Marcellin, or completely on another tack, a firm, mature cheese such as Coolea, Comté, Doddington or St. Gall. All will have to be in season. Indeed, if you purchase from a good cheesemonger (such as the two above), you won't be allowed to buy cheese that isn't in season.

With wonderful produce like this, all you have to do is to find a fine piece of wood, or a good-looking china platter, to arrange the cheese on; bring it to cool room temperature; offer some excellent bread (you've already got this anyway) but no butter (the cheese is 'fat' enough); a decent knife that will cut the cheese without destroying it; and, of course, some good wine to drink with it. Bear in mind that red wine is not always the answer: it's great with strong, manly cheeses, but for most of the softer cheeses, goat's cheese and washed rind cheeses, you'd be better of with a full-flavoured white wine, such as chardonnay or viognier. I think celery is too much of a bully to serve with cheese, but grapes are fine and if it's summer, then serve fresh cherries with very mild, young goat's or cow's cheese. Finally, Chateau d'Yquem is utterly perfect with blue cheeses.

prunes and blue cheese

Put a chunk of beautiful blue cheese, such as Gorgonzola, Roquefort or Cashel Blue, and a few prunes on each plate, with a few (untoasted) whole almonds, macadamias or hazelnuts. Even more chic would be to add a small shot glass of port.

And that's it – I hope I've given you lots of ideas, reassuringly simple recipes and a way to have *eight round the table* without wanting to cry.

First published in 2006 by
Quadrille Publishing Limited
Alhambra House
27-31 Charing Cross Road
London WC2H OLS

This paperback edition first published in 2007

10 9 8 7 6 5 4 3 2 1

Text © Ruth Watson 2006
Photography © Peter Cassisy 2006
Illustration © Toby Morrison
Design and layout © Quadrille Publishing Ltd

Editorial Director: Jane O'Shea
Art Director: Helen Lewis
Editor: Jenni Muir
Design: Jane Humphrey
Photography: Peter Cassidy
Food Stylist: Annie Rigg
Illustrator: Toby Morrison
Production: Bridget Fish

ISBN-13: 978 184400 507 9
ISBN-10: 1 84400 507 0

Printed and bound in China

acknowledgements

My thanks, as ever, to the splendid team at Quadrille, especially Alison Cathie; Jane O'Shea, my pragmatic and intelligent editor – huge respect; Clare Lattin (undoubtedly the best PR person I have come across); Helen Lewis; and Ian West. Special thanks to Jane Humphrey for her thoughtful and stylish design and to Jenni Muir for conscientious copy editing. The book would be so much poorer without Peter Cassidy's spirited photography and Annie Rigg's great food-styling. I love Toby Morrison's brilliant illustrations and I continue to be very thankful that Rosemary Scoular is my always honourable agent. Lastly, a big thank you to Darling, dearest Jessie and sweet Jack, for making home the best place to be.